THE CONCEPT OF STATE AND LAW IN ISLAM

By

Farooq Hassan, D. Phil.; D.I.C.L.C.;
B.A. Juris (Hons), M.A., B.Litt., (OXON);
of Lincoln's Inn, Barrister-at-Law,
Senior Advocate, Supreme Court of Pakistan,
Member, International Institute of
Strategic Studies, London.
Professor of Law, Willamette University

University Press of America™

Copyright © 1981 by

University Press of America, Inc.™

P.O. Box 19101, Washington, DC 20036

ISBN: 0-8191-1427-8 Perfect
0-8191-1426-X Case
Library of Congress Number: 80-69038

To Mehreen, Amber, and Uzma.

Divisions of the Quran

An explanation of Quranic citations may be useful for students. The Quran consists of 114 Suras of very unequal length. All Suras are numbered and also possess a title. Each Sura is divided into Ayats. Some Suras contain a few, others hundreds of Ayats. In English a Sura is usually referred to as a chapter and an Ayat as a verse. These are useful but not very accurate descriptions. The juristic and theological reasons why the English terminology is incorrect need not be gone into here. In this text, I have mostly referred to the Ayats by their number.

Abbreviations Used

There are very few abbrevitions used by me; those used are very well known. They are: U.S. = United States, U.S.S.R. = Union of Soviet Socialist Republics, U.N. = United Nations, I.L.O. = International Labor Organization, A.D. = Anno Domini, Christian Calendar's description, A.H. = Anno Higirae, Muslim Calendar's description, I.E. = id est, that is, Cf = Compare, O.A.U. = Organization of African Unity, O.A.S. = Organization of African States.

Transliteration

In the transliteration of Arabic words (or words of languages which use the Arabic Script) I have, for the sake of convenience, dropped all the punctuation marks in the English alphabet designed for phonetic accuracy.

Translation

I have used various recognized translations while quoting from the Quran. Although the best-known Quranic translations are mentioned in the Bibliography at the end, I have not restricted myself to the works mentioned there.

Acknowledgements

All of the major quotations in this book are taken from the Quran and, as such, no formal acknowledgement is necessary; the debt I owe to God for giving me the opportunity to finish this undertaking cannot be described in words. On a human plane, I would first of all thank Mary Wason, of the American University Law School, who was originally in charge of typing the manuscript. I am also very grateful to Dean Tornquist and Associate Dean Holland of the Law School for encouragement and to the Word Processing Center of Willamette University for preparing the finished final manuscript. Some of the people who were particularly helpful in this process I would specifically like to name: Jackie Walker, Carolyn Kilday, Verna Larson, Judith Jones, Ann Abbot, Teri Fitzgerald and Karen Oliver. For coordinating the activities of the many people involved, I would like to thank Anna Schmidt, who took great pains in ensuring the speedy outcome of the preparation of the manuscript. I am also grateful to two Willamette students who prepared the Index and proofread the narrative, Glenn Haese and Karen Jensen; the former is also my research assistant, who worked prodigiously in various ways in this undertaking. Finally, I want to thank Donna Parton who also read the proofs and made helpful suggestions.

The examination of the various texts necessary for the completion of this work was principally done at the Bodlein Library, Oxford, British Library, London, and the Library of Congress, Washington, D.C. I am thankful for the use of the facilities of these institutions. I also want to thank a number of scholars in Turkey and Pakistan with whom I discussed some of my thoughts while arriving at some of my conclusions. Principally on their requests, they remain anonymous; in any case, the final conclusions are mine, for which I alone am responsible.

I also want to thank many friends, colleagues, students, and members of various churches, who encouraged me to undertake the writing of this book. Two of them I would specifically name, Professor Bert Lockwood of the University of Cincinnati, and Dean Emeritus S. Reese of

Willamette University; without their moral support it would not have been possible to accomplish this task. Finally, I am grateful to Dr. T. Younger for suggesting the Biblical quotation used by me on Page vi.

* * * * * * *

Al Quran:

> "Verily Allah commands you to make over trusts to those who are trustworthy." (IV:58)
> "Verily the most respected of you in the sight of Allah is the one who is most God-fearing." (XLIX:13)

The Bible:

> "...When one rules over men in righteousness, when he rules in the fear of God." (Samuel 23:3b-4)

Table of Contents

                                                        page
Acknowledgements. v

Contents. vii

Preface ix

Chapter I. Introduction 1

Chapter II. The Crisis in Iran. 9

Chapter III. Historical Development of Islam. . . . 19

    (A) Dawn of Islam and the Arab Society. 19
    (B) The Spread of Islam 25

Chapter IV. Political Concepts of Islam 29

    (A) Concept of State. 29
    (B) Concept of Leadership 51
    (C) The Concept of an Islamic Constitution. . . 58
    (D) Concept of Legislation. 70
    (E) Concept of an Islamic Community 83

Chapter V. Legal Concepts of Islam. 93

    (A) The Shariah: Genesis of Islamic Law
           and Jurisprudence 93
    (B) Concept of Law. 110
    (C) Evolution of Eternal Law. 123

Chapter VI. Islamic States. 131

    (A) Pakistan. 132
    (B) Turkey. 146
    (C) Afghanistan . . . . , . . 152
    (D) The Communist World and Iran. 156
    (E) United States and Islam 161

Table of Contents

page

Chapter VII. Political Economy of the Islamic State . 169

   (A) The Economic Structure of Islam 169
   (B) The Structure of Taxation in Islam. 178
   (C) The Structure of Land Tenure in Islam . . . 185

Chapter VIII. The Islamic State in the
                 International Field. 193

   (A) Islamic State and International Affairs . . 193
   (B) The Impact of the Islamic State on
         Western Nations. 211

Chapter IX. Islam and Other Religions 225

   (A) The Attitude of Islam Toward
         Other Religions. 225
   (B) Islam and Christianity. 241

Chapter X. The Islamic State in the 1980's 249

Important Reference Bibliography. 264

Notes 265

Index 285

Quran, Chronological Tabulation of Citations. 307

Preface

This endeavor is in the nature of an introductory book analyzing the fundamental concepts of State and Law in Islam. Originally, it was conceived as a collection of essays on Islamic Jurisprudence and Constitutional Law. This idea was prompted by the realization that no such text was available to students in the English language; most of the books on Islamic law currently available deal only with the civil and criminal laws of Islam. During 1978-79, I delivered many lectures in different places in the United States, and felt that even amongst the educated people there was an ostensible lack of knowledge and familiarity with the historical, cultural and religious fundamentals of Islam. Yet, events in Iran had suddenly created an abundant interest in knowing what was "an Islamic State," "Islamic Law," and why Muslims wanted to recreate an ideal Islamic State in the 20th Century. In order to be of greater benefit, I rewrote the text to answer such questions.

Accordingly, as this book now appears, it is designed to be of assistance not only to students of law and comparative jurisprudence, but to undergraduates studying religion, history, political science, and international affairs. I was able to change the format of the narrative, since, it will soon be found by the reader, that, State, Law, and Religion in Islam are simply different facets of the Faith. In order to give continuity to the narrative, various international events have been briefly examined; their comprehension will also indicate whether, today, realistically, we can speak of the creation of an ideal Islamic State in the context of the foreign policy considerations of the great powers. Nevertheless, essentially seven chapters are devoted to a study of jurisprudential and religious matters, and I would consider this book as dealing mainly with questions of comparative jurisprudence. With the aim of being. useful to a large variety of students and scholars, I have provided as much information as I could within the scope envisaged by me for this undertaking. The substantive chapters referred to above represent my examination of original sources. Furthermore, my opinions and interpretations will fall in the Sunni Schools of Islamic Law. As with most books of a legal character, I had to draw upon the same source materials which have been examined earlier. However, it is hoped that my approach and analysis will present a different expose on some important specific points. Since I have been mainly concerned with finding the "real" or "true" concept of State and Law in Islam, I had to resort to the two primary sources of Islamic Jurisprudence, the Quran and the Sunnah. My observations are thus primarily based on these and I have avoided, as far as possible, references to post ninth Century authors for supporting (or opposing) a particular view.

In keeping with my aim of reaching the non-Muslim scholar or student, I have been motivated to specifically project the stronger points necessary for an understanding of the Islamic traditions. I feel this subject has been ignored for too long and an exaggerated emphasis, if any, is better than none at all. But with this qualification, I must stress that this is not an evangelistic but an analytical work. At several places, indeed, my opinion is contrary to the one projected by the classical Sunni schools.

The views expressed are mine, and I, too, will bear any blame for errors and imperfections. There are several people who helped me in making this project reach the publication stage; I am thanking them separately in the Acknowledgements. In keeping with my aim for making this text useful to students of various disciplines, an elaborate Index has been prepared. The extent and nature of this compilation will show the diversity and extent of the points covered in this narrative.

Kings College, London
August 10, 1980

Farooq Hassan
Visiting Professor of Law &
Director, Insititute of Law
Policy Abroad (American Univ.)

CHAPTER I

Introduction

Throughout its history of about 1400 years, Islam has been one of the most cherished, while at the same time, one of the most misunderstood faiths. There are a number of reasons for this misunderstanding, two of which should be particularly mentioned. First, the advent of Islam also saw the political ascendency of its adherents. Unlike its two monotheistic sister faiths, Christianity and Judaism, Islam, within years of its inception, had become the religion of the rulers of most of the known civilizations. Whereas the Christians and the Jews had to undergo prolonged persecution at the hands of their non-believing rulers, Muslims, within years of the dawn of Islam, had travelled well beyond the deserts of Arabia in search of military and political conquests. These historical events had profound consequences, not the least important of which, as Russel points out, was the total misunderstanding of some fundamentals of Islam after the awakening of Europe following the Dark Ages.

This misunderstanding came mostly from the European writers for whom it was difficult to comprehend that a handful of "moors" had subjugated most areas which had enjoyed political and intellectual glory in the past. Myths multiplied prejudice and during the Middle Ages conceptually, in the eyes of the ordinary European, Muslims were not much different from pagans. The revival of Western civilization also saw a corresponding decline in the political might of the Muslims, and in the place of a highly centralized form of government in existence during the time of the first few Caliphs and the Umayyads, there came about the emergence of separate Islamic countries, notably Turkey in the West and Persia in the East. Turkey and Persia were really not countries, but mini-empires, for they still retained other nationalities and territories in their control. Be that as it may, the political might of the Muslims contributed vastly to the Western prejudice against their faith, Islam.

The second significant reason which led to this misunderstanding was that, unlike most other faiths, Islam was not the name of a personal or inner experience of an individual alone. With the exception of Islam, all other great faiths of mankind focused their attention on the relationship of man and God. Islam also does this, but goes beyond. It also seeks to govern and direct the everyday life of not only the individual, but of the community and of all Muslims, regardless of the elements of time, place or geography. Indeed, it is through its application to practical life in its totality that Islam is apt to become the subject of conflicts and controversies. It is not the task of the theologian alone, but also of jurists and political scientists, to remove the clouds of confusion and prejudice so that the real core of what the spirit of Islam implies can be reached.

Law in every society aims at the maintenance of social control. It is a system which is primarily established to protect the rights of individuals as well as of society. The legal system in every society has its own nature, character and scope. Similarly, Islam has its own legal system known as Fiqh. Islamic law is not purely legal in the strict sense of the term; rather it embraces all the spheres of life--ethical, religious, political and economic. It has its origin in the Divine Revelation. The Revelation determined the norms and basic concepts of Islamic Law and in many respects initiated a break with the customs and the tribal legal system of pre-Islamic Arabia.

It should be noted that there are certain basic differences between the purpose and scope of law in the modern sense and in the sense of the Quran. Laws in the modern sense are specific rules governing the social, economic, and political affairs of a nation made by a competent authority and enforced by the sanctions of a state. Rules of individual moral behaviours are not covered by modern laws, although they do exist in the form of customs, social manners and mores, and are enforced to some extent by morality squads or local police, and by the sheer force of public opinion. But when public opinion accepts certain immoral individual actions, moral laxity is bound to prevail with change in the very concept of morality as may be noticed in the case of most of the highly industrialized nations of Western Europe and North America.

The scope of Quranic laws encompasses rules of human conduct in all spheres of life, ensuring man's well-being in his mundane life as well as in the hereafter. The enforcement of Islamic laws contained in the Quran is the duty of an Islamic state. The application of the individual's rules of moral conduct is governed by two important factors, namely, the Muslim society's collective responsibility to observe Islamic teachings, and the individual's relationship with his Creator as well as with society. Muslim society is supposed to be under the obligation, according to the Quran, to enforce the application of rules of moral behavior as divine commandments. The Quran repeatedly appeals to human conscience to follow the teachings of the Revelation for its own welfare as well as for the well-being of fellow human beings. Thus, the Quran, by making the observance of the rules of the Shariah a matter of human conscience, has dignified the concept of law and the ethical values of its teachings which constitute the noblest and most perfect basis of universal laws.

Jurisprudence is the normative science of the principles of law which may concern itself with law in its various aspects, namely, with its traditional analysis, with its historical origin and development, and with its ideal character. The starting point of jurisprudence, in the history of the development of law, is a phase in which law is developed from its rudimentary form and begins to be systematically constructed. At this stage, questions about the authority of law-making, the source of law and the method of reasoning arise. Therefore, law is followed by jurisprudence.

The policy or political philosophy (a term that would include constitutional law) of Islam is quite simple, but terribly complicated when viewed from the angle of western political thought or constitutional theory. For example, in the development of Western democracies, it is now, happily, beyond dispute that people are supreme and that they can, through their representatives, pass any law they wish. This is, of course, only the theory, and many instances can be easily cited which contradict this theory. Still, the sanctity of this principle is undeniable. In an Islamic environment, however, although in practice the matter may be similarly decided, the fundamental theory of public sovereignty is quite different. It is equally undeniable in Islamic jurisprudence and polity that people, or their representatives, possess no sovereign power, which belongs only to God.

The people act only in a delegated capacity and, for example, are forbidden to travel against the written word of the Quran, which, coming from God, is unalterable for all times. I have, of course, only touched the tip of the problem. For example, the question of the legal sovereign in Western democracy is really not that simple. For example, who is sovereign in the U.S.A.? The Congress? In many ways yes, but it has to act under the constitution, and in fact is incapable of amending the constitution by itself. In the 19th century and later, analytical jurists attempted to "locate" the sovereign in a Federation and, to their chagrin, encountered monumental theoretical difficulties, some of which are still unsolved. However, in a Muslim environment, such constitutional difficulties are certainly less because of the a priori hypothesis that sovereignty belongs to God. Similar intricate legal questions are connected with doctrines such as that of separation of powers and "checks and balances" in Western political and constitutional thought; again, some of the fundamental postulates of Islam help us to keep outside the realm of such difficulties.

It is an irony of history that, while rejecting the institution of organized priesthood, Islam has often fallen into the hands of priests. In the term "priest," I do not include the great saints, mystics, traditionalists, thinkers and other men of piety who form a distinct class by themselves. For centuries ill-educated Mullahs have often monopolized the pulpit. On the one hand, the Mullah has woven into Islam a crazy network of fantasy and fanaticism. On the other, he has often tried to use it as an elastic cloak for political power and expediencies. The result in both cases is chaotic. Inside the mosque, the Mullah has made Islam into a fairy tale immersed in strange superstitutions and opposed to all forces of progress. Outside the mosque, he has often made it a pliant handmaid of power politics. Islam was not born to be a captive within the four walls of mosques and castles. It is a fallacy to make it subservient to the imperfections of transient values and expendiencies. Islam is too dynamic and too eternal to be imprisoned in the requirements of a passing age. As the intellect of man develops into new

4

dimensions with the discoveries of new avenues of knowledge and science, his understanding of life and religion is bound to grow in similar proportions. What is really changeable and flexible is the human intelligence and not the basic propositions of Islam. Just as there is no finality in any given period of time, therefore, it should be our endeavor to focus on Islam the searchlight of new knowledge and thought so that the scholar in his study, the scientist in his laboratory, the tiller of soil in his cornfield, and the little schoolgirl in her classroom may all be able to understand and derive guidance from their faith in accordance with their capacity and without any conflict with the spirit of their times.

It is the aim of this endeavor to acquaint the Western jurist, lawyer and political scientist with some aspects of the concepts of law and state in Islam. The idea of writing this book came when I began preparing for teaching a course in Islamic law at an American law school. Whereas a number of books had been published as texts for students in the United Kingdom and other countries, practically none of them referred to the constitutional and legal matters of Islamic thought discussed above. It is true that most of the origins can be found in original sources, but access to them is again limited, since they are mostly in Arabic.

Pari passu with my examination of this subject, most serious events in Iran began to make the subject matter of this narrative even more meaningful. Therefore, I found it necessary to examine the concept of the Islamic Republic in light of the Iranian crisis. In order to keep the length of the volume within reasonable proportions, the following scheme has been adopted. In the earlier chapters, I have traced the origin and evolution of Islamic history, policy, and law. It is also hoped that these introductory pages will be of assistance especially to the students attempting to understand for various kinds . of courses the fundamentals of Islam. The subsequent chapters address themselves to different aspects and problems. Some parts of the book are devoted toward comprehending fundamental issues such as the concept of state in Islam, what, if any, are the ingredients of an Islamic constitution, and the concept of democracy and democratic rule in Islam. In the domain of "Law" perhaps the most burning issue in Islamic

5

countries has been to understand the dynamics of "Ijtehad"--how far, with changes in time, can we change the content of the positive law of Islam? In this context, we have other chapters dealing with the problem of legislation in an Islamic state--a problem of no mean dimensions in view of the fundamental postulate that the Law of God and the boundaries of state authority having been already laid down in the Quran and the traditions of the Prophet, the people, as agents of that authority can only act within the bounds of that mandate.

The other parts of the book deal with multifarious questions: e.g., since Islam was the religion of a vast empire, what was the position of land tenure and land ownership; the problem of taxation and the concept of Zakat, the main form of tax, envisaged by Islamic dictates of philosophy, polity, and law; the position of labor and workers and what rights they had in an Islamic society; the civic and political position of an "individual" in a Muslim "society" and the "minimum requirements" wherein a Muslim can fulfill his obligations as a member of the community concerned. Towards the end, a number of chapters are devoted to the position and impact of Islamic law on other systems and religions--these pages will bring out the crucial cross-national and cross-cultural impact of Islam in our contemporary environment. Apart from this substantive examination of Islam from the point of view of philosophy, law, and religion, some parts of the narrative address themselves to the political events now taking place in the Middle East. Tumultuous developments in Iran and Afghanistan have been analyzed in the light of the foreign policy intents of the U.S. and U.S.S.R.

The narrative which follows is not a textbook, although, as I pointed out earlier, it could serve as a coursebook for many disciplines connected with Islamic learning. The paramount aim is to present the main aspects of Islam, its laws, and its notions of statehood to a wide variety of reading public. The word "state" as well as "law" in the title has been used, conceptually, widely, so as to discuss those aspects of a modern state, which, politically, socially, and philosophically are of importance today. Each chapter and topic is self-contained and will, therefore, cater to the interests of people of different fields. I have aimed at making all the chapters except the introductory

6

ones short and laconic so as to keep the concise nature of this book intact.

CHAPTER II

The Crisis in Iran

The most important single event which has brought into focus the importance of understanding Islam is the current political turmoil in Iran. Iran, as a country, has figured very prominently since the last twenty-five years or so in the international political strategies of the Western countries. Because Iran was consistently a supporter of the foreign policies of the noncommunist countries in that region, it gained in stature, especially because of the publicity it received at the hands of the mass media. The Shah of Iran, during the time he was there, was considered to be the most faithful of allies of the Western countries. The movement which ultimately led to his ouster in January of 1979 has been called the thrust toward the establishment of an Islamic republic by the Ayatollah Khomeini. In this context, it is said that Islamic Fundamentalism means that a modern state should be so constructed in its constitutional and political aspects as to correspond to the kind of state history saw in the days of the pristine glory of Islam, i.e., during the seventh and eighth centuries. The Fundamentalists are supposed to be those who believe that in order to have a successful and prosperous state of the Muslim community today, it is essential that that state correspond to, and that it should contain, the basic ingredients of the Islamic way of life. The quintessence of that kind of Islamic way of life is, in fact, the subject matter of this book. Before we turn to that substantive expose, it is necessary to briefly examine the current turmoil in Iran.

The situation in Iran presents, in fact, nominally, at least, a struggle between two persons. On the one hand, we have Mohammed Reza Pahlavi, the former Shah of Iran. On the other, we have the Ayatollah Khomeini. It is an examination of the philosophies they represent that will show the real heart of the crisis, an event which is perhaps the most serious threat to world peace since the Cuban Missile Crisis.[1] In many ways, it is even perhaps the most grave threat and the most serious upheaval to take place since the end of World War II. How this is so will become apparent when we see that the forces which are now emerging are those which represent some eight to

9

nine hundred million Muslims in this world and the pangs of conscience which are felt by many of them in trying to create a system of government in which at least they can have a democratic share in the affairs of the government--like, perhaps, one witnesses as a matter of course in Western countries. The vast majority of Muslims per se are not basically trying to recreate an Islamic state in the sense in which it could have existed centuries ago; in fact, the desire is to create a state in which, because of religious precepts, they are given, to some extent, a voice in the affairs of state. The basic trouble here is that, unlike most Western countries where one can change the government by the ballot, there is no corresponding politically institutionalized system in the vast majority of countries where Muslims live where one could bring about a change of government by this procedure. One of the most blatant violations of the so-called democratic principles was witnessed when in early 1977, elections were held in Pakistan by the then Prime Minister Bhutto, and, as it now appears,[2] they were so massively rigged that it led to a state of near civil war and Bhutto's ultimate downfall. In this political conflict, religion was used again and again as the platform from which to put political and constitutional matters before the general public. Principles of Islamic theology and law were used to hit at the authoritarian rule of the then Prime Minister who had turned Pakistan into a police state. The real desire was, therefore, not to have strictii sensu, a religious revival, but religion being used for bringing about political changes.

Mohammed Reza Pahlavi, the former Shah of Iran, became the Emperor of Iran on September 17, 1941, when he was not yet twenty-two years old. The facts which led to his becoming the Emperor of Iran are contemporary history. During the war, his father's sympathies were well known to be toward Germany. Therefore, during the course of the war, the Soviet and British governments, because of their vast military presence in this area, were able to engineer the exile of the father of the former Shah. It was, in a way, quite ironical that the two governments, namely, the British and the Soviet, which had engineered the exile of the old Shah, had turned to his own son, a Swiss-educated young man, to provide a continuous support for London and Moscow in the years to follow. In

10

his own memoires, Mohammed Reza Pahlavi wrote that his beginning of ascension to the throne was, therefore, somewhat humiliating, since he had been put on the throne by foreign powers. Over the passing of years, Mohammed Reza Pahlavi grew in stature, style, and arrogance. With the growing support of the United States, he became more and more powerful. His title was that of Shaihen-Shah, which means "the king of kings." As the king of kings, there was only one way in front of him, namely, to behave like an emperor, which he did. As an emperor in the eyes of most of his countrymen and in the view of most neutral observers, he was a total autocrat. As an autocrat, his regime came to symbolize the most brutal form of repression of any form of dissent which tended to show its face against his authoritarian policies. During the course of years, a number of charges were leveled against him, the more serious of which were torture, corruption, and national betrayal. A word may be said about the first of these charges. As we shall later see, the problem of a tyranical ruler is specifically dealt with in Islam.

In accordance with most of the voices which brought Ayatollah Khomeini into power, it was said that the Shah was a most brutal and authoritarian ruler. He was charged with not rebuilding Iran, but of building himself and indulging in a kind of corruption which made his own fortunes and those of his friends and family run into billions and billions of dollars. This charge is not only supported by innumerable voices which were heard at different places in different parts of the world during the revolution which ultimately threw out the former Shah, but by numerous examinations and evaluations done by internationally-recognized, nongovernmental organizations like Amnesty. In a way, Mohammed Reza Pahlavi admitted it; in an interview with a journalist, he is reported to have said, "Believe me, when three-quarters of a nation doesn't know how to read or write, you can provide for reforms only by the strictest authoritativeness. Otherwise, you get nowhere."[3] The horror stories abound in giving instances of beatings, maimings, and rapes. Recently, in the wake of the hostage situation, when Pope John Paul II's emissary went to see Khomeini, he was told by Khomeini that the hostages could not be freed because the former Shah had "roasted our young people in boiling pots, set them on fire, and cut off their limbs."[4] In

11

1975, Amnesty International reported, that torture of political prisoners during Savak's interrogation appeared to be a routine practice. On December 3, 1979, Senator Edward Kennedy, in a television interview in San Francisco, said that the Shah's regime was perhaps one of the "most repressive in reported history." There is no point in multiplying the instances of torture and brutality which ultimately are found to have flourished during his regime. It is sufficient to note that political torture and victimization were the paramount charges which ultimately brought the people out onto the streets against him. In the second week of November, following the taking of the American hostages in Tehran on November 4, 1979, the then Foreign Minister of Iran, Bani Sadr, told the U.N. Secretary-General, Kurt Waldheim, that at least 100,000 people had been killed by the Shah's military and security forces. This, in a way, is a conservative number, for previously it had been said that at least 300,000 had been killed over the last twenty-five years by the Shah's forces. Torture and repression, in many ways, are flouishing today in many parts of the world. The response that is produced by such governmental activity varies. However, examples of recent memory in Pakistan, Iran, and currently in Afghanistan, definitely show that if there are local leaders who can stand and remind people of their past Islamic values, then religion, in this case Islam, becomes a formidable force for any ruling regime to contend with. In an Islamic environment, any government which has even a nominal appearance of professing Islam will be hard pressed to deny the people who are bent on agitating, as it were, an Islamic platform. In other words, the autocratic regimes in a Muslim surrounding can deal with agitations of a civil or secular kind, but once religion is involved, it is altogether a different matter. To start with, the armed forces, which are defenders of unpopular regimes, do not find it easy to shoot at demonstrators who have raised the slogan of Islam. The genuineness of this call becomes irrelevant. Once, therefore, it is on the move (i.e., agitation), it is very difficult to be stopped.

The above discussion, in a way, represents philosophically the quintessence of the Iranian crisis. In simplistic terms, it shows the classical function of religion. Great religions, like great ideas of mankind, came either to give moral support and hope when all else seemed lost, or they appeared when laxity or opulence seemed to have eroded the most elementary rules of a community's ethical norms.

It is not the aim of this narrative to revert to instances from other religions to substantiate this point. How Islam came to get rid of sociological injustices of the kind described above will become clear as we go further in this book. It is this historical reminder, this precedent which Islam has set for its disciples, which is a constant threat to those in authority that there are limits to which they can deny their Muslim subjects what is granted to them by their belief.

Since this is basically a study of philosophy and jurisprudence, a survey of contemporary political events is not contemplated except when such events are necessary for making a point within the scope of the present narrative. However, a brief comment should be made. The fact that Muslims in many places have been unable to find their true historical identity is not because Islam has been deficient, but because Muslims are not really the Muslims they once were. Furthermore, once the might of the Muslims declined, their new rulers tried hard to deny them access to means of administrative, academic, and technological opportunities · and experience by realizing their erstwhile stature. In India in the late nineteenth Century, Sir Sayyed Ahmed Khan wrote extensively on such matters to bring home the truth to the Muslims of the vast Indian subcontinent, that if they were to find their former status, they had to keep in touch with contemporary realities. However, such reformists have usually had a difficult time because the ill-educated Mullah, who has direct access to the common man, neither understands this point nor has the intellectual capability to even attempt to comprehend such progressive measures. The immense difficulty which the present President, Bani Sadr, is experiencing at the hand of the so called "orthodox clergy" in Iran only too vividly demonstrates this point. However, the struggle between the reformist element, which is by structure and composition limited, and the ill-educated orthodoxy takes place once, albeit, there is an Islamic state (at least in name) in existence. Only then can there be an argument regarding the nature of "Islamization." Before the establishment of such a state of affairs, it is the extremist, the orthodox who holds the reigns, for in agitation, in revolution which stems from a religious cause, there cannot be any moderation. The fall of Bhutto in Pakistan in 1977 was the result of such agitation, done continuously by the ordinary Mullahs after all the known leaders were jailed as was the fate of the late Shah in Iran two years later. With these thoughts in mind, let us turn briefly to look at Khomeini, who led the movement against the former monarch while personally sitting thousands of miles away, again proving the force of Islam as a de facto phenomenon of terrific momentum.

In order to understand how such a firmly entrenched a person as the former monarch was overthrown from his seat of power, one has to understand the man who did it. This man was Ayatollah Ruholla Khomeini, a seventy-nine-year-old bearded, frail man whom apparently the analysts of the Central Intelligence Agency and the State Department had been unable to evaluate or even fathom before 1978. It is said that Khomeini was born on or around May 17, 1900, in the town of Khomeini, the town from which he, in fact, got his name. After reading the theology of Islam at an early age, he became a lecturer or a teacher at the Madresa Faizieh and talked about ethics, religion, and political science. It is reported that his discussions with his avid students went on until early mornings. As a man, he seems to be totally unruffled and unconcerned. Throughout his lectures in his later life, he preached one and only one thing, and that was that neither the industrialized West nor the godless society of the communists could save his poor people. He said one thing and one thing alone, which was that in order to get salvation here and hereafter, the Muslim Community from which he came had to go back to their own religion, and it was then that they could come up with solutions to the problems which were confronting them. Because of his increased insistence on the abolition of authoritarian rule, he was exiled by the former Shah in 1963. After his exile, he went to Turkey and Iraq. From there, he preached the independence of Iranians from a government which he said had been placed by foreign imperialist powers. Unlike the former Shah, Ayatollah Khomeini lived and still lives in a most humble manner. In Qum, he still stays mostly in a small courtyard sitting on a small Persian rug on the ground. With his eyes half closed, he looks at those who come to him. Once what is said to him is finished, he will either nod or utter a few sentences by which he acknowledges what has been said to him as being something with which he agrees or disagrees.

It is not the purpose of this chapter to examine the chronology of political events which shook Iran in the winter of 1978 and throughout 1979. Instead, the only aim of the present analysis is to emphasize the juridicial, political, and philosophical forces which were highlighted as a result of the Tehranian upheaval. The rise of Khomeini and the events leading to his success fully demonstrate the validity of the philosophical and juridical principle that if the government, no matter how well entrenched, becomes unpopular at the grass roots level, it will fall sooner or later. In a number of countries, we find that the popular will is suppressed by the force of those who are in authority. In some third world countries, these dictators have a common theme. They all say that they are trying to reform the society, that they are trying to infuse a new spirit of modernization, that they want, in fact, to uproot the primitive and ancient values of the society and replace them with something which they say is "modernization." When confronted with the charge that they are in this process denying the fundamental political and civil liberties of their people, their answers are almost invariably the same. They say that the people who are illiterate have no right to have their voices heard at the governmental level, and that all these helpless, poor people want is some sort of economic betterment. These dictators say that they are, in fact, trying to give these poor people economic betterment at the expense of, admittedly, a denial of their civil and political liberties. The call for the revival of Islamic Fundamentalism has been used in this context in some countries to change the existing governments which had otherwise left no avenues for bringing about constitutional changes by any normal and regular processes. In 1977, in Pakistan, Bhutto was alleged to have rigged the general elections. That allegation was subsequently proven in the proceedings which took place before the superior courts of that country. However, Bhutto's downfall was not brought about as a result of a political movement; the people who really overthrew him eventually were those who said that Bhutto had put Islam in danger. It was maintained that the movement which started against him was a movement for safeguarding the Islamic ideology. The opposition party was composed of nine members. Its main slogan against the Bhutto government was that they would usher in an era of Islamic revival of the classical times and thus give to the people a sense of their own inherent traditional values.

What has been said above emphasizes that in countries where Muslims live, Islam is capable of being used for bringing about political changes. That is exactly what happened in the case of Iran. For years, the former Shah of Iran ruled ruthlessly and was able to suppress whatever form of revolt that took place against him. There were many instances when partisans attempted to force the former Shah to bring about constitutional changes, changes in which the rule of the monarchy would have diminished but all of these efforts proved fruitless. During the time the Shah ruled in Iran there was a parliament called the Mujlis. However, the people in this body were only those who had the blessings of the former monarch with the result that, over the span of thirty-seven years of the Shah's rule, there were only a handful of people who could be genuinely called his political opponents. Even these political opponents had to blend their political opposition with a certain degree of moderation, for otherwise they would have met a fate which they would not have liked. Compared to these political campaigns, the movement which was launched by Ayatollah Khomeini was on a different plane. Its aim was the same, namely, the ouster of the Shah as an emperor. However, the vehicle used was not "political" or what one might call of a "civic kind." The movement started and continued throughout as one aimed at bringing about "Islamic revival" in that country. It was stressed that Islam did not recognize kings and monarchs, and that Islam had given the world a sense of the true essence of the democratic principles. This movement to force the eventual ouster of the Shah from his seat of power through the mechanism of religion proved decisive.[5]

It was "Islam" and the call for its defense which the police state of the former Shah could not withstand. It was, and still is, very difficult for a non-Muslim Westerner to comprehend that religious fervor can be so powerful an influence. Yet this is the basic truth. Today in most of the Third World countries, the strongest movement is that of "nationalism," and if the country happens to have an Islamic population, then Islam spearheads this thrust of nationalism.

With these foundations in mind, we now turn to examine the character of this overriding current of conviction, namely, the Islamic conception of State, which in the past, and still today, has proved capable of accomplishing the extraordinary.

CHAPTER III

Historical Development of Islam

(A) Dawn of Islam and the Arab Society

In order to appreciate and better comprehend the contents of the ensuing narrative, a brief reference to the origin and evolution of Islam, its laws and jurisprudence, is necessary. The century which elapsed between the promulgation of Corpus Juris of Justinian (529-34 A.D.) and the death of Prophet Mohammed in 632 A.D. witnessed prolonged periods of political instability leading to great human suffering. The two civilizations of Rome and Persia (Aushirwan the Great), existing at the time, had been brought to the verge of ruin. The empires of Rome and Persia had to maintain strong defenses against Slavs, Avars, Khazars, Bulgars (for the former), and Mongols (for the latter). Each, too, was torn by internal tyranny and by repeated civil wars; the struggle between them had alternately blazed and smoldered for centuries. Antioch (540 and 611 A.D.), Caesarea (512 A.D.), Damascus (614 A.D.), Jerusalem (614 A.D.), and Alexandria (615 A.D.) were among the cities sacked by the Persians. The countryside was equally laid waste. The Romans, when they had the chance, behaved in a similar manner. These wars were not mere affairs of armies. So far as sufferings of the civil population were concerned, almost no reconstruction followed the wars and there followed in abundance plague, pestilence, famine, conflagrations, and severe hardships.

At such a juncture in history, the Arabs in Jahiliyyah (the time of Ignorance) led an almost primitive way of life on their peninsula and in the adjacent areas. Various clans of the Semitic race inhabited the sandy deserts and, except for those who lived along the coastal regions, they were mostly nomadic in habits. The main cause of their primitive culture was the scarcity of water. They had neither agricultural resources nor any other natural wealth. Whatever was sparsely produced from the soil was always insufficient to support the inhabitants. With the exception of the population of the city of Mecca and of the greenish portions in the Yemen and Syria, the desert people of Arabia were in a state of chronic starvation.[6]

19

The Arab society was generally nomadic, divided into tribes, subtribes, and families. Parentage and pedigree were the important factors given special consideration. Every tribe had a leader and every ten persons were collectively under an Arif. The leader of every hundred individuals was called Qaid. The tribes had allegorical names such as Batan, Sha'b, and others after the names of other human (bodily) organs. The word "Arab" means comprehensive and eccentric, and a stranger visiting their territory was termed "Ajami" (the dumb) to show their superiority over him. Political consciousness was at a low ebb, and every individual was not much concerned with matters of general or social interest, though there were exceptions to the rule during wars when funds were contributed collectively as a defense against the common danger.[7]

As opposed to the Greeks' love for learning and wisdom and for astronomy by the ancient Egyptians, the Arabs, especially the Quraish tribes, were interested in art and literature. Poetry and its recitations was their daily routine in life. While there were among them fine poets and litterateurs, they had also constructed a crystal palace named the Dar-ul-Qawarir in Mecca. The people ate the flesh of lizards, scorpions, snakes, and dead animals. In times of famine, they drank the blood of camels and considered their flesh the finest of all. Immediate and sudden fights were common, and robbery, looting, and arson, along with wine drinking, gambling, and use of narcotics were ordinary features of the Arab society.[8]

The religious life and culture of the pagan Arabs was quite unlike that of the Greeks and Romans. In light of the pre-Islamic conditions mentioned in the Quran (ii. 200-201), it may be said that they had some kind of fear of the next world or the life hereafter. It was their custom to praise their forefathers at the conclusion of the Pilgrimage.

The tribes generally followed many religious practices. There were people who worshipped idols. Some believed in gods, others were atheists, and others followed the Christian and Jewish faiths. It is said that "the beginning of stone worship among the sons of Ishmael was when Mecca became too small for them and they wanted more room in the country. Everyone who left the town took with him a stone from the sacred area to do honor to it. Wherever they settled they set it up and walked round it as they went round the Kaba. This led them to worship what stones they pleased and those which made an impression on them. Thus, as generations passed, they forgot their primitive faith and adopted another religion for that of Abraham and Ishmael."[9] The idols they worshipped with different religious practices included al-Lat, al-Uzza, Wudd, and others.

The Bani (tribe) Ismail were divided into two troublesome and mischievous groups. One of them consisted of trouble-makers, offenders, and evildoers. They were predominated by elements opposed to social harmony and weak in religion. They were, by habit and nature, misconceived in understanding and were not able to fully grasp the benefits of social order. They neither followed any traditions nor did they acknowledge them. Instead, the remained in a susceptible and doubtful state, and, being malicious, were afraid of the common brotherhood which hated them. Such people were considered to have been disowned by religious groups and they remained degenerate. The other group consisted of those who had become careless and ignorant and had discarded religion. The Quaraish had a majority of them. However, it cannot be denied that at a particular stage of their religion, people came to believe in one God who was considered by them to be superior to all other idol-gods and whom they often called by the name of Allah. During the time of the Prophet of Islam, these Arabs acknowledged the messengership of the earlier prophets. They accepted and admitted the principle of rewards for good deeds, tadbir-i-manzil, and other rules of religion as they became prevalent or were promulgated by the religion of Islam.[10] Moreover, the people of the Book on the basis of prophecies contained in the Torah and the Injil (Bible), had spoken about the coming of the last prophet (Prophet Muhammad, one of the fundamental Islamic tenets). When Islam came, such prophecies were relied upon by its advocates. Amongst a diversity of religious practices, there were people who performed the Hajj, respected the differences of holy months, distinguished the solar and lunar years, and planned and performed their routine work according to good or bad omens.[11]

21

The tribal loyalty and hierarchy had a great impact on the economic system of the pagan Arabs. The system was simple; labor was despised and slavery was common. Transactions, like everything else in daily life, were based on tradition and custom. In the absence of any law, custom regulated barter, contracts and sales, and usurious transactions were common. Some of the contracts were matters of form as in other primitive societies, like deals concluded by touching the commodity, or by casting mantles or giving a cloth token or throwing pebbles in a certain place. Usually no distinction was made between ancestral and self-acquired property, and proprietorship was generally individual. The owner held absolute power of disposal of property which consisted of camels, cattle, and tents, as well as lands and houses in towns.[12]

The Arab historians record a system of taxation imposed on the people of Mecca for the purpose of feeding the incoming pilgrims for the Hajj, and the savings was considered to be the asset of the chief leader. It was called Rifadah. Historically it was initiated by one Qusayy and remained prevalent among his successors. Whenever any stranger died heirless, his property was given to the tax fund. During fairs and at other times of religious rituals, the import tax and 'ushr were other methods of taxation. A stranger coming to perform the pilgrimage at the Kabah was not allowed to go round it wearing his own clothes. He had to take rounds of the Kabah either completely naked or he had to purchase a dress from the people of Mecca. This system was called Harim.[13]

Administration and Justice. Fundamentally, it should be remembered that as far as the science of linguists was concerned, the pagan Arabs stood in need of an alphabet to codify and record their transactions. In this respect, apart from short "unwritten" vowels, their language had twenty-eight sounds or consonants in the dialect spoken at Mecca; there were different scripts in use in different parts of Arabia. It was shortly before Islam that some people of Kufah (previously Hirah) introduced the "secret" or the "luxury" of writing in Mecca. Their system of alphabet was maintained at the insistance of Islam in the long run. In these circumstances, reading was done at random or by guess-work, and trade deals in cities like Mecca were commonly transacted orally. All this had a natural effect on the systems of administration and justice, which were largely regulated on the basis of traditional customs and primitive methods prevalent in a similar set-up of societies.[14]

The inhabitants of the city, or the general population, were termed Jamaah (carried forward by the Prophet) in the pagan Arabia. Since the tribe and tribal loyalty were the cornerstone of their social life, the individuals belonged to the tribe by blood-kinship, by adoption, or by affiliation or allegiance. According to Rabbihi and others, Mecca was administered through several governmental posts which were held by tribal leaders as a family heritage. These posts were called Nadwah, Mashwarah, Qiyadah, Hijadah, Siqayah, Idafah, Nasi, Qubbah, Ayanah, Rifadah, Imratul-Bait, Amwal-ul-Mahajjarah, Isharah, Kukmah, Sifarah, Uqab, Liwa, and Halwan-ul-Nafar. It is also reported that there was a public assembly or Senate in Mecca which framed rules of conduct and enforced them against violators.[15] Qusayy, the descendant of the Quraish, administered the city of Mecca in a scientific manner. The administration under him was divided into five departments: (1) Dar-un-Nadway or the consultative assembly, ordinarily constituted of members of the ruling family and citizens of over forty years of age; (2) the Liwa or banner given to the army commander; (3) the Rafadah, a poor-rate levy for feeding pilgrims of annual congregation at Minde; (4) the Seqayah or administration; and (5) the Hijabah or custody of the keys of the Kabah. Umar b. Khalid represented the Quraish with other tribes, and Harith b. Qais had charge of the public treasury. The Diyat or magistracy belonged to Abdullah b. Uthman, later named Abu Bakr. The right of calling the people to arms belonged to Khalid b. Walid, and Uthman b. Talhah had the keys of the Kabah.[16] The execution of diplomatic relations with foreign powers was also performed, and it is narrated that it was the family of Uthman that was mainly concerned with this function. In the absence of a central authority (a sovereign), during a war, lots were, as a custom, cast, and the person so appointed from among the tribal chiefs led the battle, irrespective of his age. The leader of the fighting army was given one-fourth of the war booty, and the rest was distributed among the soldiers.[17]

In the field of law, the word Hakam connotated the functions both of an assembly of elders and the government. Thus, it meant to govern and also to adjudicate disputes. The chief of each tribe was responsible to decide individual disputes and, in the case of intertribal disputes, an arbitrator was appointed who had to be non-partisan. Moreover, in the absence of any organized system of judicial machinery, it was a custom to take assistance of volunteers called Hilf-ul-Fudul who took into consideration the rights of the victims and helped them in getting redress.[18]

In a tribal set-up, offenses were generally ascribed to a tribe as a whole, and if a member of one tribe killed or wounded a member of another tribe, the injured tribe had the right to demand the surrender of the offender; failing surrender, retaliation followed or an alternative compensation was paid. The disputes were resolved by proofs, and oaths formed an important method in the procedural settlement of claims. Often the parties went to a diviner whose decision was abided by. The principal form of punishment for crimes against persons was retaliation commutable by payment of blood-money. Cutting off the hands of a thief or blackening the face of an adulteror were the other prevalent modes of punishment. Among the Jews, the revenge theory of punishment as set in the Torah was inflicted; amongst others,[19] the custom of the tribe was the determining factor.

The family structure was weak, and the status of the female was inferior. A man was father of all the children of the women of whom he had purchased the right to have offspring to be reckoned as his own kin. A usage known as Nikah al-Isti-badah provided that if a man desired a goodly seed, he might call upon his wife to cohabit with another man till she became pregnant by him. The Hajin or the son of an Ajamiyyah, a non-Arab woman, did not inherit, though the son of a captive did. Marriage took different forms, and prostitution and temporary marriages were in vogue. The consent of the females had no value. Without any ceiling on the number of wives, there was frequent and complete freedom of divorce with retaking of the divorced wife.[20]

The females were considered to be an integral part of the estate of the husband or guardian. The low economic conditions and poverty led to the custom of burying female infants at their birth. It is also reported, that devolution of widows went to the sons as a patrimony. The tribal principles led to the exclusion of the weaker relatives from inheritance and, thus, women and infants and cognates were denied succession rights. The practice of adoption was a mode of affiliation. This affiliation was in addition to the affiliation of a prostitute's child ascribed by her to one of the summoned sexual enjoyers.[21]

The pagan Arabs were possessed of group feeling and overbearing pride. They restricted themselves to such amount of food, clothing, and mode of dwelling as was just necessary for them; they were not concerned with what was beyond their necessity. They used tents of hair and wool, or houses of wood or of clay and stone, which were not elaborately furnished. The purpose was to have shade and shelter which they also took in caverns and caves. They were least willing to subordinate themselves to each other; they were rude, proud, ambitious, and eager to be leaders. All these features were to be reformed by one thing only, viz. religion, which had a great restraining influence upon their qualities of arrogance and jealousy. It made them subordinate themselves and, thus, unite in a great universal brotherhood. This was achieved by the common religion, the last system of faith--Islam.[22]

(B) The Spread of Islam

It is only after we have seen the primitive nature of the Arab society at the dawn of Islam that we can appreciate the positive role of Islam in these poor and nomadic people. Within a few years of the advent of Islam, there not only arose a powerful state in Arabia, but also an entity which possessed an efficient system of government, a system of administration of justice the likes of which the world had never seen since the days of classical Roman Law, and an army which surpassed the discipline and dedication of any which ever existed before it. In this point lies the main difference between the three major monotheistic faiths: Judaism, Christianity, and Islam. Whereas Judaism and Christianity were the faiths of the persecuted for centuries, Islam became the faith of the state itself, and soon of a vast Empire. Whereas the believers of Christianity and Judaism had to hide from their pagan rulers, the Muslims were ruled by Muslims. Herein also lies the difference between the Islamic outlook towards religion and state and the attitude of other religions mentioned above. Whereas in Judaism and Christianity the Church was in the hands of the priests and existed separately from the secular state which was in the hands of Pharaohs and Ceasars, in Islam there was no such bifurcation; religion and state were one, the religious precepts laying down the rules of conduct for both the rulers and the ruled. The closest example is provided by a fiction of the British Constitutional Law in which, even today, the sovereign is both the head of the state and the defender of the faith. The Caliphs of Islam also had this dual capacity. It was their duty and business to defend the faith and the state. Historically, as Hitti states, Islam was the third of the monotheistic faiths and also the youngest one, but, because of its history, which was entirely on account of the fervor of those who believed in it, its attitude toward such things as politics and statecraft were totally different from those of its older sister faiths.

The fundamental source for the Muslim in his conduct regarding personal affairs, his social affairs, his civic and political affairs, and his spiritual affairs, is the Quran. The Muslims believe it to be the last of the revealed books. Professor Phillip Hitti, one of the few Western scholars on Islam, and, at one time, Professor Emeritus of Semitic Studies at Princeton maintains that the Quran is easily the most widely read book ever written and one which practically every Muslim, whatever his ethnic and linguistic background, invariably reads in Arabic, in the same form in which it is believed to have been revealed to the prophet. It has been translated into almost every language. The reading of the Quran in Arabic has the support of the prophet himself. The Quran says that it was preceded by other revealed books, i.e., the gospel for the Jews and the Christians, but because of time and lack of authentic recording, the original words were lost and replaced by the words of different men, admittedly saints and disciples, but still not the words used by God. To keep the purity of the Quran intact, the prophet encouraged the believers to learn the text by heart. A person who does so is called a "hafiz." In fact, every mark of punctuation, and there are many in Arabic, is memorized, as are the total number of verses (6,236), words (77,934), and even letters (323,621).[23]

Mohammad, the prophet of Islam, was born in 571 A.D. in the tribe of Qurayash at Mecca. He was so respected for his integrity that he was called "Al-Amin,"[24] the faithful. His father died before he was born and his mother when he was six. He was, therefore, brought up by his grandfather, Abd-al-Muttalib, and later his uncle, Abu-Talib. He married a widow at the age of twenty-five, a lady who was fifteen years his senior. It is reported that he was always contemplative and dissatisfied with what he saw around him. Then, one night in A.D. 610, he heard a voice command him to a cave, Ghar-a-Hira, where God first spoke to him: "Recite thou in the name of the Lord who created . . ." (Quran 96:15). This was his first revelation, and this night came to be called the "night of power" (laylat al-qadr). His message was as prophetic as any of the Hebrew prophets, but one which soon enough changed the history of the world. It was his call to believe in one God which kept monotheism alive during the centuries when modern Europe stood in what is described as the period of the "dark ages."

It is not the purpose here to examine the details of the Arab history of that time. Suffice it to say that initially the Prophet Mohammad had the greatest difficulty in having people believe in one God. His earliest converts were from the poor. It was, perhaps, with the conversion of Umar, son of Khattab, and given the title of "Farooq," the truthful, that the impact of Islam began to be felt. Against very heavy odds, a handful of Muslims began to assert themselves, and within the life of the prophet Mohammad, the Islamic State was created. The initial establishment took place at Medina, not Mecca, though that soon followed. Thus, a group of a few thousand converts laid the foundation of not only a new faith, or of a new form of state and government, but of a kind of Pax Islamica, which had for its adherents a total outlook towards life. The ensuing pages will be devoted to examining the characteristics of this new mode of life.

27

One last word may be said in parentheses before we turn to this detailed jurisprudential, philosophical, and political analysis. As long as Mohammad lived, in tune and conformity with the postulates of Islam, the faith he brought, religion, politics and state were one. He was the spiritual as well as the temporal leader. However, spiritual leadership was qualified in the sense that Islam recognizes neither any priestly class nor any intermediary between man and God, and the prophet himself is only considered a mortal man like any other man. Thus, he was a spiritual leader in the sense that his own actions were a source of interpretation of God's will. His actions were thus binding in the sense that in common law the earlier decisions of the higher courts are binding. Thus, the actions of the prophet, called "traditions" (hadith), have a special significance in Islamic law. His actions are the second source of this law after the Quran. Once he passed away, the question was who was to succeed him in all but the spiritual sense. The head of the Islamic state was to be the Khalifah (Caliph), and he had to be elected. This was decided by Mohammad himself, who proclaimed that the leadership of the Muslim community, the Umma, was by consensus, and kinship and dynasty had no relevance. Thus, Islam, in a practical way, laid the foundations of a representative or elected government. Many early believers thought that Mohammad should have been succeeded by Ali, his closest relative and son-in-law. But that was not to be. Indeed, those who believed in Ali's rights became the first and the only major sect in Islam. They are now known as the Shiates, and today most of them are to be found in Iran. The great majority of the Muslims did not believe in this right of kinship. They constitute the vast majority of Muslims and are called Sunnis. The prophet was, thus, succeeded by Abu Bakr in 632 A.D. as the first Caliph of Islam. He was followed by Umar, 634 to 644, Uthman, 644 to 654, and finally by the fourth Caliph, Ali (the prophet's son-in-law) from 656 to 661. These first four Caliphs are called the "rashdin," or the righteous Caliphs. The Islamic State was established during this time. Umar, the second Caliph, is particularly responsible for the early expansion and conquest for the Islamic State.

CHAPTER IV

Political Concepts of Islam

(A) Concept of State

Before examining and analyzing the legal concept of the State in Islam, we should first briefly examine the problem from the view of a Western legal philosopher. However, which "one" is exactly "Western" is unclear. In the course of the last two hundred years, there have emerged a number of schools of jurisprudence, most of which take different views of a State. Their basic postulates are different and so are the theories which have been built on these foundations. Under the powerful influence of Bentham (1748-1832), there emerged the analytical or imperative school of which Austin became the most famous. On the European Continent, there emerged the historical school under Hegel which saw law differently, and so its conception of State was basically different from that of the positive theorists like Bentham and Austin. Along with these two major philosophies, there had always existed, in one form or another, the school of Natural Law. Within these three different and sometimes conflicting prognostications, there also arose a number of other schools to which we need not refer. However, their emergence does signify certain inadequacies of the major schools.

There are three ways of constructing a theory of the State. We may examine the actual functioning of the State (as in political science), the ideal of what a State ought to be (as in political philosophy), or the theoretical basis of the lawyer's approach to the State. The last method, the so-called juristic theory of the State, is not meant to present a complete picture of the actual working of a State, but rather the theoretical conceptions around which the doctrines of the law are built. In particular, the juristic theory of the State deals with the relationship of law and the State. To put the same problem in another way it asks the question whether public law is really law. Can a subject have legal rights against the State?

There are three main juristic theories of the relationship between the State and the law which can tersely be expressed thus: the State is superior to and creates law; law precedes the State and binds it when it comes into existence; law and the State are the same thing looked at from different points of view.[25]

The first theory is illustrated by the work of Austin, who defines law as the command of the sovereign. But when Austin attempts to define sovereignty and the State, he adopts a practical test. First, there must be a political society of "considerable" numbers and a superior in that society who is habitually obeyed by the bulk of the members of that community and who is not in the habit of obedience to another superior.[26] Within this community, the superior has a sovereign power to lay down the law. The relation between subject and sovereign is, therefore, one of power. The sovereign can have no legal rights against his subjects nor can he be bound by legal duties, for a legal relationship can exist between two parties only when there is above them a sovereign who will enforce the rule of law. Hence, constitutional law must be divided into two parts. As against the sovereign body as a whole, constitutional law is mere positive morality enforced by moral sanctions alone, but it may be regarded as positive law in so far as it binds particular members of the sovereign body.[27] Collectively considered, the sovereign is above the law, but a member of the House of Commons is individually bound by an Act of British Parliament though he is a member of the body which creates the law. If the sovereign consists of only one person, constitutional law is only positive morality.

As a postulate to explain the working of a legal order, the concept of sovereignty has its uses. However, the term is used with so many conflicting meanings and so easily stirs the emotions that it is better for jurisprudence to avoid its use. The "initial premise," as used by some writers, is a better and more neutral phrase: there is no need for jursiprudence to postulate sovereignty in the sense of power that is unlimited, eliminable, and indivisible. These qualities are not a priori, necessary, but depend only on particular political theories, as is demonstrated by a study of the functioning of actual states. The basis of law is legal order, the presuppositions of which are accepted by the community as determining the methods by which law is to be created, and those presuppositions will vary from one community to another.

This legal conception of the initial hypothesis does not pretend to explain the real nature of politics or the art of government.

The theory of sovereignty has been of service as a formal theory, but some writers go farther and seek to justify sovereignty as a moral necessity instead of as a convenient hypothesis. For example, Hegelianism treats the State as a supreme moral end and being a value in itself, it is not bound[28] by the rules of ethics that apply to individual men. Only in the State can man attain true self-realization; and, since the will of the State represents the real will of the individuals, the State, thus, includes the entire hierarchy of social life. This theory "grants to state absolutism the virtue of moral truth."[29] "The State is the divine idea as it exists on earth."[30] This doctrine has been carried farther by the Nazi and Fascist conceptions which regard law as but the will of the leader. (This, at least theoretically, is impossible in an Islamic State.) To attempt to bind the State (these engaging theorists tell us) is to commit treason at the bidding of out-moded liberal ideas, which, striving to protect the liberty of the subject, strike at the welfare of all. This doctrine is more understandable (if less palatable) when we see that totalitarian States, Islamic or otherwise, use this concept while defending the denial of legal human rights to all citizens.

The above analysis pinpoints the crucial importance of the Austinian school in contemporary affairs, particularly with its emphasis on sovereignty--supreme power in the State's executive as a juridical unity. As we shall later see, this contrasts fundamentally with Islamic jurisprudence.

The second theory regards law as more fundamental than, and as anterior to, the State. Hence, law may bind the State. Some turn to the medieval solution of natural law--the sovereign has absolute power over positive law but is bound by ius naturale. (In theory, close to the Islamic conception of divine origin of most Islamic laws.) In the Middle Ages, even a royal justice such as Bracton could[31] "fearlessly proclaim" that the king was bound by law. We cannot impose on the Middle Ages an Hegelian theory of the State, for the Church still exercised over the State an undefined control. Moreover, the baronage claimed vague rights of judging the king in his own court, although there were no effective means of bringing this about save by revolution. Modern constitutional theories may attempt to bind the government by the creation of a higher law which can be amended only by referendum. Declarations of rights may be inserted in constitutions to place certain interests beyond the reach of arbitrary interference by chance majorities.[32]

Ihering considered that law in the full sense was achieved only when it bound both rule and ruled. (In practical terms, this is what is aimed by Islamic law.) But as Ihering regards the State as the maker of law, we may well ask how the creator may be bound by the creature of his fancy. Ihering solved the problem by what is really a political argument: law is the intelligent policy of power, and it is easier to govern if the State voluntarily submits to the law it has created. This is merely an argument of expendiency--we can do everything with bayonets but sit on them--and, while it undoubtedly contains much truth, it is of little service to juristic theory.

In English writing, the same problem has been discussed under the heading of the rule of law. Dicey found three meanings in this phrase: firstly, the supremacy of regular law over arbitrary power; secondly, equality before the law in the sense that officials must obey it and are subject to the jurisdiction of the ordinary courts; thirdly, the fact that the law of the constitution is the result of decisions[33] of the courts as to the rights of private individuals. These are undoubtedly the characteristics of the English legal system, but they result from the political struggles of the past and are not logical deductions from a rule of law.[34] Law may have a varying content; it may protect the subject against despotism or give the most ruthless power to a tyrant. It is not enough for the democrat to demand a rule of law--everything depends on the nature of that law. Every legal order which functions has a rule of law. This applies to a Nazi state as well as a democracy. What democratic liberals desire is that the powers of government should be restrained so as to protect as far as possible the "personal freedoms." This is a noble ideal,[35] but not one that is necessarily secured by a rule of law.

32

There is, however, a growing movement among Western nations and others influenced by them, to achieve more than that and attach a more specific and demanding meaning to the phrase "rule of law." The nineteenth-century movements for constitutional reform, based in the main on eighteenth-century thinking, did not proceed on any Dician kind of notions about the rule of law. They sought to fetter governmental powers by laws which would protect individual human values. It is seen today that economic questions must be solved before such ideas can be fully implemented, that men must eat before they can enjoy freedom from tyranny.[36] Further, there has been a growing school of thought, often based on revived "natural law" notions, which seeks to find in the concept of law itself fundamental aspects requiring limits to be placed upon the exercise of power by governments of whatever kind.[37]

Kelsen illustrates the third type of theory that law and the State are really the same. The State is only the legal order looked at from another point of view. Human individuals alone can act, and legal force is imputed to their behavior only if it is in accordance with a rule of law. Just as men personified world forces and created a deity, so the jurist has personified the hierarchy of norms and created a State.[38] When we think of the abstract rules, we speak of the law; when we consider the institutions which those rules create, we speak of the State. But the practical importance of Kelsen's approach is that he emphasizes that law is a more fundamental notion than that of the State. While it is true that law cannot exist without a legal order, that order may take forms other than that of the State. Hence, the theory is wider and, therefore, more acceptable than that of Austin. A legal order may be created in the international sphere even though no super-state is set up. His emphasis on the "sanctity of law" is really close to Islamic notions as will become clear by the rest of the narrative.

The three theories relating to the relationship of law and the State have now been discussed. Logically, each may be defended, but if we examine actual States, we discover that no one solution will apply to all. Just as law may serve many purposes[39] so the relationship between law and the State may vary. It is possible to conceive of a State

33

which recognizes a fundamental law which is beyond the power of any authority to alter. Such a legal order might prove impracticable as conditions change, but an unalterable fundamental law is not beyond the bounds of imagination. At the other extreme, a sovereign parliament may have no limits whatever on its exercise of legislative powers. This is typified by the British Parliament.

What are the essential marks of the State? Salmond defined the State as an association of human beings established for the attainment of human ends, two of which are primary and essential--war and the administration of justice. These two purposes Salmond regarded as partaking of the same quality--the maintenance of right by the exercise of force. Hence, he regarded a State as a society organized so as to use force to maintain peace and justice within a given territory.[40]

In the foregoing narrative, we have seen the quintessence of the major approaches amongst the Western thinkers on the philosophy of State. That some of the greatest minds have come up with different explanations about the same subject and phenomenon shows the diversity and delicate nature of the juristic problem now being examined.

However, with these issues before us (the closeness, or otherwise, of some of them to Islamic notions was noted in parentheses), we can now move on to examine this matter from the point of view of Islamic law. By unanimous consent, political scientists and jurists agree that a State has four basic ingredients. For example, Oppenheim says that to constitute a State, four elements are essential: (1) territory, (2) population, (3) organization, and (4) sovereignty. With regard to the fourth element, the Islamic State differs fundamentally from all other States and in that occupies a unique position. Under Islamic law, sovereignty belongs to God and, as such, a State possesses no sovereignty. But it is not here that the matter ends. Since there is no sovereignty, the organs of the State possess no supreme power and, in fact, have to act within the limits set by God. Furthermore, the emphasis on defined "territoriality" loses some significance when compared to the Western or communist conceptions of State.

The Islamic State was founded by the Prophet Mohammed in the seventh century of Christian era and continued with full vigour during the Khulfa-i-Rashidin (first four Caliphs) period. Soon enough, however, its complexion changed owing to certain variations in its goals. However, certain basic ideals like equality, liberty, justice, the foundations of Islamic policy, and even toleration remained in force to a certain degree in the post-Rashidin period. But, owing to the existence of institutions like monarchy and feudalism, the basic notions of the Islamic State could not find a foot-hold in European countries, although a very energetic and glorious Islamic State was in existence in Spain for several centuries. The abolition of the institutions of monarchy and feudalism in the wake of the French Revolution, however, paved the way for the reception of some of these ideals into Europe.

The most profound change which was brought in the realm of philosophy was the ending of kingship and the legal theories which were associated with the institutions of monarchy. Indeed, the election of the first three Caliphs, Abu Bakr, Omar, and Usman, over and before Ali, the son-in-law of the Prophet, was the greatest testimony of the manifestation of the democratic principle of Islam. It was the most elegant testimony of the basic foundations of Islam that neither were there any kings, nor was there spiritual superiority of a family to the institution of hereditary right to caliphate, or a throne (the Shiate schools take a contrary view).

It is true that these postulates were not always adhered to in the centuries which followed. But, still within the realm of institutionalized government, principles of highest ideal value had been set in the life and time of the Prophet and the Khulif-a-Rashidin, all of whom, incidentally, had been the companions of the Prophet.

As already stated, in an Islamic State sovereignty belongs to God. This does not, however, mean that in an Islamic State all the laws are to be made by God himself or that the Quran provides all possible positive laws and that the people have nothing to do with sovereign functions. On the other hand, all the laws in an Islamic State are to be made by the people's representatives in light of the Quranic fundamentals. Thus, in an Islamic State, the

35

people enjoy a partial and restricted right of law-making. They cannot, of course, make any law which runs contrary to the clear Quranic injunctions meant for universal application. In this sense, the people who make the laws are not really law-makers. Nor are they above the law; they are only the executors of law and, as such, they stand at par with ordinary citizens.

The original source from which all principles and ordinances of Islam are drawn is the Holy Book, called al-Quran. According to Muslim belief, the Quran is a divinely revealed book and as such, all positive laws given therein have superiority over man-made laws. Taking into consideration the divine origin of the Quran and the purity of its text, one must regard it as the real foundation on which rests the whole super-structure of Islam. Furthermore, being the absolute and final authority in every discussion relating to the principles and laws of Islam, the Quran is the sole source from which all the teachings and practices of Islam are drawn.

There are two kinds of verses in the Quran, namely, decisive and allegorical, the latter being those which are capable of different interpretations. The decisive verses are the basis of the Book and contain the fundamental principles of religion. So, whatever may be the differences of interpretation over allegorical verses, the fundamentals of religion are not affected by them.

The Sunna or Hadith is the second and undoubtedly a secondary source from which Islamic laws are drawn. Sunna literally means a way, rule, or manner of acting. In its original sense, therefore, Sunna indicates the doings and Hadith the sayings of the Prophet. In effect, however, both cover the same ground and are applicable to his actions, practices, and sayings, Hadith being the narration and record of the Sunna but containing, in addition, various prophetical and historical elements of Islam. As the Quran generally deals with the broad principles or essentials of Islam, the details are generally considered to be supplied by the Sunna of the Prophet. Even for the two most important religious institutions of Islam, viz., prayer and Zakat, no details are to be found in the Quran. The details about these injunctions were supplied only by the practice of the Prophet. These are but two examples, but since Islam covered the whole sphere of human activities, hundreds of points had to be explained by the Prophet by example in word and deed. The explanations or decisions given by the Prophet are contained in various compilations, notably that of Bokhari and Muslim. The persons who embraced Islam thus stood in need of both the Quran and the Sunna. And, it was because the Sunna occupied such a tremendous, though a secondary, place in the super-structure of Islam that the early Muslims devoted themselves assiduously and energetically to collecting all possible traditions with every care that was humanly possible. The compilations referred to above are then very important for understanding the various interpretations of God's laws.

In judging whether a certain Hadith was spurious or genuine, the collectors not only made a thorough investigation regarding the trustworthiness of the transmitters but also applied other tests for its acceptance. No Hadith was, however, to be accepted if it was opposed to or was against the plain teachings of the Quran.

Ijtihad (exercise of judgment) is a subsidiary source from which the laws are drawn. The word itself is derived from the root Jahad, which means exerting oneself to the utmost or to the best of one's ability. Ijtihad, which literally conveys the same significance, is technically applicable to a lawyer's exerting his mental faculties to the utmost for purposes of solving difficult legal problems.

Reasoning or the exercise of judgment, in theological as well as in legal matters, plays an important part in Islam. The Quran does recognize revelation as a source of knowledge higher than reason, but it also admits that the truth of the principles established by revelation may be judged by reasoning. In doing so, it repeatedly appeals to reason and denounces those who do not use their reasoning faculty. It also recognizes the necessity of the exercise of judgment in the formulation of a decision. It was for this reason that, for example, Iqbal, one of the foremost Muslim thinkers of the twentieth century, particularly stressed that modern religion could not survive on dogma alone. In his "Reconstruction of religious thoughts in Islam," following Kant, he decried

37

the attempt by Fundamentalists to refer to the letter rather than the spirit of Islamic teachings and learning.

Ijtihad, or the exercise of judgment, is expressly recognized in the Hadith as the means by which a decision may be arrived at when there is no direction in the Quran or the Hadith. The following Hadith is regarded as the basis of Ijtihad in Islam. On being appointed Governor of Yemen, Muadh Bin Jabal was asked by the Prophet as to the rule by which he would adjudicate. He replied "by the law of the Quran." "But if you do not find any direction in the Quran, how would you decide," asked the Prophet. He replied, "I will apply the Hadith, i.c., Sunna." "But if you don't find any guidance in the Sunnah as well?" he was again asked. "I will then exercise my judgment and act on that," came the reply. The Prophet raised his hands and said, "Praise be to Allah who guides His Messenger as He pleases."[41] This Hadith shows not only that the Prophet approved of the exercise of judgment, but also that his companions were well aware of the principles and that Ijtihad was freely resorted to by his followers, when necessary, even in the Prophet's lifetime.

A similar source of Islamic law is Ijma. The word Ijma is derived from Jama which means collecting or gathering together. Ijma carries the double significance of composing and settling a thing which has been unsettled and, hence, determining and resolving an affair and agreeing or uniting in opinion. In the terminology of the Muslim Jurists, Ijma means a consensus of opinion of the Mujtahids, or an agreement of Muslim Jurists, of a particular age on a point of law. Ijma, however, is not a major source of law; it is really Ijtihad on a wider basis, and like Ijtihad, it is always open to revision.

In the second century of the Hijra arose the famous schools of the great jurists who codified the Islamic law according to the needs of the time. This codification became the chief basis of Islamic law of the future. However, owing to the degeneration that started in the Muslim society (in consequence of which it could not produce jurists of the calibre of the famous former Imams), the community as a whole began to believe that the codification, as done by those great Imams, was final, and that there was no scope for further Ijtihad. Whatever may be the justification, this belief was nevertheless contrary to the very teachings of Islam. On this point the author takes a contrary view to the one taken by some of the so-called Fundamentalists, particularly exemplified by the ordinary Mullah classes.

Since the Islamic laws are to be derived from the Quran which is regarded as a universal guide for all time, it is inevitable that Ijtihad should continue to be exercised. It is, therefore, a mistake to suppose that the door of Ijtihad was closed after the earliest four Jurists who expounded the fundamentals of Islamic law. The four Jurists after whom the four schools of law are based are Abu Hanifa, Hambal, Malik, and Shafi. In the ensuing narrative, in order to present a simple and tabulated picture, various characteristics of an Islamic State have been gathered from a reading and analysis of the sources discussed above. It is hoped that by this technique, a very elaborate and complicated subject can be easily comprehended. It has already been shown that the Quran and the Hadith have directions to the effect that the Muslim world should continue to exercise its judgment in making laws for itself. Since the ultimate test of the correctness of Hadith is the Quran itself, the conclusion is evident that Islam allows independence of thought, subject only to the requirement that the principles laid down in the Quran are not contravened. A fortiori, the expositions of the four classical schools, are entitled to the highest weight and respect but it is submitted that it is possible to offer new interpretations for new situations, or to modify existing ones in light of contemporary circumstances by those who are learned in the law.

It will, thus, be seen that the Muslim community possesses the partial and restricted right of law-making. It is, thus, a restriction imposed upon the framers of law in an Islamic State which has created a world of difference between this State and all other States.

The quintessence of the Quranic Principles is that they, being of divine origin, are equally applicable to the whole of mankind, irrespective of a person's status, position, color, race, sex, language, or nationality. If a thing is declared legal, it is legal for all in any shape or form.

There are to be no exceptions; and even if they are allowed, they are allowed for all under certain conditions and circumstances. We can, therefore, conclude that owing to the restricted right of legislation, nobody is regarded as a "legislator" (in the modern sense of the word) in an Islamic State. The authority of authorities in such a State can only be regarded as that of executors of law, basically made by God.

CHARACTERISTICS OF AN ISLAMIC STATE

(A) Fraternity

An Islamic State to begin with, must encourage social harmony. In accordance with the famous verse of the Quran (XLIX: 10), "The believers are but a single brotherhood," the first characteristic of the Islamic State is fraternity. This verse asserts that Muslims, whatever their country, race, color, or language, are members of a single brotherhood. Among the believers, white and black, rich and poor, master and servant, Arab and non-Arab, all stand together and enjoy equal rights and bear equal responsibilities in running the State. The force of Islamic brotherhood is such that even blood relationship counts for nothing. A non-believer, thus, even if connected with a believer by blood ties, falls into a totally different category.

Regarding the division of the believers into nations and tribes, the Quran says: "And we made you into nations and tribes, that ye may recognize each other. Verily the most honoured of you with Allah is he who is the most righteous of you" (XLIX: 13). This verse emphasizes that all regional and tribal distinctions are merely of a geographical nature. Islamic attitude towards international law is, therefore, very different from the one taken by Western writers. Neither can they form the basis for the classification of rights of a superior nature of one tribe or nationality over other tribes or groups. Among the believers, if any distinction is to be made at all, it should be on the basis of Taqwa or piety. The flowering of Islamic fraternity perhaps reached its climax on the occasion of Hijrat when the Prophet knitted one Muhajir and one Ansari together in the brotherhood of Islam and they lived under the same roof as brothers.

40

(B) Equality

The Islamic notion of equality is unique and realistic. It distinguishes legal equality from an abstract or hypothetical norm proclaiming a "real" equality; for at best, such an abstraction is a hope, at worst, hypocrisy. It is, therefore, a mistaken notion that Islam sanctions absolute equality among its votaries. Absolute equality is denied by nature as no two persons are equal in every respect. Any amount of effort on the part of a State to equalize the mental faculties or even physical gifts of different persons will prove fruitless.[42] Consequently, a well-known verse of the Quran says: "Verily we have given preference to some over others." However, the question then arises: What is the concept of equality in Islam? It means equality before law and in matters of civic rights and obligations to the State. Above all, it means affording of equal opportunities to all, irrespective of caste, color, race, sex, or birth. It also connotes social equality, a principle which even some of the most progressive and democratic states in the world have not been able to enthrone even in the present age. Only merit, character, and devotion to the cause of Islam, and duty towards one's profession and fellow beings should enable a person to occupy the highest position in the State. A person's worth should not be judged by birth, but by efficiency, character, and service to the cause of Islam, his society, and community.

(C) Liberty

The third characteristic of an Islamic State is liberty which in its truest perspective in historical terms, was initially presented by Islam to humanity. The greatest of individual liberties is involved in that very "Kalima" which every believer is required to pronounce while declaring his or her faith. The pronouncement of the "Kalima" that "there is no god but one God" excluded all other authority but that of God. A Muslim is free as he is not required to obey any other authority but that of God. In other words, this means that he is free within the limits prescribed by Shariah. No one can encroach upon the rights of others but, at the same time, one can feel free within his or her own rights. Freedom of expression and liberty of conscience are the two cornerstones of Islamic polity. Even an ordinary citizen of the State can criticize the highest in the State and call him to account. Early Islamic history is full of many instances of such accountability. However, license in the name of liberty is not allowed; none enjoys the right to slander the people or to sabotage the authorities. It is, however, the obligation of the Islamic State not to deprive any citizen of the liberty Islam confers upon him without proving his crime in a court of law and without giving him full opportunity and facilities for his defense.

(D) Justice

The fourth characteristic of an Islamic State is justice. Justice in an Islamic State should be impartial. Islam is no respecter of persons, whether high or low, prince or peasant, white or black, Muslim or non-Muslim. The Quran enjoins upon Muslims to decide a case on the basis of equity, justice, and upright testimony. As such, the entire Muslim community is to be held responsible for the administration of justice.

The following verses of the Quran sum up the conception of justice in an Islamic State:

"O ye who believe be (firm) maintainers of justice, bearers of witnesses for Allah's sake, even though it be against your own selves, or your parents or your kindred and whether it be against rich or poor. For Allah can best protect both. Follow not the lusts (of your hearts), lest ye swerve; and if ye distort (justice) or decline to do justice, verily Allah is well-acquainted with all that ye do." (IV: 134)

"If (O Muhammad;) thou judgest (concerning the affairs of non-Muslims), judge in equity between them (however hostile may be their attitude towards these). For Allah loveth those who judge in equity." (V: 46)

Thus, the Quran has emphasized again and again that however hostile, mischievous, or cruel may be the person with whom authorities have to deal, it is not permissible for them to deviate even slightly from the path of absolute justice.

In the light of the above Quranic injuctions, it becomes incumbent upon the Head of the State to provide free impartial justice to all, irrespective of caste, creed, color, nationality, race, status, or sex.

According to Islamic notions, the Head of the Islamic State has a two-fold judicial function, one positive and the other negative. His positive functions relate to the establishment of peace in the State, maintenance of concord among the various sections of the people, and the protection of the weak against the strong. His negative functions concern punishment of the evil-doers and the restitution of the rights of the injured. For the dispensation of justice, the Head of the State has to appoint Qadis (judges), well-versed in Shariah law, God-fearing, and of irreproachable character and sterling piety. The Qadis who apply divine law consider themselves responsible not only to the Head of the State but also to God Almighty and, as such, should dispense justice equitably and speedily. Since the Qadi's court is regarded as God's court, no preferential treatment is to be given even to the highest in the State. "The King can do no wrong" does not hold good in an Islamic State so far as the dispensation of justice is concerned. Under Islamic law, no one can claim exemption from appearance in the court or even a preferential seat in the court; recording of deposition of influential persons through commission is not allowed by Islamic law. The Islamic law lays down easy procedure for the conduct of cases, and cheap and speedy justice is to be meted out to rich and poor alike free of cost.

In particular, Islamic law lays greater emphasis on the prevention of crimes than on punishing the culprits after the offenses are committed. Modern reformist theories of penalogy also emphasize this aspect.

Seeking legal opinion from well-known scholars has been in vogue since the very inception of Islam. The authorities allowed learned scholars to give free legal advice to all. Islamic law like in Western systems also assumes (by a fiction) that every citizen knows the law, for it gives an equal opportunity to every person to know such legal details. But on intricate matters the opinion of experts is desirable. Often Qadis who were not quite sure about

43

some legal point referred the case to a Mufti and took a Fatwa from him. This is analogous to the modern Western recourse to calling an Amicus Curie in a court.

(E) Certain Identification Between Sin and Crime

The fifth characteristic feature of the Islamic State is that everyone from the Caliph down to an ordinary citizen is doubly responsible, viz., to God and to some sort of earthly authority. The fear of God and the punishment of the hereafter being common to all, the people are responsible to the Head of the State who, in turn, is himself responsible to the former. Hence, there is a double check upon all actions. The Caliph and citizens are responsible to each other as well as to God.

The content of most secular and religious laws being divine commandment, there is an absence of the distinction between a crime and sin in many spheres of Islamic law. True, the enforcement of one type of violation is by State and of the other is by God, but for the individual, the nature of the violation is of the same essence. Thus, the distinction between personal and public acts disappears altogether in an Islamic State. Furthermore, it takes the matter beyond controversy whether criminal law should be based on morality. This has been one of the most contentious matters in Western jurisprudence. The submissions of famous jurists like Hart, Devlin, and Fuller are too fresh in our memory. It is still one of the unsettled matters whether the content of the criminal law should follow the norms of morality of a given community. Hart and Devlin, following the Austinian tradition, argued that it may not: Fuller of the Harvard Law School took the opposite position. But, such controversies have no place in Islamic law. Whether the "offender" is caught or not, he is made conscious of the fact that his violation is against the law of God. The identification to a large extent of crime and the concept of sin is an important distinguishing feature of an Islamic State. Indeed, the observance of the laws of God (whether they are in the realm of criminal law or morality) falls on the "community" of Muslims. All the community is made conscious of the fact that their God is keeping a vigilant eye over them and they shall not escape his scrutiny.

44

(F) Toleration

In accordance with a verse of the Quran, "It is he who hath created you, and of you are some that are unbelievers and some that are believers" (LXIV: 2), the population in an Islamic State is divided between believers and nonbelievers. Among the believers, there are two kinds; Muslims who believe in all the revealed religions and their Prophets and also in Islam as the last religion and the Prophet Muhammad, and those who believe in their own revealed books and Prophets but not in Islam or its Prophet Muhammad. Since the Islamic State is an ideological State, it is but natural that its administration should primarily be entrusted to those who believe in its ideology. They have to agree to give preference to the interests of the State over their own and so make it a success. In order to defend the frontiers of the Islamic State and to promote the cause of its ideology, military service is made compulsory upon all the able-bodied Muslims without any exception. In return, they are guaranteed maintenance allowance from the State.

The second group of believers, viz., the followers of the revealed books who believe in the existence of God and their Prophets, but do not believe in Islam or its ideology, are governed in accordance with the famous verse of the Quran: "Let there be no compulsion in matters of faith: Truth stands out clear from error" (II: 257).

The Islamic State regards them as Dhimmis or its own responsibility, and guarantees them full liberty of conscience, protection of property, life and honor, and freedom of religious beliefs. Nay, it goes one step further and provides full scope for the growth of their culture and traditions and the administration of their civil affairs in accordance with their own religious laws. Christians and Jews, therefore, occupy a special position in an Islamic State.

An Islamic State does not believe in forcing its own culture and traditions on others or in adopting coercive measures to get the culture of the Dhimmis submerged into that of the Muslims, as it is usually seen under a nationalistic dispensation. As the Dhimmis are not obliged to defend the Islamic State, they are required to pay a small tax in

45

return, called Jizia. If they offer themselves for military service, they are exempted from that tax.

No distinction is made between the Muslims and the followers of other revealed books in matters of civil rights, and the latter could qualify themselves for all offices of the State except the religious ones.

(G) Nature of the Islamic State: Religious and Temporal

As all the guiding principles of the Islamic State are derived from the Quran which, according to Muslim belief, is a divinely revealed book, some people assert that it is a religious institution. In reality, the Islamic State is not a religious institution in the sense of Medieval Western Theocracy in which certain ecclesiastical authorities claimed for themselves the right of law-making. Others assert that the Islamic State is temporal as it is required to administer affairs which are temporal in character and not spiritual. It is, however, not temporal in the modern sense of the terms, since the modern State is not guided by religion, and it usually lacks moral conscience and a moral basis for administration and application of its laws. Since the fundamental ingredients of an Islamic State are derived from the Quran, it becomes a little difficult to separate religious from temporal functions. Since its chief function is to protect Islam and to promote its cause both within and without, and to administer both religious and temporal affairs in accordance with the Quran and the Sunna, this State may be regarded as religious as well as temporal. It should, however, be made clear that the State religion of the Islamic State must be Islam for whose protection and maintenance it is called into existence and continues to exist.

It will be a fallacy to compare the Islamic State with any modern State, as it differs fundamentally from all of them and stands in a class by itself. Since it is based on Quranic principles and has a definite mission to perform, it may be regarded as an ideological state. In the words of some writers, it may, however, be termed as Theo-Democracy,[43] for in such a State, under the sovereignty and paramountcy of God, a limited popular sovereignty has been conferred on the believers.

46

Since the Islamic State encompasses both the religious and the temporal spheres and comes into existence through an arrangement between the (elected) Amir or Caliph (Head of State), and the general Umma (community), it is nothing but a device to fulfill the aspirations of the individuals themselves collectively and, to a certain extent, individually. This State is, thus, not marked theoretically by any serious controversy between the State and the individual. According to Islamic polity, the State, the Amir, and the Milla (Nation) are all animated by an ethical ideal, and it is the duty of each one of them to strive towards this ideal. Accordingly, the personal liberty of the individual is guaranteed to a very large extent under this system, and political power is not concentrated in the hands of one person.

(H) Administration and Government

Another important feature of the Islamic State is to carry on the administration through mutual consultation. The Quran says: "And those who conduct their affairs by mutual consultation" and "O Muhammad consult them, i.e., the companions in the affairs. Then when thou hast taken a decision, put thy trust in Allah. For Allah loves those who put their trust in (Him)" (III: 153).

Thus, there should exist in an Islamic State a Majlis-i-Shura or Council (or Parliament) consisting of representatives of the people reflecting the total legal wisdom of the entire community. The appointment of this Council can be made by the Amir or it can be elected by the people from among the various sections of the public, the only criteria for appointment or election being their intimate knowledge of the Shariah, their previous services to the cause of Islam, and their character. The Amir or Caliph administers the State with their consent. Since the final authority is the Quran and the Sunna, pleas should be based on, and in accordance with, their principles. The decision is that of the majority; the Amir and the Mujlis are under collective responsibility (in the sense of British Constitutional Law).

47

(I) Separation of Powers

The Islamic State possesses separation of powers. Although the Qadis (judges) are to be appointed by the Amir, the highest executive official in the State, in consultation with Mujlis, yet judiciary is completely independent of the executive. The fact is that a Qadi can accept a suit against the very person of the Amir without any previous permission and can try him in an open court. This feature of Islamic judiciary is an index of the independence of judiciary in an Islamic State. Nor is the Amir exempted from personal appearance or to be given any preferential seat in the court. The question of taking deposition of great and prominent personalities by means of commission does not arise in an Islamic State. As far as legislation is concerned, the principle appears to be that to the extent that law making can be done by the State, legislation in some matters is centralized; in others localized. The nature of the subject will determine whether, on a given subject the central legislature can pass a law.[44] The nature of the Islamic State which is based on Quranic principles demands that there should be uniformity in important legislation. It is only the Central Legislative Assembly which can legislate in connection with matters touching the fundamental religious or political aspects of life or the common problems of the State such as foreign policy, taxation, justice, and constitution. However, in matters of local administration, much should be left with the local authorities. An examination of the first two hundred years of Islamic state amply proves this point. In cases of provincial revenues and expenditure, the Provincial treasuries can work as independent units: the Provincial Bait ul-Mal (treasury) is to receive and disburse the amounts realized. In early Islam, Zakat, also, realized from a certain place, used to be spent on the needs of the local people. The balance, if any, in the Provincial treasury used to be deposited with the Central Treasury, whereas deficit, if any, in the Provincial Treasury was met from the Central Bait ul-Mal.

(J) Economic Policy

This matter will be analyzed in greater detail in a later chapter, but certain doctrinal matters should be mentioned here. The economic policy of the Islamic State is based on some positive injunctions in the Quran. It lays down: "So that the wealth should not circulate only among the rich from among you." Hence, the distribution of wealth among all classes of believers has been emphasized by the institution of a "property" tax, known as Zakat, to the extent of two and one-half percent on surplus property, cash, jewels, and commercial capital; also there are restrictions on the process of testamentary disposition by laws of inheritance, and a clear prohibition on usury. In June, 1980, Pakistan became one of the first countries with Western traditions of law to enforce Zakat tax; however, this is in addition to the existing framework of taxation.

The ideal Islamic State believes in the imposition of minimum taxation and the provision of maximum benefits for the people. The believers are supposed to pay less tax than the Dhimmis. However, they may be required to pay all their surplus wealth to the State in case of emergency. Since the believers have to stake their lives and property for the defense and the maintenance of the State, they are secured. The Dhimmis are also guaranteed food, shelter, and other necessaries of life, but nothing is expected of Dhimmis in return.

In an Islamic State, there is no classlessness, nor does it undertake a complete socialization or taking over of the basic instruments of production and distribution. It does allow the individuals to acquire private property so that their incentive may not be lost, but, it does not allow the concentration of wealth into a few hands in order to perpetuate capitalism in its purest form. The economic system in an Islamic State, thus, stands midway between the two antagonistic systems in the present world, Capitalism and Communism. According to the Quran, the objective of the Islamic State is to "establish prayer and pay Zakat, and enjoin good upon the people and to restrain them from committing wrong" (XXII: 42).

Such verses in the Quran sum up the chief objectives of the Islamic State regarding the economic national duties of the Muslims. The first part of this verse relates to prayers and Zakat to enable Muslims to practice, in actual life, the principles of equality, liberty, fraternity, and justice. The second part of this verse regards the Muslims as basically capable of wrongdoing; there is no arrogation that Muslims are the best people or the chosen ones. They are, therefore, required to persuade others to do good and restrain them from committing wrong. This express Quranic injunction thrusts enormous responsibilities upon the Head of the State as well as upon its people. This obliges the State not only to carry out these orders within its own jurisdiction, but also beyond it if occasion should arise.

The above discussion on the nature and concept of State in Islam and on a few aspects of Western jurisprudence have amply demonstrated some of the fundamental differences between the two approaches. The basic foundations of the common law and civil law were stated not to show the superiority of these systems in comparison to the Islamic system, or vice versa, but to focus our attention on the basic foundations, and a priori hypothesis, to enable us to clearly understand the point of view of different legal systems. In a world where doctrinal controversies are rampant and political ideologies outweigh juristic considerations, perhaps, there is still time to reflect on the course which was charted for mankind by the Great Messengers of humanity.

To sum up, therefore, the main characteristics of the concept of State in Islam would be: (1) sovereignty belongs to God and does not vest in the State; (2) all basic laws, organic or ordinary, are laid down by the Quran and the Sunna for all times; (3) subject to the previous restriction, a limited right of legislation vests in the legislature; (4) Ijtihad is to be used to vary "abstracted" legal rules to meet the changes in time; (5) an identification between sin and crime in most areas provides for the "moral" basis of all laws and the State; (6) the State is to ensure equality, fraternity, and liberty to all citizens; (7) administration of justice is the prime responsibility of State; (8) no difference between religious and temporal matters exists since an Islamic State is an ideological entity; (9) administration is to be run by consultation, with those who are learned and who have served Islam; (10) there is separation of powers and a unitary centralized form of government; (11) in economy private property is to be protected; the economic system is midway between Capitalism and Communism; and (12) the

State is to foster the ties among Umma, the international community of Muslims.

(B)   Concept of Leadership

The Problem of the Righteous and the Unrighteous Ruler

To the jurist trained in the Western systems of jurisprudence, i.e., in both civil and common law, the very notion of "righteousness" in the government would appear to be somewhat anomalous.[45]   It is true that at the root of the theories of social contract, both Locke and Rousseau stressed the concept of popular sovereignty over delegated government, but this had no connection with any conceptions of being morally right.   The only recourse was via the doctrine of mandate if the chosen government went against the wishes of the electorate.   This, however, was a political method to reassert the fundamental postulate of popular sovereignty.   It could not be asserted during the life of the elected government by legal methods.   So clear was this constitutional position that it led Dicey to assert that during the life of a parliament, there was indeed the dictatorship of the Cabinet in England, especially since there did not exist any higher organic law in that country to serve as a yardstick for evaluation of the government's performance in the legal sense.   In the U.S., popularity on righteous grounds, or lack of it, is no ground for removal of a President during his constitutional term of four years.   The process of impeachment, jurisprudentially, is different and used in constitutionally identified situations.   Perhaps the closest (yet not on grounds of righteousness) is the British constitutional law rule of "no confidence" against a government.   Be that as it may, it should be reiterated that all these political, philosophical, and legal theories have nothing to do with any "righteousness" in the executive.

The existence of the Islamic State and its mode of government was explained by early Muslim theologians and jurists in light of certain metaphysical concepts.   By deduction from these principles, they built up an elaborate theoretical structure, the basis of this being the Umma, the community of believers, who accepted both the Shariah and the rule of their leader, the Caliph.   This basis and this acceptance were, thus, given so that the validity of

51

the assumptions underlying them could not be questioned, and political speculation was accordingly limited to the means by which the unquestioned ends of the community's existence might be realized. In these circumstances, it was inevitable that dogmatic theory and apologetics should receive more attention than political thought and that the latter should exercise relatively little influence on political activity.

To the extent that the Islamic community was forced to provide for the administrative needs of an extensive empire, certain problems inherent in the Islamic conception of the State were accentuated. Among these was the problem of the unrighteous ruler, which was never really faced by the main body of Islamic opinion, either Sunni or Shiia.[46] It is true that the principle was laid down in the Hadith that there is no obedience in sin, that is to say, that obedience is not due to a sinful ruler. But since no means were indicated by which an unrighteous ruler might be deposed, the dilemma remained. With the incorporation into the Islamic theory of State ideas derived from the Persian conception of absolute monarchy, it became even more acute than before, for there had, of course, been a gap between the ideal and the actual practice even in that early age. The main result of this was not to bring about a reappraisal of fundamentals, but rather to create a situation in which the religious life on the one hand and political and social on the other were lived on different planes. As such, the pious became increasingly reluctant to participate in the affairs of government, lest they should thereby jeopardize their eternal salvation.

Mawardi, writing in the middle of the fifth/eleventh century (Islamic calendar is described by the letters A.H., i.e., After Hijrat--Prophet's leaving Mecca for Medina; since there is a difference of six centuries between the Christian and Muslim calendars, fifth century A.H. is the same as eleventh century A.D.), sought to justify the historical development of the caliphate, interpreting the sources of [47] revelation in the light of political developments. Ghazali, writing much later, attempted to reintegrate the political and religious life of the community by restating [48] the relationship of the caliphate and sultanate. But, his attempt was only temporarily successful. The caliphate ceased eventually to have even

52

institutional power. The position which the jurists were finally forced to acknowledge after the extinction of the caliphate, though it had, thus, in fact, existed before that event, is described by Ibn Jamaa (d.1333 A.D.) in the following words: "The sovereign has a right to govern until another and stronger shall oust him from power and rule in his stead. The latter will rule by the same title and will have to be acknowledged on the same grounds; for a government, however objectionable, is better than none at all."[49] The purpose of government remained in theory, primarily the maintenance of the religion of Islam and the establishment of conditions in which a Muslim could fulfill his true destiny. From the beginning, it had been recognized that coercive force was needed to achieve these ends, but when all attempts to legitimatize this coercive force were abandoned, it was inevitable that the people and officials should be increasingly subject to the caprice of the ruler and the arbitrary exercise of power, even more so since the theory that the caliph was the Shadow of God upon Earth had been adapted to the person of the temporal ruler. A stage had, thus, been reached when it was no longer possible for the jurists either to give validity to the rule of the sultan or to preserve historical continuity. Clearly, in these circumstances, their expositions exercised less and less influence on the conduct of affairs. Their place in medieval Persia was, to some extent, taken by the works of the type known in Europe as "Mirrors of Princes." In such writings, although the ideal State portrayed differed considerably from the idealized community of Medina and was based largely on practical considerations, they exhibited an attempt to conform to Islam. These "Mirrors of Princes" were produced for the guidance of rulers and others, and almost certainly influenced the conduct of the official classes by their insistence on an ideal and their emphasis on the responsibility of the ruler of God for the well-being of his flock.

It was perhaps because no means had been devised of controlling or limiting the increasingly absolute power of the ruler that the main emphasis in these works was laid on justice (adl) and, to a lesser extent, its concomitant, discretionary punishment (siyasat). Whereas, the earlier jurists were concerned with defending the Islamic State against unorthodoxy, the philosophers and the authors of

53

"Mirrors of Princes" were concerned with limiting tyranny (zulm). The only way they saw of doing this was to exhort the ruler to justice, which they came to regard as the sole, or at least the main, quality necessary to a ruler, the basis of temporal prosperity, and the cause of safety from the wrath of God in the world to come. Attention was almost wholly focused on the ruler and his functions, especially his dispensation of justice to his subjects. Insofar as the latter had "rights," they were moral and ethical, and the implication is that they were enjoyed by grace rather than by right. It is important, however, that Husayn Vaiz Kashifi in the Akhlaq-i-Muhsini (composed in 1494-5 A.D.) states that the fundamental reason for kingship was not the satisfaction of the king and his entourage, but rather to care for the people (riayat-iibad) and the development of the kingdom.[50] Najm ud-Din Razi (d.1256 A.D.) also mentions the obligation of the ruler to show care for the rights of the people and the kingdom (riayat-i huquq-i ibad va bilad),[51] while Shihab un-Din Ali b. Muhammad al-Hamadani (d.1385 A.D.) lists twenty matters which the believer had a right to demand of the ruler.[52] These, although termed rights (huquq), were rather pious hopes that the ruler would perform certain duties, mainly of an ethical nature. More often, however, the place given to a ruler's subjects was secondary, and any mention of their "rights" was excluded in favor of reflections on the qualities and functions of the ruler himself. Many writers, following the example of Abu Yusuf, compared the ruler to a shepherd and his subjects to a flock. The favorite simile of the philosophers and the writers of "Mirrors of Princes" was that of the soul and the body, the ruler being likened to the soul and the various classes of his subjects to the members of the body (similar to the metaphors used in twelfth and thirteenth century European writings).

From the preceding narrative, it would appear that by actual practices the injunctions regarding rulers were not always obeyed. The self-interest of the governors led them to assert with great vigor their military might over their subjects. Despite this long and protected history, however, none of the rulers was able to even slightly modify the basic doctrine that the ruled could disobey a ruler who indulged in "Zulm" (tyranny and cruelty) and that the said ruler was subject to a "removal" by the people.

By placing the powers of removal on grounds of righteousness and by placing no limits on the mode of the exercise of this power, prime facie, it would appear that under Islamic jurisprudence, the ruler can be removed at any time. The method would depend, it is submitted by the present author, upon the society in which the removal has to take place. But could it be argued that reliance on such a doctrine is potentially most dangerous as it could mean a state of perpetual insurrection? This argument is only pedantic, for the Shariah is explicit that the right to disobey the ruler is merely an inchoate right and becomes exercisable only when the ruler has become a "zalim" (tyrant). In other words, the stage where the people have the right to overthrow a government (in contemporary language and sense) is only on rare occasions. In 1977, when the "legal" government of Bhutto was ousted by the army, there had been many calls by the religious leaders and by the Bar Associations in Pakistan said that, inter alia, Bhutto lost the right to govern since he had become a "zalim."[53] The emphasis, therefore, is on the stage of "irresponsibility" indulged in by the ruler. It would be a legal precondition to change the status from righteous to the unrighteous.

We must now advert more deeply to the concept of the word "righteous." That this is not the same thing as being unconstitutional or illegal is abundantly clear. The Shariah uses different words to describe acts which are illegal in the modern sense. We find clear references to the acts which are illegal and the further indication that they are to be decided by the regular courts. Therefore, when we talk of the "unrighteous," we are clearly in the realm of ethics and public morality. The ruler is enjoined not only to obey the letter and spirit of the law, but he has to abide by the norms of the "society" and the guidelines of good governance laid down by God.

To understand these issues further, let us see what, historically, was expected of the Islamic rulers. If we closely study the conventions of the Caliphs to obtain guidance on this point, we will notice that the Amir was the only person to whom obedience and loyalty were enjoined and to whom the people delegated in the fullest possible measure their right of making decisions in all matters concerning their collective existence. His status was, therefore, entirely different from the status of the British Monarch or the French President or the British Prime Minister or the American President. In the modern sense, he was not only the President of the State but also its Prime Minister. He attended the parliament himself and presided over all its sittings. He used to take the fullest part in its discussions and was responsible not only for his own acts and opinions but also for all the decisions of his government. As soon as he became "impious," however, the assembly automatically turned into opposition. Every member of his parliament had full freedom to vote for or against him on any point and even his ministers were free to oppose him if they felt impelled to do so honestly and sincerely. The Caliph was not only answerable before the parliament, but also before the people, not only for his public acts, but also for his private and personal conduct. Five times every day he had to face the people in the mosque, and he had to address them every week on Fridays. Each and every member of the public had the right to stop him in the streets of Medina to question him on his conduct or to demand any of his rights, and he would do so at all times and at all hours. The general proclamation of the Head of the Islamic State was: "Assist me when I act rightly; but if I go wrong, put me on the right path. Obey me as long as I remain loyal to Allah and His Prophet; but if I disobey Allah and His Prophet, then none is under the slightest obligation to accord obedience to me."[54]

The above oath of office suggests that obedience to the dictates of the word of God and His Prophet were essential to obtain the obedience of the population. This all-embracing emphasis to follow not only the written word of God, but also the traditions of the Prophet and the examples he set in his lifetime indicates the demands which Islamic polity places on its rulers. The Shariah contains many qualifications and characteristics of those who are to rule. A few of them should be mentioned. The Quran says:

(1) "Verily Allah commands you to make over trusts (i.e., positions of responsibility) to those who are trustworthy."[55]

56

(2) "Verily the most respectable of you in the sight of Allah is the one who is most God-fearing."[56]

(3) "And obey not a person whose heart We have permitted to become unmindful of Our remembrance, one who is following the dictates of his own desires and his case is that in which due limits are transgressed."[57]

The Prophet says:

(4) "Whosoever honors and reveres an innovator (in religion), helps in bringing down the edifice of Islam."[58]

(5) "By God, we do not assign the affairs of our government to any one who aspires for it or is greedy in respect of it."[59]

(6) "We consider the seeker after a post (of trust and responsibility) as the most untrustworthy."[60]

By some writers, the duty of consultation is enjoined upon the ruler. Husayn Vaiz rests this recommendation on the practice of the Prophet. But as the element of absolutism increased, so the duty and practice of consultation tended to be forgotten. In any case, consultation between a ruler whose powers were unlimited and ministers whose appointment and dismissal depended upon his caprice was hardly likely to be effective.

The history of Islam after its initial days of glory was no different from that of other races and peoples who had fallen into bad times. Nevertheless, even in the worst of times, no Muslim ruler was able to openly proclaim a departure from the original obligations meant to regulate the conduct of the rulers. The effect of this basic postulate of an Islamic community, or this grundnorm, was that it survived in both philosophy and religion, the onslaughts and vicissitudes of changing times, and managed to have its echo heard right up to our own times.

The failure to face the problem of the unrighteous ruler was, thus, in part, responsible for the misuse of power by some Muslim rulers. This resulted in a tyrannous oppression of their subjects. It might well have provoked them to rebellion more often than it did had it not been for the fact that (1) rebellion against the ruler was regarded as tantamount to rebellion against God, and (2) within Muslim society in the Middle Ages, there developed a number of lesser institutions, guilds, fraternities, and groups to which the subjects came generally to accord a more intimate loyalty than any commanded by even the most virtuous of kings. These associations had invariably, if not a religious origin and object, at least a religious form, and so strong a hold had they over their adherents, and, on the whole, so beneficient was their influence, that the real life of the communities concerned came to be centered in them. The consequence in Persia was that the State, headed by the ruler, became a comparatively unreal and superficial thing and much more ephemeral. Thus, the problem of the unrighteous ruler ceased to be of overwhelming urgency. In that country, it was, indeed, not until the nineteenth century when the scope and effect of governmental activities increased causing the tyranny and caprice of the ruler to be more widely felt, that attention was again seriously given to this problem. The misery of the Iranian people increased when their nationalist aspirations, including their Constitution of 1906, was sabotaged by the U.K. and Russia both of whom finally placed a sergeant and a former camel driver by the name of Mohammad Reza as the constitutional Head of State in 1921. Two years later, he proclaimed himself to be a monarch. After his forced exile during World War II, his son was similarly placed on the throne by the Allies; he took the title of the "King of Kings." What happened later is a part of the history of our own times.

Today, perhaps more than ever before, this doctrine is important. Apart from its crucial importance as an absolute norm for the Muslim communities in many countries of the world, its psychological check on absolutism is quite manifest.

(C) The Concept of an Islamic Constitution

A constitution normally is a document having a special legal sanctity which sets out the framework and the principal functions of the organs of government of a state. It declares the principles governing the operation of those organs. Such a document is implemented by decisions of the judicial organ, normally the highest court of the state, which has power to interpret its contents. In addition, there gradually develop a number of conventional rules and practices. These serve to attune the operation of the constitution to changing conditions and thereby avoid, for the most part, alterations to a written document which is designed to be permanent in its operation. It is thus that today a document framed in 1787 remains in force with few important amendments, as the Constitution of the United States of America.

The birth of Pakistan as an independent state gave a great thrust to the idea of an Islamic constitution. However, most people had in mind merely a vague notion that Islamic laws should be enforced in the country when they talked of an Islamic constitution. Others, roughly, fell into two contending groups. One group claimed that every conceivable element of a modern constitution was to be found in the Quran, the primary source of Muslim law. The second group asserted that the idea of an Islamic constitution was an illusion and that no such concept could be derived from the Quranic injunctions. Both theories probably embodied a partial truth.

In the late eighteenth century when the Constitution of the United States of America was drawn up, the definition of powers of government was regarded as all important and was embodied in a formal document which was, and is, unalterable except by a process which differs entirely from the method of enacting ordinary legislation. The provision of a constitutional code is a sine qua non of every new state, and the principal States of the world have adopted constitutions in the form of definite and comprehensive enactments during the last one hundred and sixty years. Great Britain is still without a constitution in this sense. Those statutes which are regarded as part of the British constitutional law are not sections of a code. If a collection were made of all the extant enactments from the Coronation Charter of Henry I to the present day which deal with the form and functions of government, the result would be a most imperfect constitution. Moreover, each and every enactment can be repealed by the simple expedient of an Act of Parliament. This is unlike formal constitutions which contemplate no radical changes and usually can only be varied by processes more elaborate than that of passing ordinary statutes.

A constitution does not usually or necessarily contain the detailed rules upon which the working of the institutions of government depends. Legal processes, rules for elections, and the mode of implementing services provided by the state, insofar as they are matters for enactment, are to be found not in the constitution, but in ordinary statutes made by the legislature within the limits set by the constitution itself. Such statutes can be altered by the same method as that by which they were originally enacted, whereas changes in the constitution call for a more elaborate process. This is to ensure that it shall not be in the power of those who for the time being can command control of the legislative organ to vary without special consultations and, maybe, direct reference to the electors, the system and principles of government which have been set up with solemn formalities by agreement between all major political interests in the state.[61]

It was observed that, in recent times the question of having an Islamic constitution was forcefully raised when Pakistan was created in 1947. However, despite many attempts, in thirty years it has not been possible to replace the fundamental laws (based on common law and American constitutional traditions). Today, there are over eight hundred million Muslims in some fifty countries, and the idea is canvassed from time to time of having an Islamic constitution in the twentieth century which embodies the principles of goverance of the golden age of Islam of fourteen hundred years ago. Some of the important countries where Muslims live in any sizeable number are:

Afghanistan	Mali
Albania	Mauritania
Algeria	Morocco
Bahrain	Niger
Bangladesh	Nigeria
Bulgaria	Oman
Burma	Pakistan
Cameroon	Philippines
Cent. Africa Empire	Qatar
Chad	Saudi Arabia
China	Senegal
Dahomey	Sierra Leone
Egypt	Sudan
Ethiopia	Syria
Fiji	Tanzania
Indonesia	Thailand
India	Togo
Iran	Tunisia
Iraq	Turkey
Ivory Coast	Union of Arab
Jordan	Emirates (UAE)
Kuwait	Upper Volta
Lebanon	U.S.S.R.
Malaysia	Yemen
Libya	Yugoslavia
Maldivie Islands	

Thus, if an attempt were made to develop such a document by keeping in view the changes in time and space which have occurred since the advent of Islam, how would one proceed? Iran proclaimed an "Islamic Constitution" in 1979. But because of political crises of several kinds, it is impossible to evaluate, at present, its true significance. An abstract model so produced from the classical sources of Islamic jurisprudence would, it is submitted, produce a document of the kind described below.

First of all, we must turn to the Quran since, hypothetically, being the word of God, it has precedence over all other basic sources.

The Quran, however, is not a book of legal doctrine. It emphasizes the spiritual and moral aspect of human life more than anything else. The strictly legal provisions contained in it are few in number and are confined to a small category of topics. There is no set pattern of a constitution as understood in modern political science laid down in the Quran. For what is a constitution? As already pointed out, normally it means a document having a special legal sanctity, setting out the framework and principal functions of the organs of state together with the principles governing the operation of those organs. Even a cursory reading of the Quran would convince one that rules pertaining to the constitutional structure of a state are not to be found in it. At the same time, certain fundamental principles that ought to govern collective conduct in the interests of integrating Islamic ideology into a definite way of life are specified in the Quran, such as could provide an essential basis for an Islamic polity.

A few countries, as we shall later see, have attempted to incorporate some of the classical ideals of an ideal Islamic State into their constitutional law.[62]

The ultimate spiritual basis of all life as conceived by Islam is eternal and reveals itself in variety and change. A society based on such a conception of reality must reconcile in its life the categories of permanence and change. It must possess eternal principles to regulate its collective life, for the eternal gives us a foothold in the world of perpetual change. But eternal principles, when they are understood to exclude all possibilities of change, which according to the Quran is one of the greatest "signs" of God, tend to immobilize what is essentially mobile in nature.

Islam takes a comprehensive view of life--the dichotomy of Church and State which corresponds to the quality of mind and body in Western philosophical and religious thought is really foreign to the spirit of Islam. Even the so-called secular is also made sacred with a spiritualized attitude of mind. In this all-embracing system of thought, perfection could not be hoped for if no scope existed for accommodating changes necessitated by the evolutionary processes of life. A wise Providence has, therefore, confined the divine ordinances to unalterable fundamental principles, leaving the question of their application to differing circumstances and the details of subordinate legislation to be worked out in consonance with the needs, knowledge, and experience of successive ages. This is really the genesis of Ijtihad, which enables independent judgment to be formed on legal questions from time to time and which Iqbal calls the principles of movement in Islam. This dynamic view of Islamic thought is not an innovative theory of the so-called modernists in Islam as some Western writers seem to think, but rather is part of the intellectual heritage of the Muslim community. Its true import was, however, obscured by the historical process in a period of political and social decay. The State structure in Islam, therefore, is a human institution which must not run counter in any way to the essential basic principles of Islamic polity if it is to deserve the appellation of "Islamic." Subject to this restriction, it can assume various forms in its constitutional details. This brings us to a consideration of the basic principles which must underlie such a structure. Following the style and scheme of this book, below is tabled in simple terms these principles to which we refer.

(1) Time and again, the Quran reiterates that sovereignty belongs to God alone. This principle militates against the possibility of human dictatorship, absolute monarchy, or autocracy in an Islamic State. The allegiance of the Muslim subject is primarily owed to the Law of God, to which even the Head of the State must be subservient, and not to human fiat. It is only in this limited sense that an Islamic State can be described as a theocracy, and not in the sense of a priestly class ruling in the name of the Lord and claiming infallibility in their interpretation of divine injunctions. There is, in fact, no recognized priesthood in Islam which stresses individual responsibility for actions and denies the existence of an intermediary between man and his Maker.

(2) The fundamental doctrine of the unity of God as expounded by the Quran clearly implies the equality of all mankind. The essence of Tauhid (unity of God) as a working idea is equality, solidarity, and freedom. Considerations for race, tribe, color, language, profession, or country cannot vitiate this principle, for it is declared that the most honored in the eye of God is one who fears God most. The common bond is provided by belief in a common ideology. In Sura (verse) 24 (An-Nur): 54, we find a promise being held out that all those who believe and do good deeds shall be made

successors in the earth. It is significant that the promise is collectively given to the Muminoon (the righteous) and not to their leader for the time being. Power, therefore, will vest in the community according to this principle, though it may, of course, delegate its functions to an individual or a representative body as it may deem fit. Such delegation is neither expressly nor impliedly prohibited and would, therefore, be valid. The Quranic injunction calling for obedience being rendered, inter alia, to rulers, that is, the "holders of authority from among you," points in the same direction. Clearly, therefore, a democratic set up is visualized in the Quranic system.

(3) The chapter Ash-Shura designates the method of deliberation. The decision on questions has to be made by mutual consultation among those who believe, though the machinery or exact form of such consultation is nowhere laid down. This leaves a large scope for evolution of democratic forms of government, subject to the limitation that the eternal principles enunciated by the Quran cannot be abrogated. The modern representative assembly elected on universal suffrage may be one such form.

(4) Each individual, man or woman, is, according to the Quran, entitled to keep what he or she earns or inherits, and this guarantees the fundamental right to hold and dispose of property subject to the injunctions which provide for payment of a share in taxes or charity and the principles of the law of inheritance.

(5) Complete freedom to profess any particular faith or adopt any form of worship must exist in an Islamic State. The Quranic injunction, "there is no compulsion in religion," is a cardinal principle in this behalf. The Quran enjoins equal respect for all Prophets named and unnamed. The minorities living in an Islamic regime must have full protection of their culture. One can enter the Islamic fold only with one's free consent after accepting its ideology. Life and liberty must be inviolate except when the law is contravened.

(6) Men and women have mutual, though not identical rights against one another. One school of thought would apparently deny women any right to participate in active politics or to stand for election to a representative

assembly. Reliance is placed in this connection on the verse, "Men are guardians over, or supporters of women." The more orthodox view is that men are legally the "guardians" of women in their families. However, the reformist view is the one generally adopted. According to this view it is a fact of ordinary (but not invariable) reality that more men "support," because of various sociological reasons, women in their families. In some countries, men may have, in a sociological sense, higher status than women, but that does not affect the principle of representation based on rights. It is interesting to note that the advocates of the orthodox school have suggested that there should be a separate assembly for women so that their opinion on problems peculiar to them could be obtained and considered by the men's assembly.[63] Surely, that is an indirect admission that women should have a voice in a representative assembly that controls permissible legislation. We must remember the Quranic injunction occurring in the Sura al Baqara--"And they (the women) have rights similar to those of men over them."

(7) The independence of the judiciary must be a principle of the constitution. No person in an Islamic State, not even the elected Head, can be above the law, and he is as much subject to the Hudud (punishments for major crimes) as anyone else. The Quran repeatedly enjoins the administration of justice in an impartial manner, even though the decision may go against a judge's own kinsmen or his own community.

(8) The Islamic State should have all the incidents of a modern welfare state (examined in greater detail later) in which the weak and the disabled become the responsibility of the State. The moral and material welfare of the inhabitants of the State as a whole ought to be its first concern.

(9) Integrity of family life and its privacy must be assured. Entry into a house must be with the permission of the owner thereof and at times convenient to him.

(10) In the international field, an Islamic State will scrupulously observe all freely accepted convenants and treaties and cannot treat them as mere scraps of paper under the cover of a specious pretext. Indeed, since

Islamic scholars produced great works on Islamic conceptions of international law nearly a thousand years before
writers like Grotius and Vittoria undertook their treaties,
the Islamic State's regard for this field would be profound.

The spirit of a truly Islamic polity does not countenance
measures which tend to accumulate wealth or property in a
few hands.   The Quranic laws of inheritance, the
provisions against hoarding, profiteering, and usury, and
laws regarding taxes and charities which a good Muslim is
enjoined to honor in thought and deed, appear to be
designed towards that end.   Certain fundamental limits to
legislation are prescribed in the interest of stability and
collective good.   It is, thus, that an Islamic State would
strike the middle path between the extremes of anarchism
and totalitarianism, of undiluted capitalism and communism
or fascism, and avoid bitter class wars such as dialectical
materialism considers inevitable and almost predestined.

It has not been considered necessary to burden this
account with a detailed discussion of quotations from the
Quran which could be cited in support of the above views
in ample measure.   One criticism is sometimes voiced that
such an Islamic State may exist in the idealistic
conceptions of modern Muslims but that there is little
evidence of its materialization in history.   Undoubtedly,
the regime of the Khulafa-i-Rashidin, in the context of
their times, was the nearest approach to such an ideal,
but it is submitted by the author that we cannot blindly
copy that relatively simple and undeveloped system in the
much more complex conditions of today.   In light of the
Quranic eternal principles and the history of previous
attempts at their realization, each Islamic community will
have to work out its own solutions to its problems in
accordance with the dictates of its own temporal and social
environment.

Although each community will have to work out its own
adaptation, the basic principles mentioned above must be
accommodated.   In this evolutionary process, the
community will evolve, to use Hegel's terminology, its own
volksgeist.

These are, therefore, some of the salient features of the Islamic government which existed at the time of its inception. Indeed, these principles were the philosophic basis of the spread of Islamic ideology well beyond the deserts of Arabia. Their quintessence has to be reincarnated for any meaningful future attempt in making an Islamic constitution.

At the outset, we had said that in attempting to locate the essential ingredients of an Islamic constitution, we have first to turn to the Quran. Before concluding, however, we may refer briefly to three other sources whose examination is necessary (after the Quran) for deducing the essential ingredients of the framework of a constitution which could be termed as Islamic.

The Sunnah (Sunna)

This is the second source of Islamic law. It shows the way in which the Prophet translated the ideology of Islam in light of Quranic guidance into practical shape, developed it into a positive social order, and finally elevated it to a full-fledged Islamic State. These things we can learn only from the Sunnah. It will also guide us in ascertaining the precise sense, purport, and meaning of the Quranic directives. In other words, the Sunnah is the practical application of the Quranic principles to the various problems of life. Therefore, it contains invaluable precedents and very important material relating to the constitutional practices and conventions.

The Precedents of Khulf-a-Rashdin

These precedents and conventions should constitute the third source of an Islamic constitution. How the first four caliphs managed the Islamic State after the passing away of the Prophet is easily found in the books of history. It has been accepted in Islam from the very beginning that interpretations of the Quran and the Sunnah having the unanimous approval of all the Companions (technically known as Ijma), and the decisions of the Caliphs relating to constitutional and judicial problems accepted by the Companions are binding on all for all times. In other words, such interpretations and such decisions must be accepted in toto because the consensus of opinion of the

Companions on any matter is tantamount to an authoritative exposition of the law. Where there has been a difference of opinion among the companions, that is sufficient proof of the fact that two or even more interpretations are actually possible and any one of them can be preferred to the other on the basis of sound reasoning. But where there is a general consensus of opinion among them, it shows that one and only one interpretation or decision is the correct and authoritative one.

The Rulings of Great Jurists

These rulings which should comprise the fourth source are the opinions of acknowledged jurists regarding various constitutional problems of their times. They may not be conclusive on this subject, yet it cannot be gainsaid that they contain fundamentally the best guidance for a proper understanding of the spirit and principles of an Islamic constitution.

It is, thus, submitted that these are the four major sources of an Islamic constitution. Whenever an attempt is made to make the constitution of an Islamic State, one will have to collect relevant material from all of them in the same way as the people of England, were they inclined to make their constitution into written form, would have to refer to the Common Law, their constitutional conventions, various statutory provisions, and infer a number of points from the judgments of their courts relating to constitutional problems.

We must, however, end this discussion by the caveat that although there has been much talk in international political forums of Muslims about this subject, only a few Islamic countries have made a dedicated attempt to have such a constitution. The nearest we come in this respect to a devised attempt is to examine the case of Pakistan. Attempts have been made towards this direction but, unfortunately, in a diluted form up to 1977. The result is that the Constitution (now of 1973) calls the country an "Islamic Republic," and there is a chapter dealing with State policy where lip service has been paid to Islam. Before the present regime, however, these provisions were not enforceable in law.[64]

Unfortunately, with the exception of a few countries, most of which lie in Western Europe and North America, the vast majority of mankind finds itself ruled by despotic governments of one form or another. The countries where we have such governments in control include Muslim as well as non-Muslim areas. Any attempt towards the formation of an Islamic constitution, therefore, must contain an emphasis to incorporate the following two basic conceptions: a guarantee against despotism and a declaration of the rights of the citizens.[65] What must also be stressed, therefore, is its corollary, the principle of judicial intervention (as opposed to executive adjudication) in matters relating to fundamental human freedoms. The enforcement mechanism of human rights is too detailed a subject to be dealt with here at any length. In recent times since the incorporation of the American Bill of Rights, it is beyond controversy that independent courts must examine any encroachment of the citizen's rights by the executive. The Islamic constitution should ensure this. A word might also be said about the concept of absence of despotism in Islamic polity and jurisprudence.

Even a brief look at the early history of Islam will show that despotism has no place for the simple reason that juridically as a matter of religious belief there is no ruler nor ruled in an Islamic system of government. There are only "Ul-il-Amr," i.e., persons placed in authority to discharge the duties entrusted to them in accordance with the injunctions of the Quran and to render account to the people for their actions.

From the basic juridical grundnorm that sovereignty belongs to God, the further consequence invariably results that those who are entrusted with the functions of the government are simply trustees of a sacred trust. Their individual status is the same as that of the rest of the populace. The only difference is one of function. This principle is enshrined in many constitutions of Islamic countries. For example, the 1973 Constitution of Pakistan declares: "Sovereignty over the entire Universe belongs to Almighty Allah alone, and the authority to be exercised by the people of Pakistan within the limits prescribed by Him is a sacred trust."[66] In the same context, reference

69

may also be made to the historical last Sermon of the Prophet delivered at Arafat which, inter alia, emphasized:

(1) That a colored person has no preference over a white man nor a white person over a colored one nor an Arab over a non-Arab nor a non-Arab over an Arab except through righteousness.[67]

(2) Every believer is a brother of another believer and all Muslims are brothers unto one and another.

(3) The lives and properties of the people are to be respected by one another till the Day of Reckoning; they are to be respected in the way one respects and the month of Zul-Hajj.

(4) People are all equal as the teeth of a comb.

(5) Whatever you eat, you give to those in your service also to eat; whatever you wear, you are also to give them to wear.

(D) Concept of Legislation

Major Problems

The previous chapters should have brought into focus one of the most peculiar problems that jurisprudence can envisage. First, if laws were for most matters created fourteen hundred years ago, how can we meet the exigencies of our own age? And, secondly, if legal sovereignty belongs to God, what is the nature of the limited right of legislation which would vest in a legislature? It need not be stressed that the second question already assumes and clearly implies that at least the Dician notion of the omnipotence of the Parliament is absent from the confines of Islamic jurisprudence. What has been said earlier should have established that the only really meaningful legislation which can take place is where we find some scope for applying rules of interpretation or where we have a newly emerging situation. In any case, such exercises can only be undertaken by those learned in the law and not by lay parliamentarians as assumed by Western political thought.

70

Position of the Caliph

While dealing with the problems of a legislature, we have initially to refer to the position of the formal head of government, vis-a-vis, the law-making institution. This is necessary because, comparatively speaking, in terms of modern political science, both under a presidential as well as under a parliamentary system, e.g., the U.S. and U.K. respectively, the power enjoyed by such an official in legislative matters is different from the one given to such an official under classical Islamic law.

The examination of the nature of a legislature in an Islamic State in juridical terms would stem from the a priori postulate that, legally, sovereignty belongs to God. Once that step is taken, the rest would follow logically. The next question, therefore, which we have to raise is about the location of the political sovereign. Unhesitatingly, the reply would be that political sovereignty too, as a matter of law, belongs to God and God alone. Whatever human agency is constructed to enforce the political system of Islam in a state will not possess sovereignty in the legal and political sense of the term, because not only does it not possess de jure sovereignty, but because its powers are limited and circumscribed by a supreme law which it can neither alter nor interfere with. The true position of this agency has been described by the Quran itself. The term used by the Quran for this agency is "Khilafat," which means that such an agency is not sovereign in itself but is rather the viceregent or representative of the de jure and the de facto sovereign, viz., God Almighty.

The word "viceregent" should be distinguished from the medieval legal doctrine about the divine right of the kings and from the Catholic notions about Papacy. The legal notion regarding the divine right of kingship meant that the king had been appointed by God and, as such, the people or subjects had to obey him as a matter of faith, and the king needed no further legitimacy to the throne. Before jurists like Bracton[68] attempted to dilute this theory, it was frequently invoked by various monarchs in Europe. By using his famous aphorism that "the king rules under God and Law," Bracton and the jurists who followed him tried to put both legal and political curbs on the King's authority. Similarly, the institution of Pope is related to the spiritual guidance originally provided by Peter, a disciple and follower of Jesus. Viceregency has nothing to do with providing a direct link of administering the people on behalf of God who under Islamic beliefs retains all power. It also importantly does not vest the incumbent viceregent or Caliph with any infallibility of a spiritual kind, make him different in the eyes of God from the rest of the people, or place him any closer to the Almighty on whose behalf he is supposed to act. Furthermore, it may be pointed out that the word "viceregent" is an English translation by which all that is legally aimed to be transmitted is the concept of a representative with authority to act but who holds the representation on trust for God. Since many texts in English use this word, the same is being used here, with the caveat mentioned heretofore as to its meaning.

According to the Quran, the viceregency of God is not the exclusive birthright of any individual or clan or class of people; it is the collective right of all those who accept and admit God's absolute sovereignty over themselves and adopt the divine code, conveyed through the Prophet, as the law above all laws and regulations. It says:

> "Allah has promised such of you as have become believers and done good deeds that He will most surely make them His viceregents on the earth."[69]

The institution of Khalifa, or Caliph, is based directly on this principle. In technical terms, the Caliphate, or Khalifat, was the form of government which came into vogue after the death of the Prophet. The first four caliphs were elected, but later on, the caliphate became hereditary in various dynasties. The introduction of dynasty was clearly opposed to the principles of Islamic jurisprudence. However, despite this departure, the institution of the caliph continued to reflect the juridical connotations emphasized here. In other words, the caliph was supposed to act in administering the affairs of State as a trustee of the powers conferred upon him. The restrictions on the powers of the legislature and the caliph, in fact, mean that these are fetters on the State itself.

In the 1979 Constitution of Iran, the country is called "Islamic Republic" and Khomeini has been named Fagahi (trustee) for life. In a small way, it is a similar position to the position of the Turkish caliphs. As Fagahi he has the power under this Constitution to remove even the highest officials of the State. However, Khomeini has no direct administrative post. The institution of the caliph, therefore, is one of the most unique contributions of Islam to the constitutional law of all nations. In theory, particularly as evidenced in the time of the first four caliphs, the incumbent caliph was the Head of the State, its spiritual defender, and yet answerable (and also removable) to all the citizens of the State directly and personally. In view of the stringent fetters on his powers and discretion, it can be said that not only the actions of kings, but that of despots is alien to Islamic Jurisprudence. In legislation, he had no special power. As far as interpretation was concerned, this power vested with the judges; as far as finding new rules of law was concerned, that vested with the council of advisors (or similar body) which again consisted of those who were learned in the law.

Therefore, it would be well to remember that, in a way, the State itself was the institution whose ultimate majesty was set within prescribed limits. The theory of law based on these hypotheses was supposed to be a crucial bulwark against despotism.

Limitations

Under Islamic Jurisprudence the State can act only within the framework of these limitations and is not empowered to infringe or overstep them. This is not only an inference deduced from the acceptance of God's sovereignty; the Quran emphasizes it directly and warns repeatedly in clear words:

> "These are the limits ordained by God; so do not transgress them.
>
> If any do transgress the limits ordained by God, such persons are the unjust."[70]

Another positive and comprehensive principle which the Quran lays down in this respect is:

"O you who believe, obey Allah and obey His Messenger and those from among yourselves who hold authority; then if there is any dispute between you concerning any matter, refer it to Allah and His Messenger, if you (really) believe in Allah and the Last Day. This is the best course (in itself) and better as regards the result."[71]

According to the above injunction, obedience to the State is subject to the obedience to God and His Prophet and not independent of it, which clearly means that on insisting to violate the commands of God and the limitations prescribed by the Prophet in his preachings, the State loses the right of claiming obedience from the people. This very truth has been explained by the Prophet in these words:

"There is no obedience for him who disobeys God."[72]

"There is no obedience to any creature if it involves disobedience to the Creator."[73]

The other principle which follows from the above injunction of the Quran is that whatever dispute and difference of opinion may arise in the Muslim society, be it between individuals or groups, or between the people and the State, it should be referred to that fundamental law which God and His Prophet have given to us. Thus, the very nature of this principle demands that there should be an institution in the state which should undertake to adjudicate strictly in accordance with the Book of God and the Sunnah of the Prophet.

Because of, a priori, fetters on government and state, the judicial branch assumes great importance. The judiciary, therefore, occupies such a pivotal place in an Islamic community that its importance cannot be overemphasized. It further establishes that the executive or the legislature cannot abridge or take away this power. In Pakistan, for example, at least the High Court at Lahore has held that this is even true today. Speaking generally, however, the position of judiciary in many Islamic states today is nowhere near what is envisaged for it in classical law and forcefully evidenced by Islamic history. Strong tendencies, unfortunately, in governmental authority, usually supported by rubber stamp parliaments (like that under the former Shah) have tended to curtail and restrict the otherwise enormous powers available to judges under Islamic Jurisprudence. In fairness, however, it may also be equally emphasized that the mettle of judges in many Islamic states is, perhaps, not what is demanded by the Quran and the Sunnah. In many areas, judgeships are more the result of political favoritism than of legal acumen or piety (taqwah) so particularly demanded by Islam.

With these observations serving as a preface, we can now move on to see the allotted role for legislature by the postulates of Islamic Jurisprudence.

Functions of the Legislature

The legislature in Fiqh was known as the "Body which resolves and prescribes" (Ahl al-hal waal-aqd). It is quite clear that a State established on the basis of God's de jure sovereignty cannot legislate in contravention of the Quran and the Sunnah. A divine commandment is clear that no Muslim[74] has any right to decide on the basis of his own opinion, and that those who do not decide in accordance with the divine code are unbelievers.[75] It automatically follows from these injunctions that it is beyond the purview of any legislature of an Islamic State to legislate in contravention of the directives of God and His Prophet, and all such pieces of legislation, even though approved by the legislature, would ipso facto be considered void.

If this is the state of affairs in an Islamic Polity, what is the function and scope of a legislature? The answer is that, in spite of this limitation, the legislature in an Islamic State does have a number of functions to perform:

(1) Where the explicit directives of God and His Prophet are available, although the legislature cannot alter or amend them, the legislature alone will be competent to enact them in the shape of sections, devise relevant definitions and details, and make rules and regulations for the purpose of enforcing them.

75

(2) Where the directives of the Quran and the Sunnah are capable of more than one interpretation, the legislature will decide which of these interpretations should be placed on the Statute Book. To this end, it is indispensable that the legislature should consist of a body of such learned men who have the ability and the capacity to interpret Quranic injunctions and who, in giving decisions, will keep before them the spirit and the letter of the Shariah. Fundamentally, it will have to be accepted that, for the purposes of legislation, a legislature has the authority to accord preference to one or the other of the various interpretations and to enact the one preferred by it into law, provided, of course, that it is only an interpretation and not a perversion or camouflaged deviation from the law.

(3) Wherever there is no explicit provision in the Quran or Sunnah, the function of the legislature will be to enact laws relating to the same, of course, always keeping in view the general spirit of Islam, and where previously enacted laws are present in the books of Fiqh, to adopt any one of them.

(4) Wherever and in whatever matters basic guidance is not available from the Quran, the Sunnah, or the conventions of the Righteous Caliphs, it will be taken to mean that God has left the people free to legislate on those points according to their wishes. In such cases, therefore, the legislature can formulate laws without restriction, provided such legislation is not in contravention of the letter and the spirit of the Shariah--the principle herein being that whatever has not been disallowed is allowed.

Question of Legislation on Existing Laws

The broad canvas in which the legislature can function is, thus, quite simple. But we must now proceed to examine the problems of legislation with regard to those areas in which there does exist some law. By "law" here is meant a certain interpretation put on a matter by the classical schools of law or the collection of rules or precedents on various subjects.

The collection of rules, regulations, and precepts which make up what is called "Islamic Law" had taken shape already in earlier centuries. As far as the Sunni form of Islamic law is concerned, they have been dealt with extensively in various standard works and commentaries of the four schools. It is believed in many places that the work done by those earlier authorities of the four schools is final. According to it, the door of Ijtihad is closed. The scope of all following generations is confined to the handing down of the accepted legal material, to interpret it in the sense of the earlier authorities, and at most to extend it to such cases for which an express rule has not yet been laid down.

It is, however, an indisputable fact that legislative or rule making activity in the world of Islam in the recent past, particularly since the beginning of the present century, has once again been resumed and has led partly to quite surprising results. As early as in the seventies of the last century, the so-called Mejielle was published in Turkey, and the Code Qudri Pasha was enacted in Egypt. Both were attempts to codify the law of the obligations, particularly the personal law of the Hanafite School. In the beginning of this century, the Code Santillana was worked out in Tunisia, while in Algeria the Code Morand was enacted. In Turkey, the Code Familiale Ottomane followed in 1917. In Egypt, a series of important reforms, mainly of the matrimonial law, were brought about in the 20's by a number of ordinances and edicts. After World War II followed the proclamation of a Code Civil (1948) and the abolition of Waqf Ahli (1952). On the Indian Subcontinent, too, reformatory tendencies in the field of Islamic Law have been perceptible for quite some time. By enacting, for instance, the Dissolution of Muslim Marriages Act of 1939, the wife was conceded the right to effect the dissolution of marriage on the ground of certain grievances. An attempt to restrict the validity of pure family endowments and to abolish them altogether, however, had to be abandoned and were more or less revoked by the Mussalman Wakf Validating Act of 1930.

In the above legislative measures, two tendencies are discernable. On the one hand, they are prompted by the desire to be put in the order of paragraphs, numbers, sections, etc., to express accurately, and to compile in the shape of a manual which is binding on all, the legal material which is contained in an extensive literature and which can be looked into only with difficulty. In other words, it is an attempt to codify the Islamic Law, or to be more precise, the most important parts of the Islamic Law for particular territories. On the other hand, in some laws the legislative measures aim at essential reforms. They serve the purpose of checking and, if possible, of eliminating grievances with regard to marriage, divorce, inheritance, bequests and endowments, etc. The two tendencies can sometimes be clearly seen in the same enactment.

For both cases--for the attempts to codify and for the attempts to redress grievances by individual laws through reform--it is characteristic that such laws have not developed out of the Islamic tradition, but that they are the result of external influences. Behind all attempts to codify and to reform is the will to transform the existing legal order where Muslims live into an instrument which in every respect meets the challenges and requirements of human society in a modern State. The fact that in the new legal arrangements early authorities of Islamic Law are being referred to most frequently seems to contradict this assertion. In reality, however, these references to earlier authorities do not in the first instance serve the purpose of proving the respective innovations, but are rather an attempt to justify them subsequently. It is submitted that an innovation, after its necessity has been generally realized, can be brought formally and actually into harmony with Islamic legal tradition under the doctrine of Ijtihad. There is no need for anologies so long as a Quranic injunction is not mainfestly violated in letter or in spirit. There surely must be evolution or dynamism of this kind available. One cannot apply eighth century solutions to twentieth century problems. There may have been a time when man was indistinguisable from the anthropoid ape, but that is no reason now to define man as to include the anthropoid ape. Those who cling to eighth century solutions and those who are unaware of the progress of Islamic thought in subsequent centuries are usually the ill-educated Mulla class whose education and understanding are both superficial and limited.

The facts which have been briefly pointed out here have a negative as well as a positive side. They are negative inasmuch as they show that the Islamic Law in its traditional form does not meet, in every respect, the requirements of modern life. Such a realization may be painful for many pious Muslims. Large portions of the population of Muslim countries will resist this opinion and may not want to be able to realize this fact. They may still be convinced that the Islamic Law meets even today all requirements, or at least that the Islamic Law can perpetually rejuvenate itself out of its own substance. The members of the legislative bodies will have to take into consideration this widely spread conception and conviction which has taken deep root in the population. Again, unfortunately, it is supported more by the sayings of Mullahs than by trained jurists or scholars of law. Indeed, this is one of the principal differences in the role and functions of clergy in, say, Christianity and those who profess this role in Islam. "Profess" applies since Islam has no priestly class. Whereas priests in the Christian faith are, as a class, formally trained and have university backgrounds, the ordinary Mullah, one who calls the people to the mosque, has no such training. In all probability, he has memorized the Quran since childhood and has piled up various dogmatic assertions while on his way to becoming a Mullah. The impact such ill-equipped kind of clergy has on the life of the ordinary twentieth century Muslim is not always healthy or progressive.

The very fact that in the recent past legal reforms have taken place in many Islamic countries would show that, at the governmental level at least, the efforts of the ordinary Mullah have failed. It is some proof that in the world of Islam a period of rejuvenation and new orientation has set in. It is with surprise and astonishment that we see something come into existence and grow which only half a century ago was considered impossible. In those days, the Dutch scholar Snouck Hurgronje was of the opinion that codification would do violence to the Islamic Law and would, therefore, be impossible. In the meantime, however, attempts to codify the law of Islam have been made, so far successfully, in a number of countries: in Turkey, in Egypt, in Jordan and elsewhere.

There is no doubt that Turkey, by secularizing law, has perhaps left the circle of the Islamic states (properly so-called in the Austinian sense), but the Turks in their overwhelming majority have nevertheless not ceased to profess Islam; indeed, the Turks are among the most devout Muslims. Here, we have an extreme case--a bold attempt to remove the religion of Islam from public and official life and to restrict it to the private sphere. Examples of the opposite extreme are Saudi Arabia and some of the Gulf states: the almost complete maintenance of the traditional Islamic order of law and life. The remaining Islamic states should be placed, as far as legislation is concerned, in the wide field between these two extremes. Egypt has recently enacted legal reforms which are almost radically modernistic. In Pakistan, which owes its existence to a pronounced Islamic conception, perhaps less radical reforms are to be expected, since its entire judicial system is based on the common law mould.[76]

The above analysis and discussion regarding legislation in Islam has amply shown that the problem and its treatment are really quite different from anything similar in other countries. Not only is the juristic and philosophic nature of legislation different from non-Muslim countries, there are also severe limitations on the powers of its parliament or whatever else it may be called. However, it is equally clear that apart from the few Arab states in and around Saudi Arabia, in practical terms Muslim states have not really bothered to ensure conformity with this fundamental priority of Islamic Constitutional Law. Even a formalistic compliance has not been attempted. So, apart from the political events of the last decade, it could be said that for centuries we do not find much conformity with the expose presented here. This, in some ways, is also due to the effect of the colonization of Muslim areas by European states. But even after their departure, it has not been easy to change that trend. However, changes of the nature demanded by classical Islamic Law have been appearing in the past three or four years in countries like Libya, Pakistan, and Iran. In these states, efforts have been made to change the laws and make new ones in accordance with classical Islamic tenets. How this goes or if it is successful remains to be seen.

Composition

Before concluding, a word should be said about the composition of the legislature. Strictly speaking, in Islamic Jurisprudence, unlike modern democratic principles, every citizen is not really "qualified" to sit in a law-making body. Only those people are qualified to decide legislative matters who are legally knowledgeable and understand the law. To understand this aspect, we must briefly look at the early Islamic history. Moreover, it should be noted that, as already pointed out, legally speaking, there is no "legislature" in the sense of Western political thought. Islamic Jurisprudence only envisages a consultative assembly or body for giving advice to the executive. The early Islamic history clearly provides the answer as to why this is so.

Islam arose in Mecca as an ideological movement. It is an inherent feature of all ideological movements that those persons who first accept that movement are counted as the true companions and friends as well as advisers of the leader of that movement. Similarly, in Islam, persons who were the first to associate themselves with the Prophet and his movement automatically became his advisers with whom he invariably consulted in all cases wherever clear and definite injunctions of the Quran were not available. When new people entered the Islamic body politic and the struggle with the opposing forces increased, those who rendered outstanding service by virtue of their sacrifices, insight, and wisdom, naturally became prominent without any conscious effort on their part. The "election," therefore, took place not by means of votes, but by virtue of practical tests and performances; indisputably, a more meaningful and reliable method. Thus, even before the Prophet migrated to Medina, two kinds of people had already become members of his consultative assembly, viz., (a) those who had been associated with him from the very beginning, and (b) those who subsequently became prominent by virture of their sacrifices, insight, and ability. The members of both these groups also enjoyed the confidence of the Muslim masses to the same extent to which they enjoyed the confidence of the Prophet himself. Then occurred the historical event of migration (hijrat), and it took shape in the following way. A year or two before migration, cer-

81

tain influential personalities of Medina had embraced Islam, and through their labors, Islam had established a secure foothold in that city among the tribes of Aus and Khazraj. It was at the insistence and request of these people of Medina that, leaving their hearths and homes, the Prophet and his followers migrated to that city where the Islamic movement eventually grew into a political organization and blossomed into a full-fledged state. It was, therefore, inevitable that these very people, with whose services Islam had prospered and progressed in Medina, should be the leaders of the newly-formed society and its political organization. Consequently, it was inevitable that these very people should be included in the Consultative Assembly of the Prophet along with his very first associates and tested colleagues from Mecca.

Thus, in true accord with this history, a legislature in an Islamic State must be composed of people who have three qualifications: (1) knowledge of law, (2) respected for piety, and (3) service to Islam. The appropriate name should also be a "Consultative Assembly;" its main function would be to "advise" the enforcement organ, the executive, as to what the real Islamic law is which has to be enforced. The word "legislature" itself, signifies a law-making capacity which, as described earlier, is an attribute of Western parliaments, "strictii sensu." Since Islam procedes on different premises, it would be better to call such a body "Consultative Assembly." The eligibility suggested may appear to be "undemocratic," but is in essence essential to a proper working of an Islamic State. It is not necessary to go into the merits and demerits of this methodology. Suffice it to say that even in Western democracies, although theoretically everyone is entitled to be elected, yet the ones who are actually elected are those who possess the necessary influence. Often this deprives the nation of the truly worthy and humble representatives. At the same time, it fosters a class of professional politicians--something which classical Islamic thought cautiously avoids.

(E)   Concept of an Islamic Community

<u>The Umma</u>

In understanding this concept lies a proper realization of many phenomena of the Muslim world.   Herein, Islam distinguishes itself from many religions.

It is a truism that in Islam all men are equal; but the believers are members of the Umma, bound together in community by ties, not of kinship or race, but of religion: the acknowledgement of one God and the apostolic mission of His Prophet Mohammad.   There is, of course, differentiation of function of individuals in society, but before God all are equal without reference to rank, class, or race.   The only nobility in Islam is that of the pious.   Although variably expressed, even spiritually, because of different embodiments in societies separated by space and time, this basic conviction has tenaciously characterized all Islamic societies.   Furthermore, a pious non-Muslim is considered higher than a non-pious Muslim. Thus, unlike the Christian belief of some kind of "automatic" salvation for those who believe in Jesus, Islam stresses action as the basis of salvation and the life hereafter.

In describing the cultural development of the Western Middle Ages, analysts show an interplay and amalgamation of Christianity, classical heritage, and the traditions of the Germanic peoples.   For an analogous formula to describe the development of the Muslim Middle Ages, one must look to the cultural amalgam of the period as a precipitator of the Arab heritage, Islam, and the traditions of the countries conquered by and for the new religion.

The traditions of the Germanic tribes and nations maintained relative uniformity, whereas the traditions that came to interact with Arabism and Islam, revealed a fundamental diversity.   This difference in uniformity accounts for the multiplicity of cultural manifestations which are evidenced in the medieval Islamic world from India and Central Asia to the Atlantic coastline, while an almost monolithic appearance is apparent in the contemporary West.

An additional component of unification to the civilizations of the Muslim world which has likewise affected all the civilizations of Asia, Africa, and the Americas, is the recent reconstitution of Europe under the combined impulses of science, liberalism, and denationalism, along with the developments that have resulted from their impact, i.e., European Economic Community, etc. At first glance, the response to this development would seem to eliminate some of the traditional diverse cultural differences within the Islamic world, but in reality local reactions have actually demonstrated a reaffirmation of their distinctive characteristics. These units maintaining cultural differences can be found to exist as nation states. As a precondition of the self-realization toward which they are striving as a result of their contact with the West, these nation states have been forced to come to terms with this Western phenomenon.

In this chapter our primary concern is with the meaning for the individual of his self-identification as a Muslim and, hence, as one of the Muslim civilization, rather than with the ideology or material content of the civilization of Islam. One important contrast between the structure of the Christian and the Muslim community or communities must be noted. When a religious and a cultural affiliation are equated the implication of a judgment of both the claims of the faith and the nature of the civilization arises. Although for the sake of descriptive convenience they may be dealt with independently, subjectively they are inseparable.

For many centuries the articulate Muslim has attempted to underplay the distinctive local or popular elements in his religious beliefs and practices as well as in his way of life altogether. Religious fervor and conformity to the social-juridical structure which are implicit in both the Quran and the Canon Law, do not always correspond. This was not denied, but rather it was accounted for in terms of ignorance, weakness, or ethnic and social discrepancies. Thus, it is clear that the only effective way to maintain a pan-Islamic unity in which all member societies, regardless of their deviations from the authoritative precept, could feel protected and fortified, is to depreciate deviations from "standard" religious and cultural practice. The important function of literary use

84

of Arabic in preference to the vernaculars becomes apparent in this light.

Identification as a Muslim thus emerges as a highly abstract notion, and it must be such in order to remain largely independent of the accidental, historical, and social influences that surround the individual. A native of Asia or Africa may consider himself not only a Muslim, but a good Muslim, regardless of his matrilineal organization. This is true even though his version of Muslim piety may be "Wahhabi" and was so at a time when the majority of the Islamic world was reluctant to include the Wahhabis in the "orthodox" fold. Despite the knowledge that customs of which he disapproves are followed in proximate areas, the Muslim will not exclude the deviants from the Muslim community as he understands it. Correspondingly, the inhabitants of the other villages will not consider him a non-believer. It is conceded that in actual day-to-day living, this is perhaps only partially true or even merely a disposition, but, beyond its factual presence which must be evaluated on a case to case basis, there is no doubt that it represents an attitude, a determination, an ideal. In the wake of the Iranian hostage crisis, even a rumor that the U.S. was perhaps associated (not true) with the taking over of the Grand Mosque in Mecca, sparked demonstrations, spontaneously, against the U.S. embassies from North Africa through Asia and up to the Philippines. And, to be at all effective, let alone realizable, the ideal must be abstract, neglectful of many of the actualities of Chinese or, say, Egyptian Islam; in fact, of Islam as it is alive anywhere. This is so in spite of the inner need to relate every action, every occurrence to that abstract ideal, to base its acceptance or rejection on it, to justify every thought from it, and to use it as the absolute standard of evaluation.

The emotions of the individual are controlled by the accidental historical situation in which he finds himself. These emotions will be resolved according to a pattern which he will consider Islamic, but which may, in fact, differ sharply from the normal patterns experienced by other groups whose acceptance, nevertheless, will again be explained in the name of Islam. In one sense, Islam is actually none of the patterns; in another, it includes all of them. Subjectively, Islam is the acceptance by one community of the decisions of other communities regarding their own ways of thinking and living, without excluding them from the larger body because of their differences. Conversely, the subcommittees choose to maintain their identification with the larger body despite their insistence on retaining these individual patterns.

There is a small common denominator which may not be relinquished, the belief in the unity of God and in the historical person of Mohammad as His last Prophet, agreement on certain practices and on the inadmissibility of others, and on the existence of an "Islamic" way of life, but its elements are not many. More important perhaps, there is in large sections of that body an agreement as to the method by which, in case of doubt, solutions could and should be reached, there largely as a result of shared historical and spiritual experience, shared preference in resolving situations that require choices. And there is, of course, almost everywhere, the non-Muslim to assist in a certain limitation (which may be tantamount to a definition) of what is immediately identified as Islamic. The facts of early Muslim history, the known precepts and various practices that need not be based on genuine tradition, will serve as passwords to identify the fellow-Muslim. Their essential function is not to form part of an index listing of what Islam is, but to be symbols of a socio-religious unity that is essentially quite independent of their being believed or their being practiced. They give to the community the sense of structural permanence or continuity, even where such continuity has not in fact existed. They inject into time, accident, and imperfection the element of the timeless universal and Divinely Willed Justice which prompts the "fallible" group to fall in the "infallible" community of True Believers.

The Umma which is, by conviction, one and indivisible, is able to maintain a perpetual readiness for its universal mission as a result of the volitional character of Muslims in their collective affiliation with that of the Umma. This has resulted in Islam remaining an "open" system of integration which is achieved, or at least initiated, by an act of will or by a commitment by an individual or society to place itself within the Muslim community. The validity of the decision is independent of the precise knowledge of the ways and beliefs of the Muslim community that motivates and accompanies it, yet it implies the realization that it is irrevocable and binding on future generations as well. It will be said that the apostate is condemned not on the ground of doctrinal error but, to put it in modern terms, because of "high treason" to the Umma. When summoned to recant, it is not his theological views that he is asked to reconsider; he is offered a chance to resume his membership in the community to renew the act of will which will reconstitute him as a Muslim.

Once one reflects on the strident differences in cultural level among those that compose the Umma which extend beyond the core of monotheism and prophetism, the indistinctness of what constitutes an Islamic doctrine combined with the consciousness that Islam provides or contains the possibility of an existence guided entirely by divine directive, emerges as an indispensable premise.

This is another way of saying that the abstractness of the identification renders possible a sense of belonging together among peoples that in their actual mentality and way of life have very little in common and that, on the strictly cultural plane, they may regard each other with contempt or even hostility. It also keeps alive the sense of supernational values and obligations which national loyalties are apt to obliterate, something of infinite value to international law and for the development of transnational ideals.

This approach to the Muslim identity is one of the principal factors which has made Islam so successful in its transcultural expansion in recent and not so recent times. In the last century and a half, the advance of Islam may have been helped by a feeling on the part of many of the

Asian and African populations that Christianity was typically the faith of their alien rulers or would-be rulers, and that affiliation with the Muslim community meant, therefore, not only an advancement toward truth, but an advance in political dignity. It signified an admission to an intercultural body whose spiritual resources would ultimately be adequate to prevent absorptive submission to the Western-Christian world. This reaction represents a total misreading of the Universalism of the Christian message, but, however erroneous it may be, it is symptomatic of the fact that, in part, perhaps because of its insistence on a less "abstract" identification, Christianity during the last two hundred years has probably not been more effective transculturally as Islam, although many European Christian states have been politically ascendant in many areas of the world. Furthermore, while there does exist a cross-comprehension among the major Christian communities and nations, due partly to their identification with the cultural life of the successors of the Roman and Byzantine churches, the Christian states do not, in their aggregate, constitute a single socio-political community in which a mere declaration of intention to belong will secure not only a sense of belonging, but a knowledge of being accepted as well. From an abstract viewpoint, this Islamic sense of "unity," though unique, may not necessarily be a desirable thing. The Christian communities of North America and Western Europe in the wake of their constitutional and rational developments have indeed consciously struggled to separate the religion of the people from the political life of their community. The Protestant communities, particularly, can take pride in having achieved this in the last three or four hundred years. On the other hand, the Roman Catholic Church, particularly because of the institution of papacy, which provides a focal point for all Catholics, loosely resembles in practice, through not in doctrine, the "unity" of Islamic communities we are discussing here.

The cohesion experienced by the West renders it less dependent on a religious symbol than is the Islamic world. This stems from a shared heritage whose origin may be found in pre-socratic thought. This heritage is an unreflected acquisition of life's meaning and purpose which induces "Western man" to undertake infinite tasks without relinquishing the consciousness of his finiteness. The description may gain in accuracy if modified to emphasize the aspirational character of the existential experience which is the world as function and product of subjective operations of the establishment by reason of interpretative contexts that render possible increasingly adequate apprehension of natural structure, this apprehension (and, hence, the world) as process, and human achievement as eternally provisional and self-devouring in a symptomatic approximation to that absoluteness which reason postulates while proving it beyond its reach. Whatever its origin, every concept and every socially effective emotion in the West has had to relate itself to the drives inherent in its basic heritage. In this sense again, the heritage, rather than its doctrinal and organizational vehicles should be regarded as the foundation of Western unity, and here we have one precise reason for the limited transferability of the Western ethos.

In consequence, then, of the peculiar structure of the Muslim Umma, within the circle of those united by the common act of will that identifies them as Muslims, the separateness of the national, linguistic, cultural existence, the pride of domination, and the humiliation of servitude are accompanied by a sense of community that, to a certain extent, enters even into the constituents of their discreteness.

The Turk, as a member of the Turkish nation, is precisely located in space and organization; his language and history are as precisely unique, and his cultural and political aspirations are clearly distinctive over and against those of other comparable groups within the traditional orbit of Muslim civilization. The Turkish nation has defined itself as organized in a secular state. In terms of its political structure, the religious affiliation of the individual Turkish citizen is held immaterial. Yet, in terms of his self-identification, not as a Turkish citizen but as a Turk, the fact of his membership in the Muslim Umma is anything but immaterial. Ignorant perhaps of the tenets of the faith and unobserving of the prescribed practices, tolerant even of participation in public life of non-Muslims on a basis of equality, his affiliation with a community whose views and injunctions he may well consider obsolete remains an essential and highly prized constituent of his self-identification. To be a full Turk, one has to be a

Muslim as well, even though his civic rights may not be affected by belonging to a particular faith.

In the less determinedly "secular" societies of the Muslim orbit (and beyond), a certain upsurge of religion as a point of national concentration has occurred within a few years after the attainment of independence, regardless of the attitude to religion of the government of the day. In this context, the re-won freedom tends to mean, among other things, of course, liberty to revert, openly and with a demonstratively good conscience, to forms of spiritual integration that, in the days of alien rulership or paramountcy had been widely experienced as out of date, retrogressive and, at any rate, inadequate for the achievement of modernization and political advance.

By contrast, one could not predict a comparable development in those Western-Christian countries that have attained their national self-realization during the last century, even though, for example, in Greece and, to some extent, in Poland, the Church had proved to be the repository and the symbol of natural identity. Nor would the Austrian Protestant or the English Catholic be refuted his position as a "full-fledged" Austrian or Englishman; what mild discrimination he may occasionally suffer is merely incidental, being similar to that of a person who, socially, belongs to the "wrong" clique.

There is then perhaps in our day a no more striking illustration of the existential effectiveness than the selfview of the Turk, the Pakistani, the Muslims of Arab tongue, etc. Nothing but what I have called its abstractness and volitional character could have allowed the persistence of a sense of unity among individuals and especially among societies whose structure, tradition, and current aspirations are, if not incompatible, at least too different to provide significant points to contact a sense of unity that need not be directly effective in societal action, yet survives even in the face of a collective self-identification that expressly disclaims it. It is, then, anything but the profound determination to belong with others equally determined that dominates the consciousness of him who identifies himself as a Muslim, regardless of the concrete content which the Islamic ideal has taken on the segment of the Umma in which, by the accident of birth, he is to spend his earthly life.

The philosophical and, consequently, the juridical foundation of the notion of Umma is perhaps a unique mark of distinction in the Islamic conceptions of law and state. It is this single, easy-to-comprehend conception which makes Islamic postulates universal in application. The feeling of fraternity enabled Muslims to survive even when they found themselves in different and far-flung regions of the world.

Theoretically and ideally, of course, in Islamic society, the Umma is supreme, and any executive of the Islamic State must rule in accordance with its wishes and precepts. Actually and historically, however, as most scholars acknowledge, this moral authority and duty, accepted in principle by all good Muslims, did not get translated into civic authority and duty that would create political institutions through which the moral principles of the Umma could be effectively articulated. The reasons for this are complex--beyond our present concern--but were nonetheless effective in preventing the development of means for this fulfillment of Islamic democratic principles. For such means, Islamic peoples still wait in hope and expectation. It is a tribute to the reality and truth embodied in the Shariah that these principles, however frustrated in political articulation, were tenaciously applied throughout Islamic history and succeeded partially in taming and mitigating those forces which made for despotism and tyranny.

This is well summarized by Gibb in the conclusion of his essay on Islamic constitutional organization. Speaking of later expositions of Islamic political thought with the terms in which, e.g., Abu Yusuf addressed Harun al-Rashid, he says that we cannot help but be struck with the remarkable consistency (and perhaps tenacity) with which the Muslim thinkers had pursued this objective as integral to a Muslim's conception of life. He adds that although the historic caliphate had lost its power, and military conquerors had imposed their rule over every Muslim people, a rigid class structure had replaced the fluid social order of the early days, but through all vicissitudes, the principles of Muslim government and polity remained unchanged. It was on these same principles that, for example, both the Ottoman and the Mughal sultans continued to organize their administrations in the centuries that followed, until internal weaknesses brought the intrusion of new social and political ideas based upon an alien philosophy.[77]

CHAPTER V
Legal Concepts of Islam

(A) The Shariah: Genesis of Islamic Law and Jurisprudence

A literally unique aspect of Islam is the conception of the "Shariah." The ensuing pages will examine this conception. Broadly speaking, what does it mean? In a way, it means the rules of conduct of life in its totality. It, therefore, contains the sources of the Islamic law and jurisprudence, but also much more. The extent to which a Muslim is governed by the Shariah will become clear from the following narrative.

Nature of Shariah

If there is one quality distinguishing, above all others, the reformatory work of Islam, it is the spirit of moderation. Truth lay in the middle course, and the Quran declared: "Thus have we made you a middle nation" (ii. 137). In the unswerving adherance of millions lies the proof of the Mission of the Prophet as a practical guide for human conduct. It also furnishes the explanation of its permanence; for nearly fourteen centuries have survived the political, cultural, religious, legal, and social institutions framed by him in light of God's laws. The entirety of mandates and injunctions of God affecting human conduct is the Shariah. Islam still remains, for all practical purposes, the same as it was at its advent.[78]

The Reformation

The essence of Islam and its institutions lies in the full identification of its origin and in the personality of the Prophet. The steps he took affected the lives of Muslims, from small details to important matters. Herein lies the principal difference between Islam and other major religions. Whereas other religions, especially those connected with the person of Jesus, admit to various degrees the scope of religion in the private lives of its adherents, in Islam the effect of this faith in the life of a believer is total. One of the foremost effects of this totality is the amalgamation of the so-called "church" and "state" for a Muslim. Recent evangelist movements in America are attempting to approximate this Islamic conception for the Christians of, particularly, the United States.

The early development of canon law in Europe, particularly in the twelfth and thirteenth centuries, therefore, followed a diametrically opposite evolution. On one hand, the very notion of canon law was based on it being different from ordinary law. On the other hand, Islamic law is the canon law (for Muslims) and the ordinary law. For a believer, Islamic law connotes regulation of all his actions by religious precepts and rules.

The actions of the Prophet encompassed a very wide field. For example, he condemned slavery and urged its prohibition, breathed among the faithful a spirit of charity and friendliness, upheld the moral as opposed to legal authority of the husband over his family as the surest safeguard of the honor and happiness of all. At the same time, he expounded the commandments of God on complex issues regarding government, its functions, its powers, and its duties.

The religion of Islam, for the purpose of introducing a purer faith and healthier organization among the people, did not entirely overlook the exigencies of society and the requirements of human habits by denouncing all existing institutions; the inevitable result of such a step would have been to reduce everything to a state of chaos. For this reason, many exisiting institutions were tolerated with amendments, modifications, and repeals that brought them into harmony with a progressive society and the needs of individual social progress.[79] Mankind, by origin, is a single people or nation (see Quran, iv. 1, ii. 213), and after the corruption of the older revelations, the message of Islam came through the Quran with a twofold objective: (1) to confirm the true and original message and (2) to guard it or act as a check to its interpretation.[80] The days of Jahiliyyah were days of tribalism, feuds, and selfish accentuation of differences in man. Islamic reformation lifted man from that malicious attitude towards a true attitude of unity. God gave religion for the material and spiritual necessities of man (Quran, xiv. 31-34). For such reasons, the Islamic Jurisprudence set down the mandates regarding the principles of belief, acts of worship, transactions, penal affairs, family organization, democratic principles, and many other things. In other words, the reformative principles of Islam are concerned with a system of directions for human welfare (seeking justice, good deeds, equality, human rights, and brotherhood and aimed at forbidding aggression and providing defense thereto), improving the status of the weaker sex and the weak, upholding the sanctity of private ownership, fulfilling contracts and outlawing deceit, and distinguishing the public and private rights in penal matters.

The Quran explained the above principles from the history of Arabia and the neighboring lands. Even abstract notions were illustrated from the past history or Arabian traditions like that of Ad and the Thamud, from Egypt, the Roman Empire, Iraq or Iran, or from the history of the Jewish people. The Quran made a clear distinction between ancient monarchies and other nations and dealt with the main causes of their decline so that it would be an objective lesson for the forthcoming generations. Giving instances from the nation of Israel, the Quran described how God had granted them all His favors and how they had violated their covenants. There are generalizations of the causes of the decline of nations without any reference to any particular government: "God does not change the condition of a people until they have themselves changed their psychology" (Quran, xviii. 11). Since the laws of the universe are not unjust in themselves, all peoples are endowed with a measure of correct conduct, and it is only after their transgression that they are wiped out and replaced by another nation (see Quran, x. 14). It is in this sense that, like the human species which is of the essence of a state, the people (and this would include Muslims) should also have their rise and fall, and when once the national ailments have become incurable, the people, like the human body, die because of the application of preordained laws, giving place to a new and a more vigorous race (see Quran, x. 50).[81] This divine method of operation has been laid down for all times and places according to the nature of man and the limits of his capacities. It leads to the reason of the revelation in Islam which[82] for mankind, is a unique and an easy and effective path.

It should be remembered that in reality "religion" is one. An important message of Islam is that all the prophets are of the same opinion and that they believe in the "unity of God" and the worship of one God. There is unanimity on the principles of moral values and religious fundamentals which relate to piety, worship, fasting, almsgiving, Hajj (pilgrimage) revealed books, etc. With the passage of time, under corrupt leadership, the aims and purposes of religion were lost and, for that reason, a new prophet was sent to reform the corrupt society and bring back the life of the people in accordance with the original principles of religion. Under these principles, the mission of the last Prophet of God, Mohammad, was to reform the deteriorated condition of humanity. The message he brought forth was for the achievement of the natural demand of time and for the reformation of humanity back to the principles given by God. The pre-Islamic era had an accretion of time and happenings. Out of the many original institutions, evils crept up to confuse the original message of God for mankind. The worship of God, the path directed by Him, and the principles of Ibadat and Salat, obedience and goodness, were not followed. The Prophet of Islam saw all these evil conditions, examined as a whole the misguided people, prohibited the unlawful and permitted the lawful or modified or amended the conduct of the people and their modes of belief back to the original message of God.

He reorganized the set-up of the society. In different areas of human life, in all relations of man in worldly affairs, and in his relation to the Creator of the universal system, he introduced far-reaching changes. He gave to the people the laws of God, rearranged the conflicts in the interest of their welfare, taught them to be peaceful, lawful, righteous, and just, and led them to the worship of God, who is One, eternal, and incomparable.[83]

Islam--What It Is

The word Islam is derived from the word Aslama, which literally means "complete surrender" to the will of God. The din or religion, which means "submission," is a divine institution for the guidance of rational beings and for ensuring salvation here and hereafter. Inclusive of belief and action in Islam, there is external and internal submission to the will of the Almighty.[84] The will of God is that mankind should pursue Husn, i.e., beauty of life and character as expressed in revelations from time to time, culminating in the final revelation by the Quran and the Sunnah of the Prophet Muhammad.

The Quran and Islam

The Quran is quite explicit on the religion of Islam. It says: "Lo! religion with Allah is the surrender to His will and guidance" (III. 19). Morever, a religion or din is only a religion which is final and complete, on the clear maxim that since God is One, His standard religion is one. The Quran makes the point clear and says explicitly: "That is the right religion," i.e., the standard religion (din qayyim) (cf. xxx, 30). It is based on human nature, for every individual, by birth, remains a Muslim, since inclined towards a belief in one God, but later the parents bring him into the fold of other beliefs. Bukhari (Sahih, I 34) mentions the text of a hadith on the issue which says: "The Prophet Mohammad said, Every infant is born in the natural state; it is his parents who make him a Jew or a Christian or a Magian." Therefore, according to this theory, God has created only one religion which has only one major message. It is contained in Islam, which is just a submission to the will of God.[85] It implies faith, doing right and justice, being an example for others with power to enforce righteousness, eschewing wrong and being a model for others. These principles of Islam are for mankind and are forever. The more sectarian and divided a people become, the greater the necessity of the message of Islam which preaches between warring factions as the religion of peace and unity. Islam is a privilege of much value, and by accepting it, there is no favor on the preacher of the community. If the acceptance is from the heart, it is a great favor done to those who accept the light of God; it signifies that they have received guidance.[86] Those who listen to the message find God's grace at each stage and travel farther on the path of truth and righteousness. Islam means peace and tranquility. It includes a sense of security and permanence, soundness and freedom from defects, and perfection as the word Salam in the Quran (xix. 62) denotes. It is preservation, salvation, deliverance, salutation, resignation, and freedom from jarring elements. All these shades of meaning are there in Islam with reliance on God. The reign of peace is preached by it (Quran, viii. 61) with humility and perseverance for the welfare of mankind. The message of Islam was given by God through the medium of Mohammad, the last of the prophets (Quran, xxxiii. 40), who was sent as a favor to believers (Quran, iii. 164, iv. 170), as a mercy to them and to all creatures (Quran, ix. 61, xxi. 107) and as the Universal Messenger to men (Quran, xxxiv. 28).[87]

Thus, the law of Islam is framed on human nature (Quran, xxx. 30), and man has been created as a social being. Social life is indispensable for human beings. Human beings have been directed to be just and righteous. They are to do good deeds. For example, the Quran directs man to believe in God, the Last Day, the Angels, the Prophets, to spend money on the needy and the poor; and to remain patient for their welfare. To the same extent are the traditions or the Sunnah of the Prophet.[88] Religion is not a mere ideological vision. It is a practical system of life, for it balances human requirements, reason and spirit, and resolves conflicts in the interest of society between spiritual and temporal, and economic and social principles with its independent existence. The Quran says: "This day have I perfected your religion for you, completed my favor upon you, and have chosen for you Islam as your religion" (v. 4). It sufficiently proves that the principles and institutions of Islam are all-comprehensive. They include the whole of human existence, emotions, thoughts, actions, worship, economic deals, social relationships, bodily urges, spiritual demands, and every other value which is based on the rules of hikmah or wisdom for the welfare and betterment of mankind.[89]

The fundamental principles of Islam, morever, provide: "Let there be no compulsion in religion" (see the Quran, ii. 256). The reason for the above is clear. It lies in the fact that compulsion is incompatible with religion, because religion depends upon faith and will, which would be meaningless if induced by the use of force. Since God is the Creator, His protection is continuous and His plan is always to lead mankind from the depths of darkness into the clearest light. In the light of the qualities and principles of religion, it is clear that for the wise there is no hindrance which hampers or stops him from his belief in religion, for it is capable of intelligent comprehension. As God is Malik-ul-Mulk, Rabb-il-Alimin, Khair-ul-Hakimin, or the All-Powerful Sovereign, under His mercy, He leaves it to the people to come to the right way.

Every religion puts before the people a system of humanity. Being framed on human reason, there is imperfection in the nature and methods of operation of the rules which work for the welfare of mankind. If one judges other prevalent systems, one finds there is a continued thirst for perfection. The reason is simple and lies in the fact that they are man-made. The principles preached one day are substituted the next day by another ideology. Man-made ideologies work through the method of imposition and, remaining external in operation, do not bind people together. The spiritual aspects not being complete, there arises the need for modification. Other principles are imposed by the authority which believes in them. There arises group feeling and the desire to impose particular ideology. The theory of forcible implementation comes into existence and, under state power, a particular principle is imposed. With the decrease in the authority of imperative principles, another principle is substituted which asserts itself and gains control. However, this theory, in turn, withers away with the withering away of its authority. All these principles are transitory; Islam never works by these methods. It operates through external and internal manifestations, and having been ordained by the Almighty, its principles are inherent in human nature. It not only binds human acts, but its preachings penetrate the soul and spirit; every Muslim feels what he should do, and religion guides his actions from inside his mind and body.

Islam works as a complete code of life. The Muslim life consists of no dichotomy. In what a Muslim has to do in secular transactions, in his actions for social dealings, individual interest, national demands, international brotherhood, nay, in all relations of human civilization, there is a complete direction contained in the institutions which he follows. For these reasons, Islam is a religion of human nature, a religion of conduct of life. The name given to this entire system is Shariah.

Islam, as we have seen in the previous pages, is not simply a religion; it is a living form and expression or manner of existence. High spiritual aspiration, valuable outward moral and religious discipline, with rules of conduct in every minute area of human life here and hereafter, is the essence of the character of the teachings of Islam. Its laws are a part of the whole system which God has devised for the entire universe. It is concerned first and foremost with the relation between God and the human soul. The individual is given paramount consideration in this scheme, as man is called the greatest of His creations.

The word "Shariah" is used in the Quran itself. The Quran says: "Then we put thee on the right way of religion: so follow . . . Shariah" (xlv. 18). The religion of the Shariah given by God is the same, in essence, as that revealed, for example, to Noah, Abraham, Moses or Jesus, or to Mohammad, the Prophet of Islam. The source of unity is the revelation from God, and in Islam, it is established as an institution (Quran, xlii. 15) for guidance with reference to conduct, and light with reference to insight into the higher realm of the spirit (Quran, v. 47). The Islamic dispensation is one which would not have been known had there not been a divine revelation. It includes the revelations made by Allah to earlier prophets of Bani (tribe) Israel and the Nasara as confirmed by the last revelation through the Prophet of Islam. The revelation, as it came to the Prophet, is the Shariah par excellence. It implies that it is only what is stated in the divine messages, or inferred from them, that come properly under the Shariah. It means, in other words, that matters determined by intellectual processes are outside the scope of the Sacred Law. The totality of God's commandments relating to the activities of man, as given by Him, are based upon His will bounded by no limit. The duty of mankind is to follow it[90] and not to judge it for causes through human intellect.

The words "al-Sirat-ul-Mustaqim," or the "straight path," as used in Islam, are contained in the Shariah which is al-hidayah, or "the guide." The word "hidayah" means directions to reach the goal intended by God; in other words, the guide which leads to the goal. The former is used for the light provided by God, and the latter is contained in the way provided by the Prophet of Islam.

The directions contained in the Shariah serve as guides for the establishment of Shariah values, called Ahkam al-Shari, i.e., the qualities determined as a result of revelations. The evidences of the Shariah, or "Adilat al-Shariah," are four in number, viz., the Quran, the Sunnah, the Ijma, and the Qiyas.

The legal science which derives the norms and values from the Shariah is called Fiqh, or "Ilm-ul-Fiqh" (Islamic Jurisprudence). It is a method of deduction of the Shariah rules relating to conduct from their various particular or tafsili evidences. Since the four Shariah evidences or sources are too general, or ijmali, they need a particular science as a basis to establish the Shariah rules in particular cases or problems. This particular science, which prepares its premises for Fiqh, in order to derive the Shariah norms and rules from the Shariah evidences, is called "Usul-ul-Fiqh," which may also be termed as the science of the bases of Fiqh, resting on the four Shariah sources.[91]

Since the Quran and the Sunnah are the principal sources from which the precepts of the Shariah have been drawn, the rules so deduced are the principal subjects of Islamic Jurisprudence. God, the only legislator, has shown the way of felicity to the people, and in order to enable them to walk in that way, He has shown the precepts which are found partly in the eternal Quran and partly in the sayings and doings of the Prophet. They were transmitted to posterity by the Companions of the Prophet and preserved in the Sunnah and the rules thereof called Ahkam. Hukam (pl. Ahkam) is established by communication from God, and it deals with religious belief in the unity of God as Kalam and moral principles and human acts as Awamir wa Nawahi. The relations with the Creator are basically obligations of the creatures as the rights of God and are called Ibddat or Huquq Allah, i.e., the service to or the rights of God. The affairs of mankind and transactions (muamalat), i.e., the rights of God's creatures, are called Huquq-ul-ibad. They cover the whole field of human life and conduct under the framework provided by the Shariah. In the whole system of the sacred principles, God, being the sole Lawgiver, is the Supreme Sovereign or Hakim. The principle is simple that Hukam needs a Hakim, which implies the existence of persons for whom its imposition is in existence in relation to their actions and deals. The Hakim, hence, is God Who is All Powerful and Malik-ul-Mulk, or the Rabb-ul-Alimin, and the creatures or the people on whom the Hukam is imposed are called Mahkum Alaihi.

The principles of the Shariah imply that all commands or Ahkam, being divine, are as much for worldly prosperity as for future reward. These features are based upon certain axiomatic, acute, and intricate rules of metaphysics and divinity. The body of the science of Fiqh, which teaches the knowledge of various branches of human conduct in detailed application, is called "Ilm-ul-Faru." Its scope remains wide to incorporate each and every aspect of human life. The injunctions of the Shariah uniquely and positively bind the Muslim's act, his conscience, and, irrespective of what else or wherever he may be, the commandments of religion are always present to guide his actions and dealings. Timely consideration or self-indulgence may hamper the spirit, but the control of din (faith) is always present in the faithful heart. For this reason, Islam, regulating each[92] and every area of human life, is a complete code of life.

The message of Islam, as provided in the Shariah, works for the avoidance of difficulties (or Adam Harj) from human life (see the Quran, ii. 185: "God desires you ease and good and not hardship"), for the Quran says: "God is Rahman or Rahim" (i. 1, 3). Everything based on wisdom and benefit is provided for man and his social life, by God. The Quran explains the same: "We have turned about for men in this Quran every parable . . ." (xvii. 91) as details of everyday life. Moreover, the Shariah is a guide for the lessening of difficulties (qillat-i-taklif), for mankind which is one nation. By a gradual process (tadrij), a model state for the accomplishment of the ideals given by it is clearly provided. Everything based upon human nature is contained as a feature of justice and righteousness. God, who is Adil (just), made mankind into an Umma who follow His guidance and abide by His Ahkam. The commandments of God on the basis of this theory are just and beneficial for mankind. Ahkam are divided into Fard or Wajib, i.e., expressly commanded by Quran or categorically commanded by traditions. The acts

102

fall into five categories: Mustahab (desirable), Jaiz (permitted), Mubah (indifferent), Mukruh (reprobated) and Haram (absolutely forbidden). All these show the depth of the principles of the Shariah. It not only tells what is required under penalty, but also what is recommended or disliked though without reward or penalty. In other words, all human acts are permitted, or indifferent, unless and until some authority can be discovered in the Shariah which raises or lowers them in points of validity. Nevertheless, in cases of justified excuses, the strict principles of the Shariah, termed azimat, provide a concession by way of equity or rukhsat; the same is well illustrated in the concession on fasting on a journey or while sick.[93]

Not a Theocracy

It should be kept in mind that what has been discussed above are completely unique principles of the Islamic system. Islam is not a "theocracy", which is from the Greek word theos, meaning God, and which is a government or state governed by God directly or through a priestly class. In the Shariah, God is God and man is man, and even the Prophet is mentioned as man (Quran, xviii. 110: "Say: I am only mortal like you") and the caliph is a mere representative of the people.[94]

Man is a social being; he is not able to live alone, like other creatures[95] and has the need of mutual assistance and joint action. By reason of the fact that there remains the need for practical rules of conduct under which man may live, God has provided practical propositions[96] of the Shariah which refer either to the matter of future life as ibadat or to matters of life on this earth. In this way, God decreed the continuation of this world until the appointed time. This requires the perpetuation of man which depends upon his concept of the rules of conduct for his progress and welfare and for his prosperous and peaceful life spiritually and materially in earth's civilization.[97]

The Shariah, supposedly contains a complete code of life, though many of its principles have still to be uncovered by man. The progress of man is dependent upon his imperfection and the unfolding of mysteries of the universe. The Shariah is a constant invitation, for action in this direction.

Shariah's Economic System (see also Chapter VII)

From the very beginning, it should be remembered that God has organized the system of a happy life on the basis of the needs of the people. The Shariah evidences (especially the Quran and the Sunnah) have laid down principles for each and every area of man's life, and, thus, the rules and methods have been enunciated relating to ibad, manner of living, muamalat, State affairs, etc. Let us now take up briefly the principles which relate to the Islamic economic system to show that even this matter, in its essential emphasis, is covered by the Shariah.

The principles of economic realities have been enumerated in the Quran.[98] At first, man's living or livelihood is guaranteed by God and He has promised to provide a living for every creature. The Quran says: "Your sustenance is also that which ye are promised" (li. 21). It is elaborated: "There is no moving creature on earth but its sustenance dependeth on God: He knoweth the time and place of its definite abode" (xi. 6). The gift of sustenance may be different to creatures, but inequality is not the divine intention. The Quran says: "God has bestowed His gifts of sustenance more freely on some of you than on others: those more favored are not going to throw back their gifts to those whom their right hands possess so as to be equal in that respect. Will they deny the favor of God?" (xvi. 71). It means that it is the duty of those who are rich to come to the help of the needy and, thus, to equalize the necessities of every individual. Under this principle, the State has the duty to see to the sustenance and maintenance of every one of its citizens, the poor having a special right for maintenance. The surplus properties of the richer class were distributed to the poorer class during the republican period of Islam. The great caliphs Omar and Ali acted according to the directions of the original principles of the Quran and the Sunnah, and a system of social security[99] perhaps for the first time in human history was adopted.

The Islamic economic system further disapproves of accumulation of wealth in a few hands, as this ultimately paralyzes the whole social fabric. There may, however, be difference in the scale of people's riches and wealth. The Quran says: "Woe to every kind of scandal-monger and backbiter, who pile up wealth and layeth it by" (civ. 2). Similarly, the passion for seeking increase in wealth affects individuals, societies, and nations (see Quran, civ. 1, 2). The Book of God provides that goods and wealth should be circulated and distributed among all classes of society. In Surah Hashr (7), Baqarah (177), and at many other places, severe punishment for hoarders and monopolists is provided. Lawful, necessary, and individual and social spending of wealth has been regularized, and the State is made to adopt the directions of the Quran. Charity and almsgiving have religious sanction, and the unity of the principles of Fiqh is a proof for the economy in the Shariah system. The third principle prohibits unlawful deals, interest taking, undue and excessive profit, unfair trade practices and similar transactions, by laying down what is lawful and beneficial for individual and social interests. The Shariah provides economic principles relating to individual earning, what is to be earned, what is to be spent, and on what it should be spent. The rules of law and justiciability are enunciated, and man is directed to act lawfully and for the welfare of others. Under social principles, he is to enter into transactions of trade and business, work, and other means of earning a livelihood (see Surahs Baqarah, Bani Israil, Nahl, Inam, Jumuah, Muminin, etc.).

The Shariah provides for the economy to be based upon social principles for all mankind. The Quran says: "Ye are the best of people, evolved for mankind, enjoying what is right, forbidding what is wrong, and believing in God" (iii. 110).

The economic structure of the Shariah under the general principles stated above comes to a practical application when examined empirically. Based upon democratic principles, the State is administered under a social security system providing full and equal economic rights for all members of the society, without discrimination and without any bias. To benefit umemployed and the needy, the institutions of awqaf, zakat, inheritance, and taxation are provided. Suppression of usury, monopolies, hoarding, smuggling, and other unfair trade practices is made the underlying policy, with social control on means of production as against individual interests. There is the system of collective bargaining over individual profits in trade and business and equal distribution of profit-sharing for the capitalist and the labor classes. Individual ownership is subject to the principle of social welfare by implementation of methods controlling the accumulation of individual's wealth. The institutions for the welfare of the general public or common man, however, must effectively safeguard and promote individual property rights.[101] In other words, the principles of the Shariah provide a kind of social solidarity. There is freedom and right to work, to own property, and to enjoy other property rights. Nevertheless, these principles are bound by the larger interests of the community in Islam. In fact, right of private ownership in the Shariah is governed by the theory that as all property is owned by God, man is only to enjoy its benefits. In other words, his title is limited to the benefits accruing on the property, but the legal title vests in God. The exercise of this right is circumscribed by the larger interests of the community and, thus, the principles of social solidarity prohibit exploitation.

The Shariah has always placed equal emphasis on the rights of the individual and the rights of the Umma. The individual is the central element in the social edifice, and a general responsibility towards him is one of the basic concepts of the Muslim system. To keep a balance, an individual also has obligations towards the community. This system is intended to achieve social justice.

Shariah and Political Science

Prophet Mohammad showed a path to mankind, the path of a universal law, i.e., the Shariah. Contrary to the rigid limitations of race, national frontiers, language, and geographical configuration, it contains many commandments[102] about the political setup of an ideal Islamic community.

According to the Shariah, sovereignty belongs to God, and the attributes of His sovereignty can be best ascertained from His names: Rabb-ul-Alimin, Malik-ul-Mulk, Malik-un-Nas, Khair-ul-Hakimin, Malik-ul-Quddus, Ankam-ul-Hakimin, etc. (see the Quran, xvii. 11; xxi. 22;

lix. 2; cxii. 1-4). He created man by breathing of His spirit, which is a faculty of knowledge, piety, and will. He made man His viceregent on earth and entrusted him with power and disposition through the medium of trust. Man is expected to use it in order that he might fulfill the obligations of the covenant entered.[103] The idea of trust implies trustees who are authorized to administer and use the power according to the injunctions of God. The Quran is the fountain of justice, and the faithful are to derive guidance of principles from it. Further guidance and specifications are provided about God's directions by the Sunnah of the Prophet and by the consensus of jurists in cases of ambiguity (see the Quran, i. 5-6, xlii. 38).

The Shariah, thus, conceives of a social and political order as a means of discovering the signs of God's will for accomplishing service to humanity. It enables the people belonging to that order to show capacity for initiative and unfold the immense possibilities latent in these signs. The society conceived is called Umma, which has to set virtues as the object of its social and political life under the framework of Taqwa, i.e., justice and righteousness.

The Quran, in this respect, directs: "Thus have We made of you an Umma justly balanced, that ye might be witnesses over the nations, and the Apostle a witness over yourself" (ii. 143). This extraterritorial concept of Umma is already explained, according to the principles of Shariah, follows the provisions of set rules.[104] Among the people wholly belonging to an Umma, the State functions as an instrument providing fields of cooperation for the righteous people. It means the setting up of standards of righteousness in all dealings and, thus, naturally, the Umma being the prerequisite of the State, the power to govern or to be a State is granted in light of the Quranic principles. The principles run: "Surely God does not love the mischiefmakers;" and, "My promise is the conduct which is prescribed for all forming the Umma and also the state." A State is simply a system, an arrangement, for furthering the goals of the Umma by applying Shariah. The real government belongs to God, and the same is administered on His behalf by the Umma as a divine trust placed in the hands of the governors (rulers), i.e., the government for the benefit of people. The foundations of the government are, thus, trust and justice, and the State must apply itself to achieve these ends. The government enjoys the right of obedience by the people so long as it conducts the affairs of the Umma according to the Islamic spirit and ideals, and as soon as the same is violated, the government, or those who form it, lose their right and the Umma may change them. The institution of Chilphate is formed on the same principles. The actual sovereign being God, the ruler of the State has to abide by the limits set up by His orders as found in the Quran, Sunnah, Ijma and Qiyas. God is Adil, and Sadiq, i.e., just, and true, (see the Quran, xxi. 47, lxxv. 8). Under His Shariah, everything is regulated by principles of justice and righteousness which are to be cherished and achieved.

The above discussion shows that in the Shariah, the conceptions of political science are based upon the principle that "sovereignty" belongs to God and the State or the government is the representative of the Umma. The community has the highest corporate existence. The administration is to be run according to the ideals provided by the evidences of the sacred principles of the Shariah contained in the Quran and other sources. These ideals are based on the principles of justice, righteousness, peace, and the prosperity of man in accordance with the nature of man's creation. Under them are provided the rules of the politico-legal science of Islam. It shows that there is no absolutism in Islam and, thus, neither the State nor the government has unlimited power. The individual has his own self-recognized, corporate, and social life, with due provision for his different fundamental rights and related claims through the principles of social solidarity.[105]

This analysis may clarify the place and method of the principles of the Shariah in matters of the rules of human conduct and government in general. The Shariah contains many principles for public, private, social, national, and international conduct; these principles govern all human action for life in this world and also for life hereafter. The messages of God, through divine means, did not come all at once. They existed and came into operation on the day man was created. The final message came through the last Prophet Mohammad for all mankind. Shariah is, thus, a complete science which is not specialized for a particular period of time, but is meant for all periods and times. It cannot be amended or modified (see the Quran, x. 64), for it is given by God, who is Perfect and Creator of the universe and all things. The principles laid down by the Shariah are above every man-made society and, being perennial, are adoptable for every new situation.

Man-made laws are always subject to amendment and are modified from time to time according to the changes in man's social life. The principles of the Shariah of Islam, which include the laws needed for society, remain perennial and fixed, in spite of changes in social situations. They cover changes which may come about in the society. They are also flexible, for they contain instructions for new rules of law arising in every society. The modern systems of law, as framed by different societies, are for a particular place and, nature being transitory, do not always fully and completely satisfy human needs. The modern systems have the welfare of the individual and society as their objective. The Shariah of Islam also has this objective in view. The modern systems, however, work only for external actions, and the modern oriented laws are binding only for the external conduct of the people. In contrast, the Shariah works not only towards binding external human actions, but also towards man's internal conscience. The role of a Qadi, or judge, in the Islamic system is concerned with external justiciability of human actions, and the Mufti has a role which is concerned with internal manifestations, man's conduct in belief, and matters relating to his conscience which are tested in accordance with the rules of the faith of Islam. The Shariah, it will be seen, has, thus, a wider scope of purpose, a fact which speaks well for its depth in content.

The principles of the law framed by the Shariah aim to do complete "justice." Justice is, of course, a much wider term than law or even equity. On the basis of the monotheistic nature of Islam, the Islamic notions of law, justice, and society are very similar. Whereas, for example, in Common law these three terms have different meanings and history, they may be used interchangeably in Islam. It's an index of Islam's predisposition towards an ethical basis of its laws. The Shariah conceives of one legislator, one law, and one justice for all. In other words, there is harmony in the principles of law and justice. In contrast, the Roman law, the English law, and all other man-made laws have a dualism in their systems. The notion of law provides one thing, but since "justice" requires other principles, to do complete justice, the State, or as in England, the Chancellor, intervenes to mellow down the rigors of law. In Western legal systems it is justice according to law; in Islam, legal justice is the same as abstract justice.

The present chapter has principally aimed at analyzing some major aspects of the Shariah: its nature, its effect on the political norms, and its insistence on economic measures to be adopted by Islamic communities. Only these have been discussed to show the comprehensiveness of Islamic law for its believers. The nature of this book has demanded the exclusion of discussion of other, perhaps less important, matters with which the Shariah deals. Accordingly, we can now turn to a discussion of the concept of law (in the Western sense) of Islam. This is also contained in its comprehensive Shariah.

(B) Concept of Law

In abstract terms, the term "law" is primarily in controversy in many modern systems. The notion of the term "law" in civilian systems is not the same as in common law in which again there are various schools. To the communist, it simply means an order of those in power. The boundaries of the term "jurisprudence" are greatly controverted, and there are systems of jurisprudence that judge and define the term "law," vis-a-vis, its application and enforcement according to a particular notion and policy. Thus, there are analytical, positivist, imperative, purist, realist, functional, sociological, teleological, comparative, and other systems that variously conceptualize law. These systems approach the law on the basis of their notions and go further to define law in terms of ethics, judicial process, purpose, social fact, imperative, or totalitarian ideals. All this controversy has a far-reaching effect on the methods of administration and application of the law and its enforcement in different communities. It has given rise to a set of different forms of states, governments, and constitutional laws. On judging these complexities, the politico-legal science in the Shariah has neither a dichotomy nor a conflict in its aims, purposes, and objects, and a unity is visible in its ideology, action, and effects. The Shariah system works through secular and religious principles and also has a method of protecting individual, social, and human interests. The Shariah, having been framed upon the inherent nature of man and constitutional elements of his creation, remains different from other systems. It is different primarily since all of its schools have common fundamentals. Law, whether secular, non-secular constitutional, public or private, must be based on and derived from the word or mandate of God as evidenced in the Quran, or from the traditions of the Prophet. "Laws" are, thus, the norms of human behavior as desired by God.

Any Western examination of the concept of law is very difficult, for we have to decide many questions of policy while talking of "authority" and "enforcement." Hart's monumental work on the concept of law abundantly proves this point. The Islamic conception of law, however, is relatively simple. There being no dispute as to its authority (by definition, it comes from God), the essence and aims of Islamic law are the protection and progress of first, the individual, and second, the community. Man-made laws (i.e., where allowed), if valid, have, and indeed must have, the same characteristics. All laws must, therefore, protect and provide the individual's normal and righteous life in a community.

The man-made systems are operative only under a rule of enforcement by a body imposing them. The Shariah system being divine is operative forever; it remains fixed and is perennial. The manufactured systems do not possess an internal manifestation but remain operative only during such time as they are kept enforced by the temporal power. The Shariah is operative by internal manifestation and works on human conscience. Therefore, where Islamic law is not a part of the positive law of a modern state for the Muslims, it is a case of the "validity" of law as against its "efficacy." Laws are there, but the system (non-Islamic) refuses to enforce them. From the preceding discussion, it is clear that in Islamic philosophy, because of this basic postulate that all "laws" must be derived from this law of God, the lexicographical problems which have been arising in Europe and common law jurisdictions become unimportant and irrelevant; of course, what "is" the word of God is a jurisprudential matter and has been minutely examined by the various schools in the evolution of Islamic law. Furthermore, the controversy which has gone on for at least the last three hundred years in the West about the nature of law amongst the various protongonists of different legal philosophies, is also of little importance in Islamic law. In Islamic law, it is, a priori, settled that "law" is a mandate of divine origin and, therefore, aims at the betterment of the society within the limits prescribed by God. The doctrine of "Ijtihad" provides the necessary "dynamics" to meet the exigencies of the changes in time. We will discuss it in greater detail later on.

In the Western political and legal theories, the origin and relationship of law and State is a matter of controversy. Some schools of law maintain that the State is superior to law and creates it, while others are of the view that law precedes the State and binds it after it comes into existence. Still others take a combined view that law and the State are one and the same thing looked at from different points of view.[106] There have also been disputes about the theory of sovereignty and forms of government. In England, Parliament has been called the Sovereign; in the United States it is the Supreme Court's interpretive power or perhaps the Congress; and in the communist countries, it is the Proletariat. In other words, the essential make-up of the State is in controversy. A set of writers accepted the State as an association of persons established for human ends in war and peace. The theory of laissez-faire curtailed the sphere of the State, while the collectivists preached for the State to be all functional and authoritative. The purists believed the State to be incorporated by international morality, while others held the State to be a juristic person endowed with the right to impose its will on the inhabitants of a given territory.[107] Compared to all these conflicting views, it may be said that the Shariah is simple. God being an absolute sovereign as the creator of all things, the roles of State, government, and law have been well settled for centuries.[108]

It follows from what has been stated that, to begin with, there is a very important distinction in the notion of State between Western political thought and Islam. From Plato and Aristotle to Rosseau, it has been maintained that the institution of State was the culmination of an evolutionary process by which a large number of people in a fixed territory formed an organization for the collective good of all. The philosophical basis for this creation was provided by different versions of the social contract theory. As a consequence of these theories, especially that of Hobbes and Locke, there emerged within the State so created two sets of entities, the rulers and the ruled.

Compared to this, Islam begins by speaking of "universality" rather than of territorial limitations. The closest notion (but in reality quite different) to this outlook, is provided by the concept of "ius gentium" and "ius naturale" of Roman law. While admitting that territorial boundaries do exist for artificial or administrative reasons, there is no place for the notion of the "rulers" and the "ruled." As a direct consequence, there is no place for the theory of social contract. The "righteous ruler" and his election by the community is provided by a divine mandate, and no philosophical basis is needed to give sophistication to an existing state of affairs. The rights of the community and "human rights" have an important place in the law of Islam.

We have seen that the message of the religion of Islam is a complete surrender to the Creator, His worship and submission to His orders. The word "Islam" also means peace. We have seen how greatly the theory of the Shariah aims at the betterment and welfare of mankind. God being the real ruler of the world, He made man His viceregent on earth, but under prescribed limits. He commanded man to do justice and practice righteousness. Man's individuality has been given special significance, and even the angels were ordered to prostrate before him; he has been influenced by God's spirit, as he was created in the best of moulds (see the Quran, xv. 29, lxxxv. 4). The brotherhood of man must be helped by the Umma as a service to God and cannot be complete without fulfillment of obligations towards mankind. The continuity of the prophets culminating in the last of the Messengers, Mohammad, leads to the conclusion that the main purpose of God is the welfare of man. The Quran says: "Verily, this brotherhood of yours is a single brotherhood" (xxiii. 52). It is clear that mankind is the highest form

113

of ideological unity above all differences of time and space. Man is given an individuality, and its free development must be allowed in relation to the brotherhood. This, in a nut shell, is the aim of all Islamic laws.

Human Rights

The development of the individual within the society became the basis of what we now call "human rights." However, it took centuries before we reached the stage wherein these rights could be legally recognized, and it has taken decades for its international enforcement since the U.N. was created in 1945. The development of modern international human rights law is currently being divided into three generations, the first being civil and political, the second being economic and social, and the third containing a number of different rights under the rubric of solidarity rights. In Islam, all of them were to be found fourteen hundred years ago in the content of the Shariah.

There is little doubt that the British Parliament is the mother of all modern parliaments. Its evolution is indeed the story of human rights. The first act on the part of the sovereign which gave recognition to the rights of the people was the grant of Magna Charta (1215 A.D.). It was followed by the Petition of Right of 1628 and the Bill of Rights of 1689. The Rights of Man received the attention of Paine, Grotius, and other philosophers in Europe, and the theory of the state of nature transformed itself to the social contract theory and the general will at different times. The French Revolution imbibed a spirit for the attainment of the rights of man, as did the famous Virginian Declaration of Human Rights. The American Declaration of Independence of 1776 was also a landmark towards the rights of man. The two world wars led to the establishment, first, of the League of Nations and then of the United Nations. Through different international agreements and conventions, the principles were adopted in the fundamental laws of national constitutions in the shape of fundamental rights. The United Nations finally adopted, in 1948, in the Universal Declaration of Human Rights, many moral principles in the shape of legal provisions.

It, therefore, appears that the rights of man in the Western world were recognized centuries after the advent of Islam. The Shariah had already provided, more exhaustively, the recognition of human rights and other principles for the welfare and protection of interests of mankind. These were laid down by the Quranic revelations, Prophetic Sunnah, and the practice and traditions of Islam in the seventh century A.D.

Aims and Essence of Islamic Law

If one were to state the essence and aims of the Islamic law, it could be laconically stated simply, the protection and promotion of human rights. The analysis of the present chapter would establish that that is the main and undeniable thrust of the Shariah. All the positive and negative injunctions frequently used from Quranic sources revolve around some aspect of the human rights philosophy. Since man (not States as in Western political theories) is the center of the universe, laws are made with a clear mandate behind them for his welfare. Therefore, inter alia, the source of human rights protection laws is the highest in Islam.

It has been stated above that man is the viceregent of God on earth. The viceregency includes many things and is a symbol of man's status and righteousness. The Quranic message says: "Mankind was one single nation" (ii. 213); man was created one, and God's message is in essence one, for unity of all peoples, regardless of their race or ethnic background. But, by selfishness, man split his kind into different nations, races, and entities of regions (see also the Quran, x. 19). The message of God provides free will for man, particularly in religious matters. It says: "If it had been thy Lord's Will, they would all have believed all who are on earth. Wilt thou compel mankind against their will to believe?" (x. 99). With full freedom and with complete rights given or delegated to him, man is an agent of God (see the Quran, vi. 165). His interests are protected in a variety of ways by the numerous laws and rules of the Shariah. Two examples will suffice for our present purpose. The Quran says: "And lower thy wing to the believers who follow thee" (xxvi. 215) asking man to be kind, gentle, and considerate to human beings (see also Quran, xv. 88 and

xvii. 24). The principles of justice mentioned at various places in the Quran ordain man to be good in his deeds, fulfilling all requirements of civilized life. The opposite of these qualities is prohibited as are also shameful actions, things unjust or injurious to others, and any rebellion against the Shariah values and ideals or man's own conscience in its most sensitive forms (compare the Quran, xvi. 90). The Prophet also stressed strict adherence to the Quranic principles. In the last sermon on Mount Arafat, the Prophet said: "O people! listen to my words as I may not be another year with you in this place. Be humane and just among yourselves. The life and property of each are sacred and inviolable to the other. Render faithfully everyone his due, as you will appear before the Lord and He will demand an account of your actions. Treat woman well; they are your helpmates and do nothing by yourselves. You have taken them from God on trust. O people! listen to my words and fix them in your memory. I have revealed to you everything; I have left to you a law which you should preserve and be firmly attached to, a law clear and positive, the Book of God and the Examples" (i.e., Hadith).[110]

The principles providing protection of human rights are thus part of the Shariah itself. The laws of conduct or rules for human behavior include the provisions of fundamental rights. A tradition says: "Abdullah b. Umar reported that the Messenger of Allah said: Behold! each one of you is a king, and each one of you will be asked about his subjects. A leader is a king over the people and he will be asked about his subjects; a man is a king over the members of his household and he will be asked about his subjects; a woman is a queen over the members of the household of her husband and of his children, and she will be asked about them; a servant of a man is a king over the property of his master, and he will be asked about it. Behold each one of you is a king and each one of you will be asked about his subjects."[111] This tradition lays down in a most comprehensive manner what the rights and duties of persons holding status in life's various departments are towards others around them. The main principle which appears in this tradition is that the meaning of law not only includes the prohibition of wrongful conduct violating others' rights but also that one should always pursue a good conduct morally for the general welfare. It, thus, provides for automatic protection of human rights. The legal conception is wider in its effect, for its operation is dependent not only on legal behavior, but also on behavior which goes to reform man in his future modes in life. Man's inner self is also bound by the rules of the Shariah which is superior to mere legal principles.

The system of the Shariah is based upon divine principles, and its institutions are sacred. The infringement of the moral rules of the system, as opposed to secular rules, includes unlawful conduct, and it is also a sin against religion and God. There is a double protection of human rights. The rules of law work not only for the prevention of injurious conduct towards others, but they also go deeper than other systems through internal conscience. It is not only an offense but is also a sin to injure or damage the rights of other individuals.

The basic and most fundamental right is the protection of life. (Article 3 of the Universal Declaration of Human Rights, 1948). The Quran declares: "If anyone slew a person unless it be for murder or for preventing mischief in the land, it would be as if he slew the whole people; and if anyone saved a life, it would be as if he saved the life of the whole people" (v. 3). Moreover, the Quran declares: "And slay not the life which Allah hath forbidden save with right" (xvii. 39). Apart from this right, Constitutional laws and various international documents attempt to guarantee other rights, like that of property, reputation or family. The provisions of the Quran in Surah Hujurat (xlix. 12) are more clear on this subject. Thus, dishonoring others, hoarding, smuggling, defamation, back biting, and destroying others' property are declared offense and sins.

The conception of freedom recognized by the Shariah is much wider than is commonly perceieved. The rules of Shariah provide for the freedom of religion, conscience, expression, speech, avocation, movement, education, assembly, etc. The Quran says: "There is no compulsion in religion" (ii. 256, also vi. 108), and it is laid down as a duty to speak for justice. The Quran also says: "Command what is right" (vii. 199). The freedom given to man is related to the establishment of right and justice.

117

The Quran makes it the duty of every individual to speak the truth without any fear. It says that "Allah loveth not the utterance of harsh speech save by one who had been wronged" (iv. 148). This freedom is given through limitations set up in public interest, and anything which disturbs the public in general is not permitted. All possible methods of demonstration against evil by expression are possible, but they must be under the limits of the rules of morality. Freedom of speech must observe the constitutional means for expression. It should not be violent and injurious and should not give rise to other evils or wrongs. Nevertheless, the Shariah makes provision for rising against authority when there is a violation of the sacred principles on its part. The traditions of the Prophet make it clear that orders or directions to do what is sinful are not to be obeyed (both Bukhari and Muslim emphasize). The Quranic injunctions also contain the same principles (see iv. 59). Since principles of Shariah are based upon eternal wisdom, the Shariah also demands human wisdom in human transactions. The Quran repeats that it should be used by the faithful upon the basis of which all creation has been brought out in existence (Quranic chapters - Baqarah (164), Romans (8), Yunus (191), Tariq (5-7), Imran (7), Hajj (46), etc.). It explains that the balancing of conflicting interests is provided by the Shariah for whose establishment the modern theory of jurisprudence of interest is now exerting.

The protection of property rights is another important principle of contemporary human rights. The Quran expressly stated this principle centuries ago in the following words: "And eat not up your property among yourselves in vanity, nor seek by it to gain the hearing of the judges that ye may knowingly devour a portion of the property of others wrongfully" (ii. 188). This passage of the Quran also mentions that bribery to gain property is as much an offense as theft, embezzlement, robbery, extortion, etc.[112]

The Islamic conception of property rights is fundamental in its practical system. Tampering with these rights is considered Haram, and it is the duty of the State to respect private property, for the principles provide[113] Lilmilkiyat al-Hurmah (i.e., property has sacredness).

Similar to the sacredness of the right to property is the freedom of contract which has a high place in the Shariah of Islam. The conception of pacta sunt servanda has a special place in any law, so the Muslims are bound by their stipulations. The Quranic rule is: "O ye who believe! fulfill your undertaking" (v. 1). It means that it is a tacit obligation for living in civil societies to execute one's agreements. The Prophet was known as Amin even before he received the message of God, and the institutions of the Shariah are based upon the principles of "justice" (Adalah) and "faithfulness" (Amanah). The social and economic rights of the community are safeguarded by the particular guarantee of freedom of contract. In addition to the secular operation of contracts between the parties, it is a divine institution. It is more often resorted to in Islam than in other systems and has a factor of flexibility and adaptability to the changing economic patterns and social life. The law of contractual transactions was evolved, and the jurists developed many principles which show that the law is protected against stagnation. In the absence of any direct text in the fundamental sources of the Shariah, the jurists (as Abu Hanifa) resorted to searching the practices of the people in their transactions for solution. Such a souce of legislative activity under the Shariah is not provided by any other system.[114] The moral sanctity in Islam of contracts makes redundant the modern international law recourse to the doctrine of pacta sunt servanda. Thus treaties, like contracts, are binding because Providence has commanded in His law to make all agreements binding.

The contemporary declarations on human rights especially provide and preach for the right to equality and equal protection of the law. In addition to Article 1 of the Universal Declaration (also Article 2), similar elements are contained in most modern constitutions. To what extent these declarations are implemented is another question. The principles of justice in the Shariah incorporate perfect observation of equality before law and equal protection thereof without any kind of discrimination whatsoever. The Quran says: "When you judge among men, judge with justice" (iv. 58). It clarifies the principles by directing: "O ye who believe! stand out firmly for justice, as witness to God, even as against yourselves, or your parents, or your kin, and whether it be against rich or poor: for

God best protects both. Follow not the lusts of your hearts lest ye swerve, and if ye distort justice or decline to do justice, verily God is well acquainted with all that ye do" (iv. 135). The exercise of justice and its principles is a vital rule of religion, and it is a duty of every Muslim to abide by these principles. The Quran further says that there is to be no discrimination between the sexes (see iv. 36; xix. 95); that man is one nation and no discrimination is allowed on the basis of race, region, caste, color, religion, etc. The traditions of the Prophet contain many principles of justice and equality in treatment of men and women (see Quran, iv. 58, 65, 105, 135; vii. 29; xvi. 90; lvii. 25). The notion of justice in the Shariah binds a Muslim not only to God, but also to his fellow men including the non-Muslims. This principle is applied not only to private matters but also in public transactions and even in international relations. There is a sacred duty to administer justice without any fear or prejudice, and the history of Islam has many remarkable examples in the dispensation of justice.[115]

The modern approaches, in protecting human rights, operate upon the principles of rights of the people. The concept of democracy which establishes a State by the people, must work for the betterment of human life. The Shariah's conception of Umma is a system which has the same goals for an Islamic State. But it was centuries before the modern notions came to be established. The Quran says: "who conduct their affairs by mutual consultation" (xlii. 38), or "and consult them in affairs of moment" (iii. 159). This principle of a State established and governed by the people was practically applied to its fullest extent by the Prophet and the Republican Islam (the period of the first four caliphs: Kulfa-i-Rashidin). Injustice, when perpetrated by the State or the ruler, is to be prevented. A tradition says: "He who sees evil should prevent it." Moreover, it is narrated that "the greatest struggling for the sake of God is a word of justice said before an unjust ruler." The principles of the Shariah lay down the limitations of any ruler. When the ruler violates the rules of the Shariah, particularly those dealing with human rights, it is a person's duty to disobey such a ruler's authority. The concepts of imamate and caliphate are based upon the theory of the trust of the public. The moment the ruler or the government violates

120

the mandate of God and His book, the change of government is essential.[116] The Quran says: "My convenant includeth not wrongdoers" (ii. 124). Similarly, the Prophet said: "Obedience is only for the lawful orders." The first sermon of Caliph Abu Bakr, at his election, is of significance; he said people should only obey him if he is just. It leads to the natural result that the Shariah principles imply the protection of human rights in a most comprehensive manner. Only some of them have been reproduced in the above pages. They are enough to show the vast field covered by the list of human rights of the Shariah.

In the above narrative, we have seen the ideals and practical principles of the law of Islam. The practical philosophy of the eternal principles is also called Majmual-ul-Ahkam al-Amaliyyat al-Mashruah fi al-Islam or alilm bil-Ahkam al-Shariat al-Amaliyyah. The sphere of operation of the principles of the Shariah is both temporal and spiritual. For the reason of a combined action, the rules of law as contained in Ahkam are applied severally by a variety of mechanisms. The Qadi is ordinarily concerned with external actions of man; the Mufti gives his opinion on matters of conscience or toward the "self" of man. This conception of the Shariah is not available in any other man-made system. The Shariah system deeply affects a person since it operates upon the nature of man's beliefs and his would-be behavior here for the hereafter.

The above analysis of the Shariah system leads us to another aspect of the situation. This system, being vitally different from other conceptions, and having been framed upon principles in accord with human beliefs, aims for a happier human existence. On a review of the legal and political history of the world, it is noticed that many good features of other systems are already a part of the Shariah. Its nature provides for the same things, and presents in a refined manner many things which are beneficial to mankind.

The system of the Shariah, in addition to preventing blameworthiness in human conduct aims for a reform of human society, provides for the recognition of the highest ideals of life for this world and for hereafter. This aspect is not present in the man-made systems which only work to prevent what is wrong or offensive in this existence. The basic conception of Western democracy restricts the government in its authority over its people. The trend in communist countries is the reverse, to increase the power of the State over its citizens. The Western formula is based on various legal and political methods. The common technique is to give the courts the power to enforce fundamental freedoms by having a kind of Bill of Rights in the Constitution. These methods endeavor to fetter governmental powers by rules and laws which would protect individual human values. Such a philosophy and new attempts by many of the human rights activists to establish a World Order of all human beings, show that man is in search of an order and a more comprehensive system, for the betterment of his species. If we compare these new thoughts with the Shariah, it may be seen that the solutions for man's problems are already available and have been so for a long time. It shows and proves that the Shariah is not only supreme and in accordance with the needs of man, but it also contains principles which are for universal application in the future as well. This basic philosophical foundation of Shariah as a guideline for all times, in secular and religious matters, is the essence of Islamic polity, its concept of law and State.

A last word in parentheses. It appears that the truly fundamental juridical difference between the concept of Islamic law and the Greco-Roman laws is with regard to origin and validity. Whereas both origin and validity have been variously examined in both common and civil law leading to many controversies, the same type of conflict is absent in Islamic law. This is so since it is, a priori, a revealed law; its origin and validity are effective as a fundamental postulate of life for a Muslim. We do not have to face the controversy or or give justification which, e.g., Hart had to do in his "Concept of Law." There are, ex hypothesi, no such problems of lexicography, jurisprudence or philosophy while examining the nature of the Islamic law.

(C) Evolution of Eternal Law

The Role of Ijtihad

Most of what has been discussed earlier falls in the realm of religion, philosophy, and jurisprudence. Ijtihad, however, presents the problems of practical law. It provides a challenge to a trained lawyer and jurist to find the law when there does not appear to be any direct authority (Quran or Sunnah) on a particular point for determination.

There has been some dispute as to the number of sources of law in the religion of Islam, but it is generally considered that there are four: the Quran, the Sunnah, Ijma, and Qiyas. Most writers have acknowledged these four sources, and have dedicated their energies to defining the precise meaning and significance of each.

Despite the general acceptance of four sources, however, writers do not rule out the possibility of a fifth source of law, Ijtihad, which some feel is, has been, or may again become a source of law. Consideration of this possibility is not merely incidental. In many countries a major issue in modern Muslim life which maintains social, political, economic, and even psychological significance, is the extent to which Ijtihad may be used to affect the law through change, modification, or adaptation to new conditions.[117] It is important that we grasp the meaning and appreciate the significance of this problem.

It has been maintained in this text that the one predominant source of Islamic law is the word of God. What does this mean? It implies the "sources" where we find that word of God are those whose "formal connection" in being the word of God is unquestioned. But, in truth and logic, this can only be maintained for the Quran; also since it was the Prophet who received the revealed word, his teachings and traditions possess this link. But what has been considered to be "Islamic law" for centuries contains more than the content of these two sources. That is the result of the human element, the matter of interrelations, about which we have already said something. It is this "human element" to which we now turn. The conclusions submitted here are at variance with

123

many orthodox views but are believed by the author to be a correct picture of the essence of Islamic law.

Initially, it must be understood that the ultimate source in Islamic law is God; God determines what man should and should not do and how society should and should not operate. The four sources of law noted above are the instruments through which His orders are revealed, as well as the means through which man derives his knowledge of the law. Thus, Muslims believe that the transcendent pattern of prescribed behavior has been disclosed through the Quran, through the behavior of the Prophet, and through various other means. This procedure for letting man know God's will is called revelation. Revelation was not required, for without it there would still be law. However, in the author's view, the absence of revelation would leave humanity without the awareness of what the law is. Nevertheless, according to the Mutazilah, who were repudiated by the community in earlier centuries, even without revelation it was possible for man, through reason, to attain an awareness of what the law is. Therefore, according to them, although revelation simplifies this process, it is not essential.

The issue, then, is one of acquiring something independent of the Quran and the other sources. God alone is al-Hakim, the Supreme law giver. The recognized sources of the law are merely the means of discernment, usul-al-fiqh, roots of fiqh. Fiqh is, therefore, not the system of rules itself, but the science of finding out what that system is, and the persons who allegedly or who in reality have discerned from the courses what the ahkam (rules, orders) are, are called the Ulema.

Thus, whereas the law is divine, jurisprudence, fiqh, ilm, is human, and whereas the law is infinite, knowledge of it is temporal. Jurisprudence is not merely human, however, for revelation has guided man in this matter. Similarly, Ijtihad is illuminated by the same principle. A mujtahid is one who attempts to ascertain the law. His Ijtihid does not change the law; rather, it is either successful or unsuccessful in revealing it. Admittedly, the Muslim community did not begin with a full knowledge of the law Even at the time of the Prophet's death, although revelation was completed, full knowledge of the law was not yet attained. It is asserted that considerable effort and time were required before complete knowledge of the law could be achieved, or, in Islamic terms, before the gate of Ijtihad could be closed. In fact, this knowledge was not considered to be complete until a couple of centuries later. It is the understanding of revelation during these centuries that is the point at issue.

God's message is contained in the Quran and the Hadith: by belief, this is the eternal law. This is the Nass, the basic principle for legislation in Islam. There is no alternative for a Muslim but to explore the Nass and apply it, and after completely grasping the denotative, connotative, and applied aspects of objects seeking verification, derive the rules of organically developing life. This is what is termed as Ijtihad with due agreement of all the Schools of Muslim thought. After twenty-three years of revelation of the Quran and the framing of the laws of Shariaat, it took nearly two hundred years of systematic development by different schools of Muslim jurisprudence to examine and codify the content of the Corpus Juris of Islam.

All the differences of opinion during the period of Ijtihad arise due to different approaches towards the exploration and understanding of Nass. Such differences are not such in their nature so as to be insoluble by the scholars. In this exploration of Nass, one fact is established, namely, the Quran and the Hadith are the basic sources for examination of all issues. The Muslim jurists are divided in their opinion whether, by the concurrence of all, the will of the Prophet can be formed by Ijma, or whether through Ijma only of jurists (Ulema) can we get at the Nass of the Prophet. There can be no doubt about the fact that if the whole Millat (nation)[118] is in agreement on a certain point, it will imply the will of the Prophet. But this is hypothetical and such a case has never arisen. The other types of Ijma have, however, been enumerated and discussed, and still attempts are being made by the jurists to find a way for the exploration of the Nass.

Some Schools of Jurisprudence have explored Nass to establish by Qiyas (analogy), Istehsan (personal inclination), and the considerations of the past precedents the basis of derivation of new rules of law. Those who do

125

not accept these bases have no consideration for them. But those who accept them do so on the authority of some Nass. However, all the schools of Muslim Jurisprudence assert that the Ijtihad is based upon the Nass, that is to say that the Nass could fulfill the human requirements today, provided it is explored and understood. This exploration depends upon the rules of that knowledge in semantics, commentaries, biographies, the Hadith, etc. The definition of Ijtihad, that it is the derivation of rules through explicit reasoning from the basic defined guidance, is not new, but its use is very much needed today.

This firm foundation of Ijtihad, it is submitted, will keep the religion flourishing:

"Whose root is firm and whose branches are high (in the skies) yielding its fruit in every season by the permission of its Lord." (14:24)

The indifference towards the Nass, if not more dangerous than the "Ijtihad versus the Nass" controversy, is not less than that. The ignorance of rules of derivation is the peril throwing a crisis over the whole of the Islamic world. Islam needs Ijtihad only in the sense that the Ijtihad takes root in the Nass with due piety (Taqwa), and not the Ijtihad which is opposed to the Nass or the Ijtihad which is indifferent towards it. The Ijtihad, of which I speak in Islam, is the exploration and understanding of the Nass with systematic reason. This is not the sole right of any particular sect or creed. Whosoever cultivates these capabilities must come forward for this task (Mujtahid). The non-Mujtahid must follow his Mujtahid and work for the betterment of his political, social, economic, and spiritual life according to the verdicts of the Mujtahid.

On the basis of the Nass, the door of Ijtihad in Islam, with full consideration of the rules of derivation, is open to everyone. The verdict of a Mujtahid is not binding upon the followers of the succeeding age. It is also not imperative to follow the past Mujtahids. This is the principle of Ijtihad which is linked to progress and the evolution of thoughts and ideas. The Mujtahids of today who fulfill all the conditions of Ijtihad are no less in capacity than the Mujtahids of the past. But the verdict of the Mujtahid is not the essential element of faith; the Nass is the essence of faith.

One can hold the belief in a changeless law in its ultimate sense while at the same time maintain a profound conviction that Ijtihad today is not only legitimate but truly necessary, for the two beliefs are not incompatible. The necessity for Ijtihad is the result of social and legal exigencies, as well as of the moral necessity that man must always strive to reveal God's law. It is not required or expected that man will discern the law totally and ultimately, for to do that is perhaps beyond both his capacity and his need. Man must strive, however, to discover the law to the extent that it applies to actual situations in his life. Thus, the principle of Ijtihad as constant and progressive is imperative. This position is even stressed in a Hadith which asserts that God is pleased with man's striving despite its ineptness, and that He is further delighted when the endeavor results in a true understanding of His law. Spiritualism, therefore, appears to be important to Ijtihad.

In the context one aspect of a religious basis of law, we may, albeit briefly, look at the spiritual life of the Western nations, where today, admittedly, religion is on the decline. With the decline in religious fervor, there has taken place a marked change in Western culture, and people's attitude towards life. At the same time, it seems open to doubt whether it is possible to form true ideas about the spiritual life of the West without giving an acknowledgement to the pre-eminent importance of freedom of thought and historical criticism, abundantly manifest in its people. It is unmistakable that freedom of thought and a critical approach have been all-important factors in the development of modern European culture and its conception of life. Spiritualism may not be always an essentail thing in law--a secular institution for it. Under the powerful impact of this current of thought and ideas, there have come about both beneficial and baneful consequences. Some results are considered desirable; others are not. But then the question is, who considers them desirable and who does not? The answer either in Islamic or in the Western states, is not easy. Nevertheless, it is clear that there will be wavering whether innovation under the influence of new thoughts, ideas, and criticisms of established religious interpretations is necessary or good.

Nobody will maintain that all fruits of this tree are equally healthy and good. To a certain extent these waverings are perfectly understandable. Some risks must be taken into the bargain, however. Perhaps Von Grunebaum, while talking of Muslims, is right in explaining hesitations of this kind as falling under the subconscious devices for self-preservation which should not be completely discarded before the new values and the old aspirations have been more convincingly attuned to each other.[119]

However this may be, the outsider cannot but feel that Islam is moving on a road from which no return is possible, and which eventually will lead to a clearer distinction of minds and an open recognition of the freedom of thought on a larger scale. No more than in Christianity is the need for such a recognition universal and compelling. Even the Roman Catholic Church, which claims to be a guardian of tradition and origin, nowadays is calling for a new theology that does not eschew the contact with modern thinking and modern science on issues of contemporary significance, such as birth conrol, women as priests, and so on.

Seen in this light, Islam is still entering upon the same crisis which beset Christianity almost two centuries ago, and against which it has been able to bear up ever since. However, out of this conflict between religion and science, a modernistic theology arose which endeavored to reconcile the doctrine of the Church with the conclusions of modern science; eventually, this modernistic theology gradually acquired its recognized place beside the old. Of course, this development did not come to pass without much struggle. Snouck Hurgronje, the well known Dutch Islamicist, said that sometimes it may happen that the general movement of spiritual progress goes almost too fast, so that one revision of the stores of religion is immediately followed by another. Then dissension is likely to arrive among the adherents of a religion; some of them come to the conclusion that there must be an end of sifting and think it better to lock up the treasures once for all and to stop dangerous inquiries; whereas, others begin to entertain doubts concerning the value even of such goods as do not yet show any trace of decay.[120]

128

These doubts concerning matters divine may or may not be followed by a forsaking of opinions acquired by birth and education, but in any event, they do not come about in a vacuum. They occur in the souls of human beings, and more often than not, they are attended with violent inward struggles and personal sufferings. No wonder, therefore, that in Western literature, quite a number of writers have been attracted towards religious doubt as a literary theme, similarly there are also many autobiographies which do not pass over this side of inner life in complete silence.

The institution of Ijtihad is necessary not only in matters of legislation, strictii sensu, but also to meet the doubts and uncertainties created or bound to be created by contemporary thinking and science. The terrific impact of new ideas, whether coming from the realm of philosophy or science, cannot be simply met by dogma. To do so would be to lose valuable contributions. The challenge of new ideological and scientific threats has to be faced by reason and logic. Ijtehad is, therefore, perhaps the single most essential institution which must be continuously nourished to keep Islam abreast of the changing times. It is also submitted that in this march, Islam would be served if ideas come from those who are learned in law, religion, philosophy, political science, and so on. To accept Ijtihad and then leave it to the Fundamentalist or to the ill-educated Mullah, is to miss the point altogether.

CHAPTER VI
Islamic States

In this chapter, we shall initially enumerate countries with Islamic backgrounds and then examine the more important ones. There are approximately 900 million Muslims living in the world today. The exact number is very difficult to ascertain since most of these countries have no exact mechanism of ascertaining figures. Consequently, the figures are based on calculations based on early censuses. It appears, nevertheless, that on the basis of available records, the world Muslim population is approximating the number mentioned above. The states in which Muslims are in a majority or in which they are to be found in considerable numbers have already been mentioned in an earlier Chapter.

The states having large populations of Muslims are found in three continents: Africa, Asia and Europe. The greatest number of Muslim countries is found in Africa, where twenty-three countries claim large populations of Muslims. These include: Algeria, Cameroon, Central African Republic, Chad, Dahomey, Egypt, Ethiopia, Ivory Coast, Libya, Maldive Islands, Mali, Mauretania, Morocoo, Niger, Nigeria, Senegal, Sierra Leone, Sudan, Tanzania, Togo, Tunisia, Uganda and Upper Volta.

Similarly, Asia claims a large number of countries which maintain substantial Muslim populations. These include: Afghanistan, Bahrain, Bangladesh, China, India, Indonesia, Iran, Iraq, Jordan, Kuwait, Lebanon, Malaysia, Oman, Pakistan, Qatar, Saudi Arabia, Syria, Turkey, Union of Arab Emirates, Yeman and the U.S.S.R.

Europe has four countries in which Muslims can be found in considerable numbers: Albania, Bulgaria, Yugoslavia and Western Turkey.

As indicated, the author does not propose to discuss all these countries, but in order to understand the thrust of the present narrative, it will be necessary to examine at least three of them. These countries are those wherein some of the issues presently being discussed have surfaced and have produced some important consequences of note.[121] Three particular issues or points directly apply to the countries discussed below. First, we notice a country created solely in the name of Islam, but continuing to maintain a secular set up, the resultant tussle being between Islamic propagandists and the so-called moderates who stress the priority of economic issues in the policies of a state.[122] Secondly, we examine the case of a country which for centuries was the heart and soul of the Islamic world, then began a concerted march towards secularism; and lastly, we will study the case of a poor country which, with apparently little else but Islamic fervour is at war with a super power. An overview of this discussion will enable us to focus our attention on the central issues of this book, what is today an ideal Islamic State and whether the twentieth century will allow such a state to exist given (1) the current international political situation, (2) the urgency to provide for the economic needs (and not religious) of the people of Muslim countries, and (3) the visible authoritarian tendancies in many countries where Muslims live.

(A) Pakistan

Without doubt, the most important state in the context of Islamic revival is the state of Pakistan, for Pakistan is clearly the first modern state to have been established anywhere in the world on the basis of religion alone. Like all movements, the movement which led to the establishment of this country had a long history, a history in which the people who struggled for it had to put up tremendous fights against heavy odds. All movements in which the aim is to put forth an idea, an idea which has as its basis change or which attempts to have an impact on the total life of a community, has to have considerable time to work for its eventual success.

Pakistan was carved out of India in 1947. The actual events which led to its establishment were that India, at that time, was governed by the British. The British government, during the World War II years, had come to realize that for its own benefit it was necessary to grant independence to India. India was the largest of the British possessions overseas, possessions which included such territories as Canada, Australia, New Zealand, and many parts of Africa.[123] However, unlike all these other territories and areas, India had a unique history. For

132

several centuries, India, a country populated mostly by people who believed in Hinduism, was ruled by a minority, Muslims, who had come through the Khyber Pass (in the northwest of India) from lands which are now modern Turkey, Iran, and Afghanistan. From time to time, Muslims had invaded India, but the dynasty which was to have an impact for centuries was the Mogul Dynasty. It produced some great rulers: e.g., Emperor Akbar who ruled about the same time as when Queen Elizabeth I ruled in England. The task which lay ahead of the Muslim rulers was no easy matter. Being only a handful of people, they were confronted by millions of their subjects, who were not only non-Muslims, but whose cultural, ethical, and social values were totally different. For example, Hinduism, unlike most modern religions, has an inbuilt system of different classes. The lowest class was, and still is, the so-called class of the untouchables. This class was, naturally, confronted with having no hope of any real status in the society in which it lived. Therefore, when Muslims became the rulers of India, it was this class which was the first to convert to Islam. Some of these untouchables also embraced Christianity. Over the years, the Muslims were able to establish a vast empire in the Indian subcontinent, even though, numerically, they were always outnumbered by about five or six to one by the majority Hindu community. At the dawn of the twentieth century, the Indian political leaders began their onslaught against British imperialism. In this march, they wanted to establish a state in which the local population had some form of autonomy. This was a long and tedious march from which two political parties eventually emerged. The majority party was the Indian Congress. Originally, it contained both Muslims and Hindus, but over the years, especially those following World War I, another major party, the Muslim League, was formed. It was a separatist party which represented the Muslims. The creation of this party was especially aimed at safeguarding the interests of the Muslims in any future constitutional arrangements to which the British might agree.

Its leader was Mohammed Ali Jinnah. He was initially in the Congress, but when the new movement started, he became its spearhead. Whereas, Mohammed Ali Jinnah was the political leader of this organization, its spiritual and thinking guidance was in the hands of perhaps the greatest Muslim thinker to come from that region in the twentieth century, Sir Mohammed Iqbal. Of all the modern thinkers of Islam, Sir Mohammed Iqbal is perhaps most well-known in the West. He is one of the few authors who attempted to write some of his ideas, not only in the local languages and Persian, but also in English. One of his works in English, "The Reconstruction of Religious Thought in Islam," contains many reformative ideas. Whereas, Mohammed Ali Jinnah led the political aspirations of the Muslim movement in India, Sir Mohammed Iqbal had much wider visions for Muslims everywhere. He was amongst the earliest Muslim thinkers in the twentieth century to project the idea that it was necessary for Muslims, wherever they lived, to form a community of republics in which Islam could have its say in a way in which the civic, political, and religious life of the people corresponded to those values which religion had provided. Iqbal said, "For the present, every Muslim nation must sink into her own deeper self, temporarily focus her vision on herself alone, until all is strong and powerful to form a living family of republics."[124]

The only modern Islamic country before Pakistan to emerge in this century which had any political significance was Turkey. However, under the influence of Kamal Ata Turk, Turkey became totally secularized following its defeat in World War I. Whereas, since 1921, Turkey followed a policy of secularization of its laws and Constitution, Pakistan clearly has become the first country which, starting with a secular background, has been gradually moving towards a religious emphasis. The secular background was that of the common law in its entirety, thus encompassing in its corpus juris the constitutional, civil, criminal, or revenue laws of England. Its legal system and its training of lawyers and judges entirely corresponded with the training of the legal community of England itself. One of the few Western observers who has been able to appreciate acutely this point is Wilfred Cantwell Smith. In his writing, he was one of the earliest to stress that the establishment of Pakistan was, in fact, the achievement of an idea to have a religiously oriented state in the twentieth century, while at the same time having as its grundnorm of corpus juris, the heritage and content of the common law.

Pakistan was, thus, started to provide a homeland where the Muslims of the Indian subcontinent could live in accordance with the tenets of Islam. The raison d'etre of the state was, in fact, Islam itself. Geographically, in India, those areas where predominently Muslims lived ultimately became Pakistan.[125] After considerable civil strife in the Summer of 1947, Pakistan was carved out by the British government from the subcontinent of India. For the creation of its new Constitution, the Indian Independence Act of 1947 was passed by the British Parliament. It provided for the creation of a Constituent Assembly, an assembly which was to pass the first Constitution of Pakistan. However, following the establishment of the Constituent Assembly, the first Constitution for various reasons, could not be passed until 1955. The first Constitution of Pakistan, therefore, was enacted in the year 1956, and it designated the country "the Islamic Republic of Pakistan." Before we examine some of the "Islamic" highlights of this Constitution, we must first recognize an important milestone in the constitution-making history of this country. This was the so-called "Objectives Resolution" passed in 1949. This Resolution, which was passed by the aforesaid assembly in Karachi on March 12, 1949, spoke of the state as a place where Islamic democracy, justice, and good will would prevail, "wherein the Muslims shall be enabled to order their lives in the individual and collective spheres in accord with the teachings and requirements of Islam as set out in the holy Quran and the Sunnah." The description provided by this Resolution may well be taken to be a definition, if such a thing is at all possible, of an Islamic State. This Resolution is historically important for two major reasons. Firstly, it was passed by an assembly which had just won a highly cherished goal--the creation of a new country. It, thus, reflected, in lexicographical terms, the hopes and aspirations of a movement for the creation of an Islamic State, the first event of such nature in modern times. Secondly, this Resolution, in terms of contemporary Islamic history was the first document of a Constitutional kind to emerge as a result of the deliberations of the scholars of this faith. In the context of modern history of Islam, it signaled a departure from the trend which had been witnessed in Turkey between the two World Wars.

Subsequent constitutional history of Pakistan does not bear[126] full justice to the ideals of this Resolution. In many ways, subsequent events dimmed the spirit of this Resolution. However, the enthusiasm about Islam, which was the underlying theme of this Resolution, has continued to surface on the national Pakistani scene from time to time.

It is not the purpose of the present narrative to examine these details of Pakistan's history; it is only to highlight some of those occasions in its evolution when Islam was used, per se, to bring forth changes of consequence. the first of such points that has been noted is that Islam was the cause behind the creation of this country and, at least initially, the foundation of its constitutionalism. As events of more recent times show, religion has again been used to affect changes of both sociological and legal character. That this has been an effective vehicle for bringing about such important changes is equally clear. The time and the phase when religion was so used was always when it appeared that, politically, the people were not able to make any headway or to make the impact of their point of view felt.[127]

An important reason for such a use has been, not only in Pakistan but in most of the countries where Muslims live, a lack of a proper or a genuine mass media system. The televisions, newspapers, and periodicals are usually owned and operated by the state. Consequently, there is always a deep-seated frustration in the intelligentsia, and, to some extent, in urban population that the mass media fails and consistently has failed to objectively report or present a realistic analysis of the contemporary situations prevailing in these various countries. Religion, thus, becomes a vehicle of dissemination of information not otherwise available. It circulates ideas, bringing some relief from a suffocating atmosphere. Shortsighted governments do not realize that when information is circulated by this method, rumors and the whim of the Mullah can play havoc with peoples' emotions, a point amply demonstrated by events in Iran and Pakistan.

While constitutional tussles were going on in the Constituent Assembly in Karachi, mostly as a result of the differences in the way in which the future federal

structure of the state was to be run (a tussle in which the provinces of West Pakistan, by and large, were on one side and the most populous province of East Pakistan was on the other), there also occurred in 1954 the first serious upheaval based on religious considerations. Before examining the major provisions of the 1956 Consitution, we must briefly advert to this episode, for in examining the issue of political impact of Islam, this occurrence has both historical and theological significance. Towards the end of 1953 in the heart of West Pakistan, in the city of Lahore, there erupted massive riots against a minority sect called the Qadianis. The Qadianis are a sect who, while believing in "Islam" (as they look at it), also believe that they have a current prophet sitting in a small village in Pakistan called Rebwah. As Islam has maintained since its inception that the institution of prophets ended with the death of the Prophet Mohammed, the Qadianis are clearly against such a fundamental Islamic postulate. This, indeed, was the cause of this trouble. The majority of the Muslims demanded that the Qadianis should not be considered or called "Muslims." This was opposed by the Qadianis sect, resulting in violence against them and in the burning of their shops and businesses in the city of Lahore. Soon, the disturbances spread to other cities, and the government was forced to proclaim martial law in that region. Ultimately, as the result of martial law and an inquiry[128] which was later conducted by a chief justice, this particular problem was partially resolved. It is not this problem which is relevant to this narrative; rather, what is of historical significance is the issue that on religious grounds there came about such a violent disturbance of the social order that it could only be solved by resorting to the extreme force available to the state, namely the proclamation of martial law. This disturbance was perhaps a forerunner of future changes which were brought about as the result of religious forces operating beyond the control of the civil governments from time to time. In Pakistan, this event brought political[129] changes--changes as a result of a religious uprising.
It was, thus, clear that religion was still a force which, if properly used (or misused), was capable of bringing about changes which otherwise might not take place at all, and if they did take place, it might take a very long time for them to have any tangible manifestation.

Theologically, this stresses that Islam still has, even in an otherwise secularized Muslim society, strong doctrinal adherence. It is still a phenomenon which is capable of producing extraordinary consequences. It continues to be a faith in which the believers will not allow any interference of a denominational nature. From one point of view, this is Islam's strength; from another, its rigidity. With these brief references to the 1953-54 riots in Lahore, let us move to a brief examination of the first Constitution of Pakistan.

The two major points which have to be examined in this constitutional document are, first, that it proclaimed Sovereignty as vesting in God and not in people; secondly, that it proclaimed that the lives of the citizens were to be allowed to be run in accordance with the dictates and demands of Islam. In Islamic constitutional law, Sovereignty does not vest in the people, as contemplated by the so-called Western systems of government. Consequently, the Constitution spoke of Sovereignty as vesting in God, and further proclaimed that the people's representatives were simply the "delegates" who had been authorized to interpret the supreme laws of God which were contained in the Book of God. However, as soon as we have said this, we are faced with, perhaps, the most monumental difficulty of constitutionalism which faces Islamic countries today. If, ex hypothesi, Sovereignty belongs to God and His laws have been laid down for all times, then obviously what an ideal national assembly or a parliament can do is to interpret those laws. If this was conceded, admittedly, the role of such a national assembly or a parliament would simply be that of a body which would be called upon to interpret existing laws or to make only those laws for certain situations on which no provision is to be found in the Book of God. Furthermore, in keeping with the same theory, this parliament would be incompetent to make any law repugnant to the spirit or the letter of the Quran since, ex hypothesi, that would be ultra vires the superior law. However, this logical system was not provided in the operational apparatus of this Constitution. Whereas, lip service was paid to provide assertions that Sovereignty belonged to God, in its actual working chapters the Constitution was no different from the constitutions of most Western countries which are admittedly secular in nature.

138

The parliament called the National Assembly, was to be elected, and it had to have a Prime Minister. The powers of the Prime Minister and the parliament were more or less the ones that we would normally find in a parliamentary form of government. There was no restriction, constitutionally speaking, on the powers of this assembly to make any law, and therefore, it was quite possible for it to make a law which might conceivably be against the letter and spirit of the Quranic law. The Fundamentalists, if they might be called such, protested against this form of government. They demanded that there be created a smaller body, composed of experts in the Quranic law, which should be able to veto, if necessary, the workings of the parliament. However, if this were allowed, a fortiori, the National Assembly would not be all powerful; instead, it would only have a semi-legislative character, and the smaller body of so-called experts would have the final say as to what is in conformity with the Quranic law. The objections of the Fundamentalists, however, were set aside, and Pakistan started its constitutional history by having a constitutional document which, while proclaiming the Islamic ideology as an ideal, was almost entirely secular in its operational character.

The second point which must be pointed out is that this Constitution provided a set of "directives of public policy." These were simply expectations that the agencies of state would encourage the teachings of Islam and provide a proper atmosphere where Islamic teachings could flourish. The fundamental tenets of Islam were, however, not made "justicible." Justicibility is a legal term connoting that the right which has been granted can be vindicated through a court of law if an aggrieved person thinks that that right has been trespassed upon. The chapter in the Constitution on a bill of rights (secular in nature), or "fundamental rights" as it was called, however, was justicible. Therefore, whereas appropriate legal proceedings could be taken in a court to vindicate the denial of an admittedly secular right, there was no provision for vindicating the denial of a religious right.

Thus, we see the anachronism. Whereas the Constitution spoke in glowing terms of Islam, it was without doubt nothing more than on the plane of dogma and polemics. It was rhetorical in its impact, since nothing was provided in the Constitution to have the religious dictates or postulates vindicated through the system of the courts.

This Constitution was of very short-lived duration since it barely survived two years. In October 1958, Field Marshall Mohammed Ayub, the Commander-in-Chief of the Armed Forces, abrogated it and proclaimed martial law. After four years, Field Marshall Mohammed Ayub enacted a new Constitution for the country. In countra-distinction to the earlier one, this provided for a presidential form of government. This Constitution, too, spoke of Pakistan "as an Islamic republic." However, in its substantive provisions regarding Islam, it was similar to the earlier Constitution.

The two points referred to above, namely a lip service or polemical assertion of Islamic ideology and a chapter containing principles of state directives, was similar to the 1956 Constitution. As in the 1956 Constitution, religious rights were not guaranteed. In other words, justicibility was that of secular rights and not admittedly of religious rights or religious precepts. Since at that time, politically, Field Marshall Mohammed Ayub was popular and was able to provide a stable government, all these points of religious or theological controversy were never agitated in the open. Ayub continued to rule the country for ten years. In 1966, the "fall" of the 1962 Constitution given to Pakistan by Field Marshall Mohammed Ayub began. This process of disintegration was begun by the former Foreign Minister of Field Marshall Ayub, Bhutto. Bhutto, sensing his country's emotions that the people were beginning to get somewhat fed up from the long authoritarian rule of the President, launched his own movement. He first formed a political party called the Pakistan People's Party. But, unlike many other parties which emphasized religion, Bhutto was quickly able to see that the first and the foremost thing the people wanted was economic betterment. He accordingly set forth before the public a program for an egalitarian overhauling of the society. He knew full well that Pakistan, like many other Third World countries, had basically a two-tiered social system. On the one hand, there were teeming millions of poor people who toiled day in and day out for a handful of returns. On the other hand, there was a small minority of people, mostly the recipients of the bounty of the colonial powers during

140

their rule in these lands, who constituted the "elite." He, therefore, on his assumption to power, first took over most of the "excess" lands from private holdings and then nationalized banks and insurance companies.[130] He also intended to take over all the basic industries in the country so that he could place the ultimate ownership in all these capital formation elements in the public. His Party manifesto did contain the assertion that the religion of the party was Islam, but in practice, he did not stress the religious aspect at all. In fact, a slogan which he coined and which got him elected was "clothes, shelter, and food," clearly emphasizing an economic rather than a religious platform.

The policy which Bhutto put before the public has this important point: that provided a politician is able to come into the foreground on his own merits, or on account of charismatic personality traits, then he need not polemically rely on religion. It is sufficient for him to put before the public a party platform more or less on the same lines which would be used before an electorate in a Western country. Long before Bhutto, Kemal Ata Turk had accomplished this successfully in Turkey. In a different way, both Nasser and Anwar Sadat have done it in Egypt.

The 1971 Bangladesh crisis and the victory of the Indian forces in the eastern part of the country brought Bhutto to power much earlier than had been envisaged. He became the Head of State in December 1971. By 1973, he had been able to formulate, with the help of all the parties in the National Assembly, a new Constitution which came into effect in the same year. Since 1956, the country for the third time had a "new" Constitution. This Constitution reversed the 1962 model of Field Marshall Ayub and went back to the 1956 formula of parliamentary democracy. Under the 1973 Constitution, Bhutto became the first Prime Minister of Pakistan which, after the 1971 creation of Bangladesh, had been reduced to half its former size.

In its essential parts regarding justicibility of rights, this Constitution again repeated the formula of the 1956 and 1962 Constitutions. In its nonoperative parts, Islam was again given a polemical significance. But, like its predecessor Constitutions, this document also did not provide for the justicibility of religious provisions.

In the years 1973 and 1974, Bhutto was popular. But, as is a common trait with many of the Third World heads of the governments, through the passage of time, he became increasingly more and more authoritarian and dictatorial. One by one, the foundations of a free society were suppressed, first the press, then the intelligentsia and student organizations, and finally the opposition parties. Having muted organized dissent to his rule, he then set up special courts under special laws, the purpose of which was to intimidate all forms of opposition. The disgruntlement and frustration against his rule was gradually growing, but there was no organized platform from which the public could project their voices or simply be heard. The first and only opportunity the people were given occurred in January of 1977. Bhutto, sensing that he had complete control over the state through its police and security forces, called for a new general election. That was his undoing. Once political activity was allowed in the country, mammouth crowds came against him in all the big cities of Pakistan, e.g., Karachi, Lahore, Lyallpur, Multan, Hydrabad, and Peshawar. Facts which have now become public knowledge as a result of a White Paper published by the subsequent government of General Zia, clearly show that Bhutto, seeing that he was faced with formidable opposition, hatched up a massive rigging plan with the help of many civil and police authorities of the country. Various devices were to be used for this purpose. Not only that, but fictitious results which were already prepared were to be announced over the radio. When the results were, thus, announced and it transpired that despite the tremendous show of opposition Bhutto had still won, there started, within seven days of the announcement, a countrywide agitation against him. During the course of this agitation, the people demanded his resignation, and also a resignation of all those who had been elected according to the results of this rigged election. But Bhutto was no saint, and he was not likely to be moved out of office by simple demands. He quickly acted; his security forces imprisoned, one by one, most of those who had dared to oppose him. After about six weeks of agitation, it appeared that Bhutto might be able to weather the storm. This was because most of the known politicians had been put away in confinement by various orders of the different authorities which were able to issue such orders.

When it seemed possible that Bhutto was about to control the situation, there began to appear a new facet of the movement; this ultimately led to his downfall. Mullahs (local priests), mostly members of the principal right wing religious party, the Jamat-a-Islami, gave a new twist to this movement: they claimed that Bhutto had put Islam in danger. At every conceivable opportunity, the principal one being the weekly Friday prayers, the priests, or the Mullahs, began their vigorous onslaught against the Bhutto government.[131] One after the other, the Bhutto government put these Mullahs in jail; but the more he jailed, the more others came out and said the same thing over and over again. Sure enough, the campaign based on religious precepts began to envelope the entire country. Bhutto tried to overcome it by imposing martial law, but there he was confronted with serious contentious litigation challenging the constitutionality of such an action. The Lahore High Court ultimately held that martial law was a limited concept and could not be used countrywide[132] to replace a civilian rule with that of the military. Thus, Bhutto was forced to negotiate with his opponents, and during these negotiations with the heads of the nine main opposition parties (known as the Pakistan National Alliance), he agreed not only to hold a new election, but also to annul the recent one and to continue for the time being as a caretaker Prime Minister. The opposition leaders had reluctantly accepted this compromise, since they thought that this was a surer way to oust Bhutto. However, the army had begun to feel that they had had too much of Bhutto. If they were to carry on the government of Bhutto and maintain law and order, thereby getting a dirty name themselves, why not throw out the wrongdoer? Thus, on the night of the fourth of July, 1977, the army moved in, and the chief of the army staff, General Mohammed Zia, proclaimed martial law by ousting Bhutto to the relief of many in the country.

We are not here concerned with events which happened after the taking over of power by General Zia. But we have to remember that soon after the imposition of martial law and the taking over of the government, General Zia realized that the reason people continued to agitate against Bhutto's rule was because they felt "Islam" had been given a "secondary" place by the former government. He, therefore, announced that his government was firmly committed toward the establishment of an Islamic rule. While promising a new general election, General Zia embarked on his own to introduce certain Islamic measures. The chief Islamic measures he took were the establishment of the Shariat benches at the level of the High Court and the Supreme Court. As a matter of law, this was a revolutionary change in the history of not only Pakistan but any modern country. These Shariat benches were, in fact, similar to a constitutional court which had been set up to examine the validity of a secular law, not vis-a-vis a higher constitutional law like a Constitution, but to test the validity of ordinary laws vis-a-vis the abstract norm of the Islamic law. In addition to setting up this very crucial and important branch in the hierarchy of the legal system of the country, General Zia also proclaimed the imposition of Islamic penalties in certain cases. It was also announced that the government of Pakistan would soon change its English system of taxation which had remained after the departure of the British, and replace it with the system of Zakat, a tax which had been initially conceived by Islamic jurisprudence. In addition to these legal measures, certain cultural and social measures were taken. The principal measures were the abolition of drinking throughout the country, prohibition against dancing in places of public entertainment, and also the abolition of gambling at places like the racetracks, etc.

While examining the case of Pakistan, I think two measures need to be stressed. In the first place, Pakistan has continuously provided a considerable bulk of the intellectual thought for Islamic revival. Not only since this country was created, but even before its inception some of the principal thinkers of the Muslims' had come from the Indian subcontinent. This is not surprising since, in terms of education and enlightenment, Pakistan, or the territory which now comprises Pakistan, and the Muslims which came from this region, had enjoyed for centuries a very high level of academic, intellectual, and philosophical heritage. It is because of this Islamic tradition that Pakistan, although it is not an Arab country, has continued to side with the Arabs in their international disputes. Since 1971, Pakistan has been reduced to half, namely, from a population of about 130 million people to just over 70 million. It has, nevertheless, continued to wield a powerful intellectual influence in the Islamic world.

The second point which should be mentioned is the place of the principal religious party in the country, namely, the Jamat-a-Islami. This party has been considered, by all accounts, to be the most well-organized party in the country. It has various tiers of administration, and the "priests" in every mosque, commonly called mullahs, are its principal workers. But despite its massive organization, this party has never been able to win, politically, any election in the history of this country. Furthermore, this party has never been able to win even a respectable representation in any representative capacity in any election at any level since the creation of Pakistan. This shows and emphasizes the point that although Pakistan has a community of very deeply religious people, yet the principal religious party has never been able to win the political approval of the electorate. This fact further aids the opinion of the author brought out in various places in this book, namely, that Islam has been used as a vehicle for political changes and not as an end in itself. As Bhutto briefly showed, religion has a normative role in the life of the people; the real concern, however, is for economic realities. People want economic solutions to their earthly problems and not merely to be fed on religious dogmas. Life, hereafter, has its attractions; but for most, life, while it lasts, presents more compelling problems. The truth of the matter, therefore, seems to be that although this party had the best organization and its founder (Maudoodi) was a scholar of great repute, the people of Pakistan had never, as a political commitment, embraced the party which professed to further Islam. In all elections which had been held, the parties which had been able to gain any form of strength in the assemblies were those which had put forth before the electorate an egalitarian philosophy. This is precisely the point and the threat which, for example, the Gulf states feel as a result of the movement launched by Khomeini. The rulers in this region are not afraid of Islam, for they are themselves Muslims and of Islamic background. What they are afraid of is that if the movement launched by Khomeini gains ground, then the first victims of such an onslaught would probably be the removal of dynastical rulers and their replacement, perhaps, by a representative government. However, on account of the wealth of these states, which, to say the least, is enormous, the common man is not that poor (as in other Islamic states) to be really motivated to contemplate such changes in the near future. Moreover, most of the small states in this region are definitely not tyrannical. The governments have generally followed, for their small populations, adequate domestic policies in terms of education, health, and welfare. Thus, the concluding observation is that, leaving polemics aside, what people want most is a solution of their economic needs. Honest leadership in Islamic countries should realize this point and remember that a hungry man is an angry man.

(B)   Turkey

Having seen the case of Pakistan, which started with a secular background and tried to transform itself on the political level to a more religiously-oriented state, we now turn to Turkey to see the manifestation of a contrary trend. Modern Turkey began after the end of World War I, which Turkey, along with Germany, lost to the Allies. The Turkish contribution to Islamic history is both magnificent and glorious. After the early Arab successes which saw the spread of Islam in all directions and in many lands, it was left to the Turks to carry on the mantle of Islamic civilization and Islamic Empire. Their first and foremost encounter of any importance was with the West, since it was the Turks who fought the Crusades against the Europeans. It was not only that they were finally able to stop the Western nations from coming into Jerusalem and other places around that area, but it was the Turks who finally created stability in the later centuries of the Islamic Empire. Not only politically but even religiously, it was left to the Turks to introduce Islam in distant lands. In the East, it was the Turks, through the Gheznevi tribe, which ultimately carried Islam into India, and it was again a Turk by the name of Babur who became the founder of the radiant and glorious Mogul Dynasty in India, the dynasty which produced famous Mogul kings who established a very big and strong Islamic state in the Indian Subcontinent. In Central Asia, it was again the Turks who were ultimately able to halt and stem the sweep of the Mongul devastation. In the area which is now modern Turkey, their most notable achievement was the final overthrow of the Roman Empire at Byzantium, the strongest force ever to have opposed the Turks in any of their encounters anywhere. After the demolition of the

Byzantium Empire, the Islamic Turks were able to take Islam and the Turkish flag to Southeastern Europe. In Northern Africa, Turkey allowed itself to be allied with the ruling houses, the Memluks, which is the longest modern dynasty to rule in Egypt. Indeed, it was the sixteenth century Ottoman Empire of Turkey which held its own against the rapidly developing might of the Western nations, especially England, France, and Spain. In the spiritual field, the Turks provided Islam with some of its most profound intellectual content; they introduced Islam to the elements of Sufiism and produced generations of Jurists who were authors of monumental works in the field of law. As Wilfred Cantwell Smith suggests, it should be reiterated that the contribution of the Turks in the field of political science and historiography and to the culture of the world is tremendous, perhaps more than any Islamic people in the entire history of the Muslim nations.[133]

Throughout the nineteenth century, the Caliph of the Ottoman Empire was called the "Sick Man of Europe." This was so because nominally Turkey did hold a vast empire even at that time, but over the seventeenth and eighteenth centuries, the political might of the Ottoman Empire was gradually declining. By the nineteenth century, consequently, the Turkish Empire was only an entity in name. The decline of the Islamic Empire of Turkey coincided with the growing spirit of secularism within the Turkish lands. But it took the jolt of World War I, the loss of its colonial possessions, and the rise of Kemal Ata Turk to finally usher in the idea of secularism in Turkey. Soon after his assumption of power, Kemal Ata Turk introduced a number of measures of very far-reaching consequence. The measures he took were not only political in nature, but touched the roots of certain conceptions of Islamic history. The most important of these was the abolition of the institution of the Caliph in 1924, which for many Islamic historians had been one of the foundation tones of their concept of international Islamic unity. In 925, he passed another law by which the various religious orders in Turkey were dissolved. In 1926, he substituted a Western based legal system for the Shariat laws of Turkey. As a matter of law, this was perhaps the most decisive blow which Kemal Ata Turk dealt to the notion of the Islamic state.

Not being content with changing the basic legal system of the country, Kemal Ata Turk was determined to deal further blows to the Islamic nature of Turkey. In 1928, he deleted a fundamental clause in the Turkish Constitution which had provided that the state religion of Turkey was Islam. Article 2 of the 1924 Turkish Constitution had read, "The religion of the Turkish state is Islam." The changing of Article 2 in the 1924 Constitution was, in terms of importance, of the most extreme gravity. It not only changed the Constitution of the Turkish Republic thereafter, but in fact brought about a fundamental change in the way of life of the Turkish people, who for centuries had held the mantle of Islamic Republic not only for the Turks, but for the rest of the Islamic community. It might be instructive at this stage to reproduce the present wording of this article to show where exactly, today, Turkey stands vis-a-vis the abstract or ideal concept of an Islamic state. Article 2 reads:

II.   Characteristic of the Republic.

ARTICLE 2 - The Turkish Republic is a national, democratic, secular and social State governed by the rule of law, based on human rights and the fundamental tenets set forth in the preamble.

Without a detailed analysis, it is clear that, legally, as a result of this change, Turkey left the ambit of "Islamic" states, properly so-called.[134] Whether it was a good thing or not depends upon one's point of view. But the contrast on this point between the case of Turkey and Pakistan is striking. Or is it really striking? Could not one say from the analysis about Pakistan presented earlier that that country too is really secular in the political sense, only nobody has had the courage to say so openly? That the label of "Islamic," etc., is merely a facade, a decorative trimming? The ultimate answer is not easy, and as the facts now stand, this is, perhaps, as far as one can justifiably go.

Kemal Ata Turk was not satisfied with the changes he had brought by 1928, and he continued with more sweeping "reforms" which aimed to secularize the Turkish Republic. The next in his list of "reforms" was the substitution of

148

the Latin alphabet for the Arabic alphabet in 1928. This was followed by another fundamental change in 1933 when he substituted a Turkish call for prayer for the Arabic one. This, in a way, was something which went far beyond the secularization of the community. Muslims, since the inception of Islam, no matter where they have lived, have always said their call to prayer and the prayer itself in the Arabic language. This, by far, has been the single unifying fact in the Islamic communities of nations wherever they have lived. This particular change brought about by Ata Turk, therefore, was very fundamental. It aimed to provide the kind of modernization which has crept into Christianity since the last two hundred to three hundred years.

In the twentieth century, Turkey provides the only example where traditionally an Islamic community was able to change by force of law not only its Islamic constitutional and legal provisions, but also some of the fundamental "mannerisms" of its people, matters relating to their social, cultural, and civic lives. The changes brought about by Kemal Ata Turk had an impact not only in Turkey, but its effect was felt throughout the Muslim world. Generally, this effect was negative.

The secularization attempts in Turkey did not have much impact by way of "reformation" of Islamic communities in other countries. In fact, in India, a movement was started to reinstall the traditional Islamic values; it initiated in other places attempts to stop the kind of reformation which had taken place in Turkey. The Turkish example was, thus, the only instance where an attempt to secularize Islam survived in its own territorial confines. However, it failed to produce the same kind of influence elsewhere; indeed, it set in motion a contrary trend. That trend and reaction stood as a bulwark against similar attempts in other countries.

This innovation in the way of Turkish life was described by a number of Islamic theologians as a crude attempt to imitate in totality the Western ways of life. It was considered that Kemal Ata Turk, in order to establish himself and to re-establish the lost morale of the Turkish people, had attempted in a very bold manner to copy the system of the Western countries regarding religion and

135

constitutional law. The intellectuals of Turkey, however, argued that this "modernization" had very little to do with their beliefs per se. It was argued that beliefs of Turkish Muslims were as fervent as those of the Muslims elsewhere, that this was merely an attempt to bring the Turkish people, for centuries the leaders of Islamic culture and thought, in line with more modern thinking of Europe.[136]

The precise problem of modernization in Islam is a question which has been attempted to be answered in other communities as well. Many facets of this controversy have been analyzed in different places of the present narrative. Perhaps the truest picture of what had occurred in Turkey was provided by Sir Mohammed Iqbal who said that, in truth, the happenings in Turkey were an aftermath of World War I. As a matter of fact, since the Turks had lost the war, they had come to believe that a catharsis of the society was necessary. In this catharsis, they turned to those values which had triumphed over them; it was followed by an adoption of the approach and the manner of thinking of the Western nations.

The attempt in Turkey towards the "reformation" of Islam has to be precisely understood. Either one must say that there was an attempt to reform Islam in the same sense that the Protestant faith was brought in to reform the Catholic beliefs, or, in the alternative, one must say that it was not Islam which was being reformed but rather that a society, basically Islamic in nature, was being transformed into secular ways of thinking. It was not that religion itself was being overhauled. Rather the approach of the society towards various matters was being altered. Some doctrinal and some practical matters were taken out of the purview of religion and placed in the domain of the "secular" and of secular law. In the author's view, what transpired in Turkey was not that Islam itself had been changed or that an attempt was made to change Islam; rather, the Turkish people were told that there was another approach in looking at the affairs of state. The fact that things like alphabets had to be changed by legislation showed that the impact of Islam and tradition in the body politic of the country was very deep. There is, however, no doubt that a number of things appertaining to the civic and social mores of the people were affected. Nevertheless, with the possible exception of changing the call to prayer from Arabic to Turkish, Islam itself was not interfered with. Therefore, it can be maintained that there did not take place any real measure which aimed at desecularizing the "content" of Islam, but instead Islam was reduced to the place of any other religion in Turkey. Moreover, the substitution of a secular constitutional law for an Islamic one would show that Islam had lost its place in matters of statecraft. This is a justified comment, since that is exactly what was intended. But, perhaps, and this is merely a suggestion of the present writer, only a change in the system of the workings of the organs of the state was accomplished and polemical references to Islam dropped. The Turkish society was asked, by changes in its Constitutional law, to have a realistic outlook towards state. Still, admittedly, contrary to the Islamic doctrines, a separation of Church and State did take place. Religion was taken away from the public sphere and placed in the private domain. Nothing, per se, was done against religion, and the Turkish people continued to remain a very religious people. They remained mostly devout and fervent Muslims. The change was simply that various religious aspects, mostly doctrinal and partly polemical, were taken out of the basic organic law of the country.

However, this conscious and dedicated attempt to take religion completely out of the affairs of state diminished with the passage of time. Soon after World War II, the Turkish government began to take measures which, by stages. brought back some aspects of religion in the public affairs of its people. For example, in 1948, the schools for the teaching of religious functionaries, namely the Imams and the Khatibs, under the patronage of the State were revived. In 1949, the University of Ankara started the Faculty of Theology, where Islam was the principal religion taught. At the same time, namely 1947 and 1948, the government allowed a number of religious weeklies to appear. In 1949, Turkey began to grant complete freedom to its citizens to go for pilgrimage at the time of the annual Hajj. From 1950, the state-run radio allowed religious programs and slowly there was a reappearance of religious ceremonies at functions (like weddings). Further, even at offical functions of a civic nature, Islamic traditions began to be seen again. Religion, then, was beginning to have a stronger influence and more ostensible note.

It, therefore, appears that in the inter-war period, as a result of Kemal Ata Turk, Islam was taken out of the affairs of State. However, since World War II, Islam has been making a slow comeback. Still, Turkey easily remains the most de-Islamicized of the Muslim countries. The people nevertheless remain very Islamic. They perform their religious functions and approach their religious events with the same fervor as one would find in other Muslim countries. Yet, the place of Islam in the organic law is not on the same footing as perhaps one would find in countries like Pakistan, Saudi Arabia, Iran, or Libya. This, therefore, is where we stand today. One last word. It appears that a religious revival, i.e., to have the religious postulates put back into the domain of the organic law, are stronger today than they have been for more than two generations. This opinion is based on numerous interviews conducted by the author in Turkey during 1980.[137]

(C) Afghanistan

The above two countries representing the two principal divergent evolutionary developments, vis-a-vis, the ideal Islamic state, were discussed.

The next state which is the center of focus is Afghanistan. Ordinarily, this country would not have been of such importance historically to have been mentioned in the context of the present discussion. However, some extraordinary events have taken place in that country in the last two years, thereby making it necessary for us to examine it within the confines of the present discussion.

Afghanistan is a country about the size of France. It lies on the northern side of Pakistan and the eastern side of Iran. To the north of it lies the Soviet Union. It has a population of about fifteen million Muslims. Its people are famous for their bravery and courage. Afghanistan, unlike most Muslim countries, has never been colonized, and remained a buffer state for centuries between the British in the south in India and the Russians in the north. For a long time it was a monarchy, but in 1974 the then King Zahir Shah was overthrown by his brother-in-law, Mohammed Daud Khan. The Daud government survived for four years. In the international field, Afghanistan was proclaimed by Daud to be a non-aligned state. Internally, Afghanistan became a republic.[139] Daud himself was its first President.

Unlike many Islamic countries, Afghanistan has, in the past twenty to thirty years, maintained strong links with its communist neighbor, the Soviet Union. Mostly on account of this alliance, Afghanistan has on more than one occasion, and by different methods, tried to disturb or interfere in Pakistani politics. Pakistan, in this context, is considered to be a potential victim for the larger Russian interests. Primarily, this interest has been to arouse factional or parochial disturbances between different provinces for eventual Russian involvement and subsequent domination. As a natural consequence, the relations between Pakistan and Afghanistan have not been happy or cordial.[138]

Daud seemed to be well entrenched, and the country was making its transformation from a monarchial system to a republican system. However, in April 1978, he was suddenly overthrown in a bloody coup led by the head of the Communist Party, one Nur Muhammad Taraki. The coup, engineered by Nur Muhammad Taraki, was backed by the Soviet Union, and the Soviet influence in the Taraki government was both ostensible and manifest. The justification behind the coup, according to Taraki, was that he thought Daud had become imperialistic. He wanted, on the contrary, to bring in socialism so that the poor people who had been first struggling, according to him, under a king and then under an autocratic government, could live a better life. For some months, the Taraki government seemed to be in control, when suddenly, towards the end of the Summer of 1978, the people of Afghanistan, especially those living outside the cities, began to feel a resentment against his government. They thought that their government had been put into power by a foreign country, namely the Soviet Union. This, by itself, was terribly upsetting to a fiercely independent people. As it has been observed, Afghanistan is one of the few countries which was never conquered or colonized. The Afghan tribesmen[140] had a proud heritage of independence through very turbulent and sometimes tempestuous times. They, therefore, resented deeply that their head of state had been installed by a foreign government, thereby compromising their centuries-old tradition of independence. But more than that was a religious conflict. The tribesmen were gradually becoming aware of the fact that communism, an ideology supported by the Taraki government, was basically opposed to a very fervently God-believing society. It, thus, became a tussle between a people who believed very devoutly in God and a government which, according to the people, was trying to make them into a godless society.

Consequently, there began countrywide disturbances. In the Fall of 1978, the disturbances had become widespread and fighting was going on in many parts of the country. It appeared on many occasions that the government would collapse, but the Soviet Union continued to help it militarily with the result that the Taraki government was able to survive the end of 1978. When the government started using air and tank attacks against the insurgents who had fled from their villages and taken shelter in the hilltops, there began a flow of large numbers of refugees into neighboring Pakistan. By the beginning of 1979, it was estimated that there were approximately 250,000 Afghan refugees living in the frontier regions of Pakistan. The civil war in Afghanistan continued and, throughout 1979, the refugee matter kept growing into an alarming problem for Pakistan and also for Iran, where some of the Afghans with the Baluchi background were running for shelter.

The Afghanistan government, in order to save face, was maintaining that both Iran and Pakistan were training guerillas to fight the Afghan government. This charge was also apparently made because both in Pakistan and in Iran there had come to exist two vocally Islamic (and so non-communist) states under the guidance of President Zia and Ayatollah Khomeini. With the growing impact of the civil war, it was a matter of conjecture as to how far the Soviet government would go on supporting the Taraki government. There were some who considered that the Soviet Union might, in its long term interests, decide it better to pull back so that it could have a friendly relation with whichever government finally came to power, assuming of course that the Taraki government was replaced. Conversely, there were some who thought that the Soviets would intervene to quickly put an end to insurgency.

However, before the Soviet Union could take either of these steps, Taraki himself was overthrown in September 1979 and replaced by one of his deputies, Hafiz-Ullah Amin. As soon as Amin took over, the civil war, instead of decreasing, became more intense. This was so because Amin's sympathies toward the Soviet Union were even more pronounced than those of his predecessor. Pari passu with these developments there began in Iran the drama of the hostages. The attention of the world was focused on the Iranian situation when, on Christmas Day and on the twenty-sixth of December 1979, the Soviet Union moved about ten to twenty thousand troops into the city of Kabul during daytime airlifts. This, for the Soviet Union, was somewhat unprecedented. The help which the Soviet Union had provided to its client states in the past which were not traditionally considered communist, had always been given in a clandestine manner. This open support of the Amin government and this remarkable escalation of open military involvement by the Soviet Union in a foreign and neighboring sovereign country was immediately condemned by many nations. Analysts were trying to study this sudden turn of events when, in the early hours of December 27, 1979, the Amin government itself was overthrown. It was reported that he had been tried and executed by the leaders of the coup. It is widely believed by intelligence experts that it was the Russians who removed Amin so as to place someone more subservient to them on the seat of authority. He was replaced by one Karmal, a diplomat in his fifties, who was known to be an even more pronounced Marxist than his two predecessors. At the moment this narrative goes to press, the civil war continues, casualties are mounting, and refugees keep fleeing to Pakistan, while the U.S.S.R. and its puppet regime seem to be bent on crushing this Islamic uprising by sophisticated military arsenal. More than seven months have passed, but this unequal battle between the armed forces of a superpower and the ill-equipped and uncoordinated insurgents, goes on unabated. In view of this manifest imbalance in the military capability of the true combatants, one cannot help but admire the conviction of the insurgents. For them, it is a "Holy war" a Jihad against infidels. This is but a brief modern glimpse of the spirit which Islam provides to those who fight for it. In many ways, both the Afghan crisis and the overthrow of the Shah demonstrate the enormous strength which is provided by Islam to those who, in its cause, fight despotism and tyranny. That is where Afghanistan stands today.

The lesson we learn from Afghanistan is an important one. It shows that a people who have an Islamic background will fiercely fight a government which they believe aims to wipe out their religious heritage. There is a special built-in antipathy of Islam towards communism, and this is a point which must always be remembered and noted by all nations in their formulations of foreign policies in regions where Muslims live.

(D)   The Communist World and Islam

The above discussion leads us to examine, albeit briefly, the place of Islam in the communist countries. Since the early 1950's, the U.S.S.R. has been very careful in the conduct of its foreign policy vis-a-vis the Muslim states because a large segment of its own population is Muslim by faith. The exact number of Muslims living in the Soviet Union is somewhat uncertain;[141] it is estimated between 50 to 70 million. The more important centers of Islamic heritage and culture in the Soviet Union are the areas of Samarkand and Bokhara. The Soviet government has been careful not to interfere in the cultural and the civil life of the people as far as Islam is concerned.

For a long time, many of these areas formed part of the Turkish Empire. As such, people have a professed strong Turkish trait in their mannerisms, attire, and languages. Since the Soviet Union has followed an overall foreign policy which has been very favorable to the Arab countries (and so pro-Islamic), it has not had to worry a great deal about antagonizing its Muslim population which largely lives on the northern side of Turkey, Afghanistan, and Iran. But the revolution which has been brought into force in Iran by Ayatollah Khomeini is something which has definitely given the Soviet Union a great deal to consider. It is inconceivable that the Soviet Union could allow a similar movement to spread in the southern part of its territories abutting Iran, Afghanistan, and Turkey, for if that were to begin, its natural consequences for the U.S.S.R. would be extremely grave. The Soviet Union has the military capacity to put down a revolt in these

156

areas but if such were the case, the toll in blood and destruction would be simply catastrophic for the government. Be that as it may, it must be kept in mind that Islam in these regions of the Soviet Union is a cause of perennial worry to the Russian policy makers in the Kremlin. Therefore, not surprisingly, the Russians have, over the years, tried in a subtle way to dilute the quintessence of the Islamic teachings in these areas. The one guarantee which, for the time being, the Soviet Union has for its security in this region, is the lack of means of communication. Furthermore, the mass media, being completely governmentally controlled, does not allow any dissemination against the Kremlin. The Russian government, by these mechanisms, has maneuvered over the years to keep the Muslim population satisfied by making them believe that, not only does the Soviet Union follow a pro-Islamic foreign policy towards the Islamic states generally, but that it is protecting the interests of Islamic communities within the Soviet Union as well.

Like all religions, Islam does not find much favor with the Soviet rulers. Because of Islamic history, its potential political impact makes the Russians perhaps even more apprehensive of this religion than of others. The teaching of Islam, like that of other religions, is officially prevented. There is no domestic law incorporating a 1962 U.N. Convention guaranteeing all parents to bring up their children in their religions. The result of this practice is to reduce the number of believers in religion in coming generations. In 1971, it was officially stated in Uchitelskaia Gazeta (Teachers' Gazette) published in Moscow:

> Communist ideology is irreconcilable with that of religion . . . [it is the duty of every Soviet teacher] to do everything possible to make atheist education a constitutional part of a Communist education, to root out with finality superstitions and prejudices among children, and to bring up every school child as a militant atheist. (November 13, 1971)

The Muslim clergy is[142] without power, and the state has effectively decreased their numbers and consequently the number of mosques. In Turkistan, alone, from 1917 to 1970, the mosques decreased from over twelve thousand to

157

under twelve hundred. In 1917, it was estimated there were nine thousand Mullahs in Bashkiria; now there are not that many in the entire U.S.S.R. These figures are an eloquent testimony to what the state has in mind for its Muslims, their religion, their institutions, and their practices.

The next Communist country in which Muslims live in large numbers is Communist China. In the case of China, we are again very severely handicapped about the exact figures of the Muslim population, but by various estimates, there should be over sixty million Muslims. Ideologically, the position of the Chinese Muslims is no different from that of the Muslims in the Soviet Union. However, in practice, China, as a friend of the Third World, particularly of the Muslim block, has not given any tangible cause of concern to indicate that it has attempted to interfere in the spiritual life of the Muslims.

Nevertheless, Islam is a religion of totality. It not only aims to govern the private life of a Muslim, but also his political and civic life. Inevitably, the civic and the political aspects of the Muslim's life cannot be realized in a communist environment. Therefore, the Muslim who lives in a communist environment is, by necessary implication, deprived of a vital part of the teachings of his faith. There is, nevertheless, one important difference in the Muslim communities in the Soviet Union and China. In the Soviet Union, the Muslims are found mostly in those areas which at one time formed part of the Turkish Empire. They are, by and large, of Turkish background and live solidly in a contiguous area almost across the Turkish, Iranian, and Afghan borders. Accordingly, because of their geographical position, the Soviet Union has to deal with them in a very careful and delicate manner. This Muslim community is not a political force yet, but because of its large numbers and since these numbers live in one continuous region, the political impact that this community could wield is manifestly visible. As a result of this, the Russian attitude toward this particular region is one of extreme caution. Compared to this, in China, the Muslims are found scattered at various places throughout the vast country. Furthermore, these Muslims, historically, were never a political force like they were elsewhere. The Muslims of China have, therefore, not been regarded as a realistic force in opposition to the Chinese government or the communist ideology.

As we leave the two largest communist states and come to the smaller communist countries, we again find that there are, in some of these countries, very large numbers of Muslims. Two of these states should briefly be mentioned.

Yugoslavia, a country with a population of twenty-two million, has reportedly at least four million Muslims. Under the constitutional law, Muslims of this multinational state are regarded as an "ethnic and equal nation." In recent years, there has never been reported any serious antagonism between the Yugoslav government and the Islamic population or its clergy. Today there are between seventeen hundred and two thousand clergymen of Islam with over two hundred religious training centers for the young where the Quran and Quranic teachings are extensively taught. For allowing this to happen, President Tito was held in high esteem throughout the Islamic world.

Neighboring Bulgaria also has a very large Muslim community. Since Bulgaria was for a long time a part of the Turkish Empire, the Muslims of this area are of Turkish origin. Bulgaria has, off and on, followed an anti-Muslim policy. Muslims have been discouraged in their religious practices and often regarded as anti-state to such an extent that in 1967, the Bulgarian government at Sophia allowed the repatriation of nearly three-quarters of a million Muslims to Turkey.

From the above brief analysis, it is quite apparent that Yugoslavia is the one country in the communist block where Islam and Muslims still have considerable "autonomy." This, in a way, is ironical, because Yugoslavia is the one communist country where the call given by Ayatollah Khomeini to have an Islamic form of government has been felt and eulogized.[143] The acceptance of Islam as one of the principal nationalities in the Yugoslav Republic has not been without battle. This battle began soon after the establishment of a communist regime in Yugoslavia and continued throughout the fifties, ending only in the early sixties. The most populous of the areas in Yugoslavia where Muslims live is the Republic of Bozynia Harzogavinia. Two to three million Muslims live there. As a result of continuous strife in this particular locality, it was in the early sixties that constitutionally the Muslims were given a status equal to, ethnically speaking, other Yugoslav populations like the Serbs, the Slovaks, and the Montenegrans. Yugoslavia is clearly the only communist country which has allowed literally hundreds of its young men to study Islamic history and the Arabic language, and to go and work in the lands where Arabs have been able to make a great deal of money from oil. As a quid pro quo to these attitudes of the Yugoslav government, consistent over the years, the Muslim countries, particularly the Arabs, have been following a very pro-Yugoslav line. The principal Islamic cleric is still the Mufti of Belgrade. He is accorded a high and important place in civic and political events.

An important point must now be mentioned. In communist states, as in the case of Yugoslavia, Islam has been portrayed not only as a religion, but as an ideology which is, in a way, quasi-socialistic in its outlook. It is portrayed principally as a faith which preaches an egalitarian outlook. This, in some ways, is true. As indicated elsewhere in this book, the economic structure of Islam is such that it aims (1) to socialize wealth and (2) to prevent the accumulation of wealth in a few hands. But it is definitely not communistic in its outlook; it simply aims at creating some kind of social responsibility in the various classes of its people. It is this "welfare" or "quasi-socialistic" outlook of Islam which, in fact, has been given a great deal of propaganda and publicity in Yugoslavia. Islam has been called, in fact, the religion of socialism. The call of Khomeini's revolution in Iran has been transcribed in Yugoslavia as "Khomeini socialism" or as "Khomeini's brotherhood;" the Yugoslavian papers and journals have maintained that what Khomeini is really preaching is that wealth should be taken from the hands of a few and distributed to the community at large. It may be quickly added that the communist countries are not the only ones to emphasize this "socialist" aspect of Islam.

As earlier indicated, this was also, indeed, the principal political plank on which Bhutto came to power in Pakistan in 1971. Unlike any of the previous political parties in that country, his was the first party which attempted to proclaim socialism as its main aim. Further, it attempted to convince and advocate that Islam within its fold had always contained a socialistic outlook as far as wealth was concerned. It was this particular emphasis which, in fact, brought him triumph in the political scene of that country. It is precisely this aspect of an Islamic ideology, this thrust, which is feared by the governments of a few Islamic states. Khomeini by himself is no threat to them. However, the idea to which he has given significance, namely, that Islam preaches brotherhood and social equality and that this can be realized through Islamic fervor, is something which terrifies those who wish to deny such consequences.

(E)   United States and Islam

In the context of the present discussion, having discussed the role of Islam in communist countries, it is now pertinent to examine the relationship of the United States, which may be taken to be the main protagonist of the non-communist world, and Islam. Historically, the United States in recent years has not followed a consistent policy or pattern of policies toward Islamic nations as a whole. It is unfortunate for America, because in times of crisis, it has been realized that Islamic states have not felt at ease or comfortable with the United States' attitude towards them. Furthermore, Islam, for the United States, or at least its policy makers, has come to mean really that part of the Muslim world which produces oil, namely, the areas around the Persian Gulf. This implies that although there are very big and important Muslim countries like Pakistan, Turkey, and Indonesia, the importance which has been given to Iran and smaller countries like Oman, Bahrain, Kuwait, and Saudi Arabia, is solely due to their capacity to produce oil. That perhaps the United States is not interested in Islam per se (but should it be?) and only in oil is a fact which is believed by many of the countries now being discussed.[144] For example, the governments of the Gulf States are heavily dependent on and rely on the United States' military support. Still, the Gulf States have felt very uncomfortable since the hostage crisis began in November of 1979. While officially they have had to agree with the manifest position in law that the taking of the hostages was illegal, they have been privately terrified of the consequences which such a support might cause in

161

their own countries. It is precisely for this reason that all the governments in the Gulf region have refrained from giving more than lip service to the support of the United States. In the working classes (mostly Palestinians and immigrants from South Asia), the United States is taken to be perhaps unfriendly to Islam itself. Even a cursory survey of the public opinion in any of these areas will make it abundantly clear that to the average man, America is only a friend of the ruling regimes. While the governments concerned wish that the United States had demonstrated more toughness in the case of Iran, and perhaps preserved the Shah from falling, yet this is something of which they have to speak very quietly. They are very sensitive to anti-American feelings in most of these regions. In fact, although admittedly, most of these nations are receiving a heavy amount of American support in terms of military equipment, publicly the leaders of these countries are hesitant to speak of the American support before their own public. This stresses the tragedy of the American foreign policy in this region. Ideologically, Islamic countries would always resist communism. But because of the continued support of a few rulers, sometimes unwillingly, by the United States, its prestige, in the eyes of the local populations, is low. Had the United States supported these countries and their people over the years and refrained from becoming involved in a personal relationship with the rulers of this region, its position today would be much more secure.

This is ironical. The United States, out of all the Western industrialized nations, has really never been an imperialistic power. However, because of a senselessness (in this aspect) in its foreign policy, first of all under J. F. Dulles in the early fifties and then mishandled by analysts of successive administrations in the sixties and early seventies, the friendship of a few rulers has been so highlighted as to give to the Third World public, including the people of the Islamic states, a totally false picture; namely, that the United States really is trying to govern these vast populations in different territories by maintaining puppet and stooge regimes.

If, in fact, the notable traditions and heritage of the American people are to be presented correctly to these vast masses of people who profess the Islamic belief, it is

162

necessary that this misunderstanding, this misconception, be corrected. To start with, the United States has to follow a policy of friendship with these states, and not exclusively with their rulers. Whether they have a king, a president, or a prime minister is the internal affair of that state. The United States must refrain from trying to manipulate or to preserve a certain dynasty or a certain man. It is in the long-term interests of the United States to be friendly to the people of these nations. The people will remain loyal and their feelings will be a more effective bulwark against communism, than a ruler who is likely to become more unpopular with the passage of time. The story of fascism and dictatorship is almost universally the same. Once the dictator gets in, he tries to become friendly with a super power, especially with the United States. Once that friendship is gained, he then tries to blackmail the United States by saying that only he can deliver the goods. The analysts in the State Department probably also think it is easier to deal with the man they know rather than to deal with somebody they do not know, with the result that the United States becomes entrenched more and more deeply in a relationship with this one man. Since, in time, this one man usually loses popularity, the United States, too, gets deeply involved in this animosity of the public against their ruler. Eventually, the authoritarian rule of this one man grows worse and there is more opposition leading finally to civil unrest and bloodshed. Even at that time, i.e., when the dictator is on his last legs against such civil disobedience and unrest, it is believed by some that America should do something to save the falling dictator. This kind of perverse advice makes the United States look bad. This is also incidentally a blatant admission that the U.S. can interfere in the internal affairs of another state.

Apart from this particular facet of the American foreign policy towards Islamic states, we must now advert briefly to another factor. It would be wrong to assume that the antipathy which the population of the Muslim countries feels towards the United States is solely due to this aspect of mishandling of the American foreign policy. A continuous reason for the antipathy felt towards the United States stems from the fact that the United States has been consistently helping Israel in its fight against the Arab nations. It is true that Arabs today do not constitute more than twenty-five percent of the world Muslim population; however, because of the concept of the Muslim brotherhood, the Umma, Muslims all over the world feel that the United States has not been friendly towards the Islamic nations generally. It is out of the purview of this book to examine the propriety of this policy in the Arab-Israeli conflict, but this fact should be remembered while examining the overall[145] attitude of Islamic states towards the United States.

It is most unfortunate that the United States, the strongest nation of the free world, should be so placed as to find itself "considered" opposed to the aspirations and[146] wishes of nearly a billion of the world's population. The widespread nature of the Islamic resentment against the United States can be seen from the sole fact that in the aftermath of events of the taking of the American hostages in November 1979 in Tehran, there were riots or demonstrations against the United States Embassies and Consulates in such diverse places as the Phillippines, Thailand and Calcutta, and, of course, in a great many of the Middle Eastern countries. That there could be resentment against the United States in countries like India, the Phillippines, and Thailand, which are non-Muslim in cultural outlook, is some indication of the depth of the feeling against the United States.

Before leaving this discussion, a word must be said briefly about a policy, particularly of the U.S., to ensure that two Islamic countries, Pakistan and recently Iraq, do not acquire nuclear capability. Although these American efforts were visible and acknowledged in the case of Pakistan during 1976-78, it has been assumed, by many, that they are directed not only against Pakistan, but against the Islamic world in general. There are innumerable references in contemporary writings of the Western press, that Pakistan, in reality, was not making something for itself, but indeed an "Islamic bomb." This point was also directly endorsed by the late Prime Minister Bhutto in his statement before the Pakistan Supreme Court during the course of his trial:

"We all know that Israel and South Africa have full nuclear capability. The Christian, Jewish, and Hindu civilizations have this capability. The communist

164

powers also possess it. Only the Islamic civilization was without it, but that position was about to change."[147]

It is not proposed to go any deeper into this matter. Nevertheless, this is an important point while examining the position of the U.S. in its dealings with the Islamic states. It is true that these American efforts have been placed into the category of "non-proliferation." However, the Islamic states do not consider it as such. It is even questionable whether it has been a practicable or a prudent far-reaching goal of American foreign policy. To the present author, given today's technology, American efforts in retrospect appear both impractical and ill-advised. It certainly did not help the U.S. in its relations with Pakistan which has had to look elsewhere for its needs.

Other Islamic Areas

We have, so far, examined three countries specifically and also the relationship of the United States and the Soviet Union with the Islamic world generally. We will now, very briefly, advert to the position of the Muslims in other parts of the world.

Generally speaking, the Muslims form of an arc of continuous population stretching from the west coast of Africa and going as far east as the Northern shores of Australia. This arc, therefore, stretches across the three continents of Africa, Europe, and Asia. The more important states, lying in the center of this crescent, have already been noted. We must, therefore, briefly examine the other states lying within this crescent. In the West, if a line were drawn somewhere from the western bulge of Africa, across toward Kenya, it will be found that almost all of the countries north of this imaginary line would be Muslim. These Muslim countries would be: Guinea, Muritania, Mali, Niger, Nigeria, Sudan, Somalia, Egypt, Libya, Algeria, Morocco, Tunisia, etc. The African peoples became Muslim in the wake of the Arab conquest beginning in the ninth and tenth centuries. By and large, Africa has therefore, remained predominantly a Muslim continent.[148] This fact often escapes the policy makers in other countries. Because of "nationalistic"

165

tendencies in its various states, the continent has been mostly concerned with questions of race, liberation, and apartheid. Still, the members of the O.A.S. have had an important bearing on the outcome of many a vote in the United Nations and other world bodies where they have consistently sided with Islamic states. Since these countries do not have strategic importance for the West (which the Middle East has), they have not yet caught the public eye. Islamic Fundamentalism (so-called) has come to the surface a few times when political exigencies have demanded its appearance. However, politically, the majority of African countries have been mainly involved in achieving domestic nationalist successes. Formerly, most of Africa consisted of colonies of Western powers, and at the time the United Nations first met in 1945, there were only four independent countries on this huge continent. Except for these four, all African countries have emerged only since 1960. The question of Islamic Fundamentalism or Islam emerging as a political force since then has not been very significant. Most important in this respect on the African continent has been an organization called the The Muslim Brotherhood. Its aim has been to create "Islamic" forms of government. It has emerged a number of times in Egypt and in surrounding lands. On all such occasions, it has been severely dealt with by the ruling governments. The Muslim Brotherhood was quite strong at the time of Nasser in Egypt. However, he soon enough put an end to its activities by either exiling its leaders or by putting them in jail. Since the revolution of Ayatollah Khomeini, there has been an emergence of the same movement in Egypt, but Anwar Sadat, like his predecessor, has for the present, put an end to the aspirations of this movement. This movement has also called, sometimes by a show of violence, for a change in existing governments in Islamic countries. So far, this organization has been mainly concerned with Egypt, but it is present in a few other countries as well, and it is now believed that it is trying to get a foothold in countries like Saudi Arabia.[149] It is also believed by some that a considerable amount of success has already been achieved in Iran by bringing Khomeini into the forefront. Other than this observation, the discussion of Islam may not have had, as yet, a political impact in Africa.

In the center of this arc or crescent of Muslim countries are the states of the Persian Gulf, Turkey, Iran, Afghanistan, and Pakistan. Since they have already been noticed, we move to the East for a look at the Islamic communities in that area. Towards the East lie such Islamic countries as Bangladesh (formerly East Pakistan), Malaysia, and Indonesia. Finally, there are also sizeable minorities of Muslims in Thailand and the Phillippines.

The Islamic faith was an important ingredient in helping some of these lands to achieve independence. Indonesia was under the Dutch. Bangladesh, formerly East Pakistan, was a part of British India, and, in fact, it was the call of the Bengali Muslims which started the movement of the Muslims towards independence in India. These eastern Islamic countries represent one important fact: that Islam is a world religion, its adherents in these regions are of totally different ethnic backgrounds from those examined or referred to so far. Whereas the people of Bangladesh are of Bengali origin, the people of Malaysia, Thailand, the Phillippines, and Indonesia are of the Indochinese racial background. In Malaysia and Indonesia, Muslims constitute large majorities of the populations. After Pakistan's dismemberment in 1971, Indonesia, with a population of one hundred and twenty million, is the biggest Islamic state in the world. However, given the present international political situation, these countries are far away from international attention or concern. Furthermore, apart from some racial tension in Malaysia, Islam has not figured prominently in any domestic or international controversy which may be mentioned here. A word might be said, however, about the Muslim minorities and their plight in Thailand and the Phillippines. In both these countries the Muslims do not form governments, but because they have been agitating for the last twenty-five to thirty years to have some form of autonomy, they have been consistently the target of government brutality. In Thailand (in the South), they have had to resort to terrorism to express their resentment against the government policies. The case of the Phillippines is more grave. The Marcos government has consistently attempted, by use of massive air and land attacks on Muslim regions,[150] to wipe out the struggle by these Muslims to form an autonomous province within the Phillippine Republic. Well-known nongovernmental organizations[151] have noted on the record the denial of human rights to the Muslims in the Phillippines and the brutality which the government has meted out to them. In their political meetings,[152] the Islamic states have from time to time also voiced serious concern over the fate of the Muslims in this country.

Within this crescent of Islamic states, we have not as yet said anything about the case of India. Muslims constitute nearly one-sixth of India's population, meaning thereby nearly one hundred to one hundred-thirty million Muslims. Historically, in the undivided India before 1947, it was the Indian Muslim who was at the intellectual vanguard of the Islamic revival in the twentieth century. It has already been observed that it was the birth of Pakistan and its creation which was the first tangible sign of Islamic revival in this century. That remark, in fact, equally applies to the Indian Muslim because it was the Indian Muslims as a nation which gave birth to the idea of Pakistan. However, all the Muslims of India could not migrate to Pakistan when the new Muslim country was formed, with the result that India still has, in fact, as many, if not more, Muslims than any other country in the world. Today, technically, the largest Muslim country is Indonesia, which has approximately one hundred-thirty million Muslims. There have been frequent communal riots in India, and at many religious festivals and occasions, there has been religious friction.[153] The Hindu majority of India resents the Indian Muslim who, for centuries[154] formed the ruling classes of the Indian subcontinent.

The position of Muslim minorities is, therefore, a subject of possible future controversies. Whether it is in India, the Phillippines, or the Soviet Union, it appears that large numbers of Muslim minorities have been subjected to one form of discrimination or another. Lack of articulate leadership and a means of access to mass media have combined to produce, more often than not, a totally wrong picture of these Muslim minorities. One tangible contribution, which the more affluent Islamic states can positively make, is to provide facilities, particularly those relating to education, through proven governmental channels, to enable these ignored minorities to become valuable citizens of their own communities.

CHAPTER VII
Political Economy of the Islamic State

(A) The Economic Structure of Islam

In a previous chapter, some reference was made to the economic system of Islam. The religion of Islam does not confine its attention to purely devotional or spiritual aspects of the life of an individual, but extends its direction to matters concerning social organization in all its aspects. It prescribes a particular pattern of social structure of which the fundamentals are ordained but the details are left for determination by the faithful according to the demands of various ages.

Some of the points of emphasis provided by Islam for its social structure lead to an economic pattern of its own. Though details are left to be worked out according to the requirements of a given time and place, a structure of continuity is bound to occur in view of the unalterable fundamental directions of policy. In view of the great importance which the Quran attaches to economic life, elaborate guidance has been given therein for building up a sound economic system together with a clear exposition of the purpose underlying it.

Chapter 11, Verse 6, contains an assertion that there is, on earth, no one moving with life, the responsibility for whose sustenance has not been assumed by Allah. Similarly, in another place, the Quran (17:31) assures mankind in particular that they should not "kill" their offspring since the responsibility of feeding His creatures is this: "Allah provides sustenance for them as well as for their offspring." The responsibility for feeding human beings could not have been assumed in clearer or more emphatic terms. Even with this solemn assurance, we still see hundreds of thousands dying of hunger and millions struggling for a scanty meal. Does this indicate non-fulfillment of the responsibility solemnly assumed by Allah? The answer is in the negative, for God also ordains that the individual must make the necessary effort. Once the effort is made, his sustenance is assured, for the Almighty in His Wisdom has provided sustenance for all His creatures, whether they are in a desert or in and around stones. This is the message of Islam.

Furthermore, God has ordained and placed a responsibility on the social order or community. The Quran, 36: 47, shows that, where human affairs are concerned, Allah's responsibility is discharged not directly but indirectly. The verse says, "When they are asked to keep open for the development of others a portion of what Allah has given them, the disbelievers ask the believers, "should we make provision for one whom Allah could provide for if He willed it?" In answering the question, the Quran says that in so thinking they are sadly mistaken. Allah does not feed the hungry directly: they are fed by the Social Order established to enforce Divine laws.

What is the mutual relationship between the individual and the Islamic Social Order? Between this Social Order and the individual members thereof, there is an unwritten agreement, the basic provision of which is that the individuals surrender to Allah their life and belongings in return for Jannat (paradise). There is undoubtedly a Jannat which will be attained after death, but, according to the Quran, the life of Jannat can also be attained in this world provided a Social Order is built up on the lines given by Allah. The main characteristics of this earthly Jannat have been cited in Chapter 20, Verse 118, that if the people build a society on Quranic lines, then "none will remain without food or clothes, none will suffer thirst nor heat (i.e., inclemencies or weather)." In other words, in the earthly Jannat, all individuals will be provided with the basic necessities of life. Therefore, under the written contract referred to above, Quranic Social Order becomes the agency for the discharge of Allah's responsibility for meeting the basic necessities of life of each and every individual.

The purpose of the Quranic Social Order, then, is to ensure for every individual the provision of the basic necessities of life so that he may be free to devote himself to the development of his personality in that social order. If, despite this promise, and after fulfilling the ordained requirements, people are hungry, then it is a Muslim's belief that that, too, is God's will. He alone knows the mysteries of the unknown, and the believer has simply to submit himself to His Wisdom and System.

With this necessary philosophical background, we can proceed to give the fundamental characteristics of the Economic Structure of Islam.

An examination and analysis of the classical sources of Islam would show that, as an economic system, Islam has the following salient features. To facilitate an easy understanding of this complicated field, these features are tabulated in seriatim below:

1. It is opposed to interest. For authority, see Verses 274-79 of the second chapter of the Quran. We shall here read only portions of Verses 275, 278, and 279 which make the whole position clear beyond any doubt:

> "Those who devour Usury. (The Arabic term, Riba, means excess or addition, so here excess or addition over the capital lent)
> Will not stand except
> As stands one whom
> The Evil One by his touch
> Hath driven to madness
> That is because they say:
> "Trade is like Usury"
> But God hath permitted trade
> And forbidden Usury
> O ye! who believe:
> Fear God and give up
> What remains of your demand
> For Usury, if ye are indeed believers
> If ye do it not,
> Take notice of war
> From God and His Apostle."

Thus, the fundamental principle of the Islamic state is to ensure that there exists an interest-free society. The question then arises, how can contemporary institutions like banks work? The answer is by allowing people to take "profit" as opposed to "interest" on their investments. In other words, deposit of money in banks will be governed by the same principles which operate when one has shares in a company. However, it must be acknowledged that this is a question of some difficulty.

Comprehensive planning is necessary to incorporate this aspect of the ideal Islamic state in the working of a modern state.[155]

2.   Islam prescribes compulsory social insurance through its system of Zakat. The order to pay Zakat occurs at least twenty-seven times in the Quran along with the order to establish prayers, besides numerous occasions when Zakat alone is enjoined. That it is something altogether different from charity is obvious from the fact that one of the items of expenditure provided for Zakat in the Quran is "those employed to administer (the funds)" (Chapter 9, Verse 60). So Zakat is something centrally or nationally organized, whose primary objective, prescribed by the Quran in the same verse, is to meet the requirements of "the poor and the needy." It is submitted that the phrase, "the poor and the needy," covers all kinds of economic weaknesses which may be the result of unemployment, old age, infirmity, or accident.

3.   Islam is opposed to the concentration of wealth in a few hands. This principle is enunciated by the Quran in a variety of ways. A good example occurs in the seventh verse of Chapter 20:

> What God has bestowed
> On His Apostle (and taken away) from the people
> Of the township belongs
> To God, to His Apostle
> And to kindred and orphans
> The needy and the wayfarer;
> In order that the wealth may not
> Make a circuit (merely)
> Between the wealthy among you.

4.   Islam stands for free enterprise. For example, the Quran says in Chapter 62, Verse 10:

> And when the prayer
> Is finished, then disperse

Ye through the land
And seek of the bounty
Of God.

According to Kanz-ul-Amal, Vol. 2, the Prophet declared:

Earning of lawful livelihood is a duty only next in importance to the duty (of prayer).

A hadith of Tirmidhi (12:4) makes the following observation about traders and merchants, who are the backbone of any system of free enterprise:

"The truthful, honest merchant is with the prophets and the truthful ones and the martyrs."

5. In this system of free enterprise, women are as much an economic entity as men. The Quran states (Chapter 4, Verse 32):

To men
Is allotted what they earn
And to women what they earn.

6. Islam is opposed to hoarding. In Chapter 9, Verses 34 and 35, of the Quran, it is said:

And there are those
Who bury Gold and Silver
And spend it not in the Way
of God: announce unto them
A most grievous penalty
On the day when heat
Will be produced out of
That (wealth) in the fire
Of Hell, and with it will be
Branded their foreheads,
Their flanks and their backs.
This is the (treasure) which ye
Buried for yourselves: taste ye
Then, the (treasure) ye buried."

7. Islam favors dispersal of wealth in the maximum number of hands. This is particularly clear from the specific portions prescribed in its inheritance law for all the relatives of the deceased. Some of the preceding discussion also tends to manifest the same goal.

8. In commerce, the practice of unethical profiteering is prohibited:

> "Whoever withholds cereals that they may become scarce and dear is a sinner." (Mishkat 12:8)

9. Employees should be properly treated:

> "It is the duty of employers to take only such work from their employees as they can easily do. They should not be made to labor so that their health is impaired." (Ibn Hazm: Muhalla Vol. 8, Ahkam-ul-Ijarat)

10. Labor should be paid proper wages and there is an injunction against slavery of free people:

> "Allah says there are three persons whose adversary in dispute I shall be on the day of Resurrection: a person who makes a promise in My name, then acts unfaithfully, and a person who sells a free person and devours his price, and a person who employs a servant and receives fully the labor due from him and then does not pay the remuneration." (Bukhari 34:106)

Furthermore, wages should be promptly paid:

> "Pay the laborer before his sweat is dry." (Ibn Majah)

11. The sanctity attached to private property is equal to that of the human person. This is expressly affirmed by the Holy Prophet in his last sermon:

174

"Your lives and property are sacred and inviolable one to another."

The right to private property, in particular, land, in accordance with Islamic traditions, is not absolute but is subject to the demands of national welfare.

12. Acquisition of private property on payment of compensation is permissible in Islam. Land was acquired for building the mosque at Medina by the Prophet on payment of compensation. This, of course, also means that expropriation without compensation is not permissible in Islam. There is, however, one exception: a gift given by the state can be expropriated, if so demanded for national welfare, as was done by Caliph Umar in the case of the bulk of the land given by the Prophet to Bilal.

13. The concept of nationalization of land is not novel for Islam. The Prophet nationalized half the land of Khaiber after its conquest, and the Caliph Umar nationalized many lands in Iraq. Therefore, it could be argued that nationalization of fundamental means of production can be done for public good. In a number of Third World countries, land has been, in fact, nationalized, e.g., Pakistan where first in 1958 and again in 1972 land in excess of certain area was taken over by the state.

The aforesaid principles may be said to constitute the core of the Islamic economic system. However, it would be manifest that these are merely "principles," and their eventual implementation will obviously have to take into account many local factors. Most of these principles are self-explanatory, but one of them needs specific emphasis. This is the position of the labor class. Both in communist as well as in non-communist systems, this subject is important because of its socioeconomic and political implications.

175

The Position of Labor and Workmen

It has already been observed that a basic and famous Islamic injunction is that labor and workmen have to be paid, even before their sweat is dry.

The above principle acknowledges that labor has to be compensated promptly. This principle, when read with its natural corollary that wages have to be fair, amply demonstrates the true importance given to both labor and the workmen in the Islamic system.

Since the formation of I.L.O. and the trade union movement, it is an accepted characteristic of contemporary international trends that the labor classes are entitled to the formation of their unions to safeguard their legitimate interests. When these movements started, there was considerable opposition to this trend. However, when we compare this aspect with the Islamic economic system and traditions, we find that even early Islam envisaged that labor and workmen could legitimately form groups for the protection of their interests. Going as far back as the time of the early Caliphate, we find that workers, craftsmen, and labor could form their separate groups or guilds. This practice was also found in vogue in many parts of the Islamic Empire later on. Professor Massignon of Paris University conducted extensive research in many Muslim areas in the first quarter of this century to trace and locate the existence and prevalence of guilds and various labor groups. His research extended from India in the East to Morocco in the West. Writing in 1927, in "Revue des Etudes Islamiques," in Paris, he said that he had found two ancient groups or guilds in the city of Lahore, going back hundreds of years in history. These groups were those of the Water-carriers and that of the Musketeers.

He went on to state that he found in the Middle East and North Africa numerous traces of the existence of many kinds of, what are today called, trade unions. It was his conclusion that it was wrongly assumed, in this particular context, that Islam would not allow the flourishing of such trends in its economic system. The Belgian review "la Nouvelle (Bruxelles, 1952-IV, pp. 171-198) has published a history of Muslim guilds and groups called "The Futuwwa" or "Craftsman Covenant," between Muslim workmen written by Professor Massignon. In this presentation, there are twelve chapters, dealing with the history and growth of some groups which he had examined in various parts of the Middle East.

The above account shows that in the course of Islamic history, there developed associations similar to modern trade unions. The economic system generated by Islam thus allowed their growth and development long before the twentieth century when, in the wake of industrialization, it became a dire necessity. It is, thus, submitted that in an Islamic state, workers and labor have definite rights to form groups to further their interests. Coupled with this is the divine mandate that God will demand an answer from those who did not treat their workers well. This postulate, like in many other fields of Islamic polity, furnishes the necessary "moral basis" for uplifting a purely secular matter to the realm of ethics and religion.

The salient features of the true economic system of Islam would, therefore, include the following ingredients: (1) a political and social order which ensures that the poor and the needy are provided the bare means of living (the genesis, perhaps, of the modern "welfare state"), (2) abolition of interest, (3) prevention of monopolies and cartels to ensure that wealth does not accumulate in few hands (once again the important economic principle which is the fore-runner of many modern anti-trust statutes in Western countries, e.g., U.S., U.K., etc.), (4) the vital protection of the labor classes with the provision that they have the right to promote and protect their interests by the formation of unions, (5) the freedom of enterprise, subject to anti-cartel laws, and (6) the right of the state to acquire the means of production of public welfare. It may be reiterated that the social welfare state of Islamic polity is to achieve its goals by the Zakat method and not by the levy of income tax on its citizens.

(B) The Structure of Taxation in Islam

Zakat, The Principal Tax

In the realm of economy and finance, the Muslims introduced revolutionary and egalitarian principles. In recorded annals, the Islamic state was, perhaps, the first in which we find that it was conceded and presumed that taxation was not meant to enrich the state or its rulers, but that whatever was collected was for the benefit of the needy. The immediate predecessors of the Muslims, namely the Romans, had ruthlessly applied state force for the collection of state taxes. The Romans, furthermore, had a variable tax formula; it could be increased or changed from time to time and, in fact, differed from province to province. As a general rule, the Eastern Roman provinces were subjected to higher taxation in which the rate[156] reached as high as seventy percent of the produce. Compared to this, the Muslims, who soon after the dawn of Islam acquired a vast empire, introduced and implemented humane principles of state levy. Indeed, the doctrine was that the levy was not for state benefit but for the poor. Under the fundamental principles of the Muslim financial theories, there is no place for the accumulation of wealth. The state is bound to ensure the circulation of wealth and to provide a living wage and relief to every individual without discrimination of race, religion, caste, or sex. In essence, it is a "welfare" state in modern terminology.

The sources of revenue of the Islamic state which are authorized by the Shariah, fall into two well-defined classes. One is the revenue collected from the Muslims; the other a secular revenue derived from the other subjects of the Muslim state. The former includes the Zakat taxes, while the secular revenue is comprised of land and poll-tax from the non-Muslims. Poll-tax is called Jizyah in Arabic.

The exact meaning of the word "Zakat" is "growth." The rate of Zakat was a uniform two and one-half percent on all property, i.e., cash jewels, or land. Being an institution of divine obligation, it was applicable to all, and consequently none was exempted. The word "Zakat" in its original sense conveys purification, hence it is used to express a portion of the property bestowed in alms[157] (as a sanctification of the remainder to the proprietor).

178

The tax has been named Zakat as it implied an increase of the property in this world and the growth of religious merit in the next. Its payment purifies the sins, says the Quran (ix. 104). In Fiqh, it is an act of piety by the giving (transferring the ownership of a thing) of a legally stated portion of one's property to a poor Muslim in a way so as to preclude for the giver any sort of benefit. It is a fard (duty) to pay this tax as it is based on the evidences furnished in the Quran, the Sunnah, and the Ijma (see Quran, ix. 11:Mishkat, Chapter 1 of Bk. VI, pp. 371-415). It is a religious and pious institution and is one of the five foundations of the practice of Islam. As distinguished from Sadaqah, which is used in voluntary aspects of charity[158] it is designated exclusively by its obligatory aspects.

The institution of Zakat should not be confused with other forms of taxes imposed by the state on its Muslims and other citizens alike. In the first place, it is not a "tax" imposed by the state, but by God; nor is it a tax destined to the state as such. The very nature of the institution requires that the part which the state is to play in the function thereof is merely one of supervision.

The difference between supervision and full control is that the latter would imply the right to increase and modify the tax, to extend or limit its scope, to suspend the imposition thereof, or even to abrogate it altogether, whereas, in its role of supervision, the right of the state is only to enforce observance of the divine law.

Let us juridically analyze this matter. It is in jurisprudential terms, an obligatory social tax which must be satisfied exclusively in the shape of surplus wealth of lasting value. This fact is clearly stated by the Quran (ii. 219): surplus wealth means whatsoever is over and above the lawful necessities of an individual and his dependents, in keeping with[159] the standard of life requisite to their position and status.

The cause or sabab of it being a wajib (duty) on the basis of presumptive evidence is the possession of full ownership of property. In other words, it is a religious duty incumbent on any person who is possessed of legal capacity and has full ownership of an estate or effects as are termed in the law nisab, i.e., a fixed amount of property, and that he has been in possession of the same for the space of one complete year. The one complete year in which the property is held in possession is termed in the law as Haul-ul-haul or the return of the duration. The nisab must be over and above what is necessary for the satisfaction of the primary necessities of life and should be free of debt (Shafi holding that indebtedness does not affect the obligation of Zakat). Property acquired in the course of the year is added to the nisab of property already existing and its Zakat is paid together when the year is complete for the nisab in question (not accepted by Shafi). Destruction before the lapse of the years does not include any liability for the Zakat that was yet to fall due on the part destroyed (according to Maliki school, willful destruction is excepted). Zakat is due upon the nisab of the possession of animals (as camels, bulls, cows, buffaloes, sheep, goats, horses, etc.), silver, gold and silver ornaments, cash, bank-notes, etc., articles of merchandise, mines or buried treasures, fruits of the earth, or any other kind of property the use of which is lawful under the religious principles.[160]

The income of Zakat goes to a special treasury and is spent only on the objects explicitly mentioned in the Quranic commandment. The Quran says: "The alms are only for the poor and the needy, and for those employed in its collection, and for those whose hearts are to be reconciled, and to free the captives and the debtors, and for the cause of God, and for the wayfarer; they are a duty imposed by God" (ix. 60). In keeping with its basic philosophy of social cohesion, Islam confined Zakat to Muslim subjects as an instrument of social justice prompted by faith and exacted in the name of God far beyond any duty which a state could impose.

Zakat was administered by the Public Treasury, by keeping a separate department. This department was responsible for looking after the needy, physically disabled, or those who were unable to earn their living. It was also the function of this department to look after the needy travellers, and prisoners of war as long as they were confined, and to provide the necessary funds for Islamic learning and preaching.

180

A person on whom the Zakat was Wajib (payable duty) could directly pay and use it for any of the directed objectives. Alternatively, the state functionaries could collect it. These state functionaries were paid employees.

The recognition of paying the wages of the staff employed in relation with the Zakat collection from that revenue is clear in that since the institution is meant for raising a public fund, it follows that the management should entirely be in the hands of a public body. However, it is lawful for the possessor to distribute his alms himself, and if he adopts this method, his statement of distribution is to be accepted. There is nothing in law, it is submitted, which prevents the use of Zakat funds in building hospitals and schools from which the people may benefit, or in the establishment of cooperative societies which can make life easier for the poorer people, or in the construction of factories which provide permanent employment to many people. In other words, though only the "needy" are entitled to receive Zakat proceeds, the fund may be used to serve a social purpose in the form of providing employment and other social welfare works in a Muslim state.

In order to understand the real significance of Zakat, it is necessary to look at the Islamic economic system as a whole, for Zakat is but one facet of this system. It is for God to provide the livelihood of every creature (Quran xi:6). However, this is one of the institutions He has ordained for fulfilling that promise. The Islamic state undertakes to fulfill this pledge by guaranteeing adequate subsistence, by Zakat collection, to every citizen. Furthermore, under Islamic law, the kith and kin of those in distress are under a duty to aid their relatives;[161] the responsibility of relatives is clearly defined in the Holy Quran. The Zakat tax-cum-subsidy scheme may be regarded as a potential measure of guarantee against the falling of any individual below or even down to the subsistence level so long as there are people with superfluous wealth around. Thus, in Islam, the poor have a quasi-right or interest in the wealth of their richer neighbors or relatives.

Zakat is, however, only the second best thing. It is against human dignity to accept even state aid, to say nothing of private charity.[162] Islam, therefore, lays great stress on earned livelihood and the dignity of labor, so much so that making an honest living for one's family is held to be equivalent to Jihad, and the status of one who works is raised to the pedestal of glory in the following words of the Prophet: "He who works is a friend of God."

Islam is not content to see a person being kept alive on a bare subsistence level, but considers it every person's right that he should have a reasonable standard of living.[163] The whole of God's creation is meant to place the gifts of nature at the disposal of man:

"It is He who has created for you whatever there is on earth." (Quran, II:29)

Nay, man is even exhorted to go around the world to seek his livelihood which is called "the bounty of God:"

"And when you complete your prayers, spread yourselves in various directions on earth, to seek the bounty of God; and remember God profusely that you may prosper." (Quran, Sura Jumua Verse 10)

Incentive to production is provided by recognizing the institutions of private property, private enterprise, and family inheritance. Yet, the system contrives simultaneously to eliminate the harmful effects of capitalism associated with each of these institutions. For this reason, Muslims can, perhaps, claim that the Islamic economic system is midway between the ideologies of capitalism and communism. That this appears to be the case would be quite clear from a number of points already made. More examples, however, may be cited. For instance, the institution of private property is unequivocally recognized in these words of the Prophet Muhammad: "Verily your blood, your wealth and your property are sacred and inviolable."[164] However, Islam also fixes a share of this property for the community in the form the Zakat taxes that may be regarded as a mild type of a capital levy which automatically liquidates an asset in about forty years if it is allowed to remain idle. Zakat, therefore, performs the dual role of putting idle wealth to productive use and, at the same time, redistributes the surplus wealth from the comparatively well-to-do, to the poor and indigent. Secondly, the connection of Zakat with religion makes it, perhaps, the best method known of taxing hoarded or invisible assets. Being in nature non-secular, it is neither of the communist type nor of the non-communist type of tax. Thirdly, the right of ownership of land and property in Islam is not to be regarded as absolute and cannot be used as a license to the detriment of other members of the society. It is subject to certain conditions, the guiding principle being the welfare of the community as a whole. There are instances in the early Islamic period when this right was actually withdrawn by the state if it was being abused by an individual or when public interest so demanded.[165]

Fourthly, while Islam approves of private enterprise in varied forms, including partnerships, it sets limits to greed for the accumulation of wealth. Consequently, while trade is permitted, the charging of interest is forbidden. Similarly, there are numerous injunctions against hoarding, profiteering, and the speculative withholding of food and essential commodities. In these matters, the state has to intervene to avoid exploitation by the rich of the poor.

Moreover, while inheritance of wealth is permitted, there are provisions against the accumulation of property in the hands of one or few. Inheritance laws, along with the Zakat taxes, tend to equalize wealth through gradual dispersion in a manner that would be least harmful to the wealth-producing activities of the owners. The shares in inheritance are so many that they increase the economic power and opportunity of more and more individuals in the Islamic economic system which aims at making every member of the community economically more prosperous so that he can participate directly or indirectly in productive activity.[166] At the same time, there are stringent anti-monopoly laws. Natural "wealth" such as forests, mines, grazing grounds, and sources of water supply are regarded as common property of the community and of the society and not the individual. This discussion again shows the social aspects of the Islamic system.

Furthermore, incentive to production under the Islamic conception of state comes by granting interest-free loans from the Baitul-Mal or Public Treasury. In the early

183

Islamic period, many other facilities conducive to development of agriculture, trade, and industry were undertaken by the state: an extensive network of roads, bridges, and irrigation projects were constructed when means of communications were comparatively poor. These are duties imposed upon the state; the welfare conception of Islamic state demands this of the rulers. There are examples from the early caliphates as well as from the Abbasides that research, education, and sometimes medical facilities were supplied free of charge to all members of the community. The Prophet made it clear to the people that even though he exhorted them to use self help, they had a right to come and have their needs ameliorated, using the public treasury if they were under any hardship.

During the reign of the second caliph, Omar (634-44 A.D.), the state revenues were augmented by the expansion of the Empire. These revenues were spent to develop what may be called a complete social security system for the members of the community; Muslims and non-Muslims, and Arabs and non-Arabs alike.[167] There are touching incidents noted in the life of the second caliph who went around personally to ensure the welfare of dependent children, including orphans and deserted minors placed under guardianship.[168] He moved from village to village, distributing the pensions to the aged, widows, and the disabled.[169] Omar even went to the extent of making inquiries into the food requirements of the rural and urban workers, and fixed food and clothing stipends accordingly, in addition to the family stipends fixed by the Prophet Muhammad.

All this may not sound extraordinary to a modern reader, but it should be remembered that these measures were taken as far back as the seventh century A.D. in the heart of the Arabian Desert. Moreover, the vivid manner in which the Prophet Mohammed and his early followers illustrated the socialistic principles of Islam are an impetus for emulation today. When the state became politically stable and wealth started pouring in from fresh conquests, Muhammad established the precedence of distributing it equitably amongst the whole population the very day it was received,[170] after deducting one fifth for welfare purposes. In short, the keynote is provided in the following verse of the Quran:

"That wealth may not form a circuit only between the rich amongst you." (Sura Hashr, Verse 7)

This simple system, however, was scrupulously followed only by the immediate successors of the Prophet, and was gradually abandoned by later caliphs. Eventually, the caliphate itself was turned into a hereditary institution, and fresh taxes were levied to meet the rising expenditures of avaricious rulers. Although it cannot be said with certitude whether during the reigns of these succeeding caliphs the proceeds of Zakat were spent strictly according to the express intent of the Quran, the payment of Zakat continued to be made under the Ummayyad and Abbaside dynasties for almost a thousand years. Finally, with the rise of the Ottoman Empire, the systemized collection of Zakat as a state institution ceased around the beginning of the sixteenth century A.D. Zakat then took the form of private charity, haphazard and disorganized, and has continued as such to this day. It, thus, left the state's functions and became a private affair.

The reintroduction of this tax after a gap of several centuries is difficult. Islamic jurists must take into account the social economic changes which have[171] occurred since the time when this tax was last imposed. This is a challenge as well as an opportunity to their genius. There is no reason, however, to think this problem will be insurmountable if the modern Islamic states approach the matter with urgency and seriousness.

(C)   The Structure of Land Tenure in Islam

It is the purpose of the ensuing pages to critically examine the position of land; that is agriculture and the resultant tenure system of an Islamic state. To understand the real problem, let us focus our attention on the main issues involved in this matter.

Throughout the history of man, agriculture has been the major form of capital and production. Even today, although there is mass production of various goods by the industrialized nations, the vast majority of mankind still relies heavily on land and its produce, i.e., agriculture, as a major means of subsistence. For the same reason, every legal system in history has endeavored to frame rules and laws in this area which truly reflect and, indeed, benefit its inhabitants. It is also a fact that in the course of history there gradually arose in every nation and in every country a few people with very large land holdings, while most people had no holdings at all. This basic fact of inequality was multiplied by every generation so that gradually there came about in most societies two classes of people: landed families and those having no land at all. It was, therefore, left to the law to work out formulae by which the interests of all, especially those whose labor resulted in production, could be adequately safeguarded. It is an examination of this problem and its solutions in the Islamic system to which we now turn.

In Islam, the right of ownership of agricultural land is, of course, unquestionable. This is, however, subject to the doctrinal qualification that everything belongs to God. But this does not presuppose the unrestricted right to let out such land on rent just as the right to own money does not imply the right to practice usury. Agriculture involves, firstly, the original and indestructible powers of land, which is a gift of nature; secondly, the initial cost of developing land, the cost of farming, i.e., the seed, manure, and implements, and the farmer's labor in tending a crop, all of which come under investment plus labor. If one analyzes the traditions of Islam, one finds a clear distinction made between the gifts of nature and the labor of man. The Prophet underlined this distinction by enjoining upon his followers the duty to respect the basic rights of others in what they did not produce with their own hands. Gifts of nature are free for the use of all; but one has a right only to such share of them as one can actually consume or put to profitable use without detriment to the legitimate share of others. This principle is fully recognized with regard to water, salt, forests, and pastures. Any undue extension of the rights of one member of the society against the rest is forbidden.

It is in conformity with this general principle that land is free and belongs to the one who cares to develop it. It is the labor and the expenditure involved in bringing the land under the plow, no matter whether incurred by the state or by an individual, which sets a price on land and determines its ownership. But once this process of buying and selling begins, a stage is soon reached in which a person owns more than he can manage by himself. The position of such a person is not different from that of a capitalist seeking the partnership of labor for the exploitation of his savings. It is natural for Islam to enact stringent restrictions on the partnership between capital and labor in the fields of commerce and to regulate the same kind of relationship in agriculture. The society of the Ansar in Medina was agricultural if the milieu at Mecca was commercial, and the evils of exploitation were as manifest in the one as in the other. Actually, we find that by and large the same prohibitions apply to both. We notice first that al-mukhatara (the advantage of a mere chance) is to be guarded[172] against in agriculture as scrupulously as in commerce. Hence, there resulted an early ban by Islam on the practice most common in the days of al-Jahiliyya, according to which land was let out with the stipulation that the produce of a particular part of it (usually that portion with the greater prospects of fertility) should go to the owner. Similarly, the practice of letting out the land on a fixed amount of produce was also declared unlawful as it stood obviously on a par with interest in business and commerce. Thus, there only remained a third method, namely the practice of letting out the land on payment of a stipulated proportion of the actual produce.[173]

It remains a fact that this practice, which is also called al-muzaraa proper, became widespread among the people. At the same time, however, there is ample evidence, direct as well as indirect, to show that grave doubts about its legality were entertained long after the death of the Prophet. Significant also is the suggestion of al-Hasan al-Basri, probably derived from the practice of Umar, that the owner of land should also take a share in investment and/or labor with the other party so that his share in the produce may not constitute a return for the gifts of nature only. Of the early great jurists, Abu Hanifa ruled out al-muzaraa as unlawful; Shafi approved of it. Later jurists approved it on account of the actual practice. They, however, did not answer the vital question of which they do show a cognizance, here and there, that al-muzaraa involved a return on the gifts of nature. A return on investment and labor is perfectly justified, but exploitation starts when one person arrogates to himself the right to charge another a price for any gift of nature. Rent of land is a clear case of unearned income with all the evils, moral and social, attendant upon it.

But if this were so, what about the practice of letting out agricultural land on a fixed sum of money? The practice was not in vogue in the days of the Prophet. Curiously enough, it grew as a way of escaping the grave doubts in regard to the admissibility of metayer tenure. Jurists like Ibn Abbas thought of relieving the conscience of the people by giving the relationship between the landowner and the tenant the form of al-Ijara, i.e., lease. But whatever the form and the name given to it, the crux of the matter is to inquire into the sanction behind this kind of relationship. Was it approved by the Prophet? Apparently not. Was it envisaged by him either as al-muzaraa or al-Ijara? The accounts given by early authors tend to show that, at least by analogy and from the example of a number of his sayings, the profit from land was not considered proper. One tradition of the Prophet is usually cited in this context. It is said that he said that if a man cannot farm his land, he should give it to his brother. In other words, renting was not forbidden, but not recommended either. (This is also a field in which, on account of unclear authority, the jurists have great latitude of construction and interpretation.) We must also recall that the cumulative result of the measures taken by Umar in regard to the administration of the conquered lands was, in the words of Welhausen, "to divert the acquisitive instinct of the Arabs from land purchases." No wonder that when the system of Umar was breached during the reign of his successors, the change proved radical[174] enough to shake the very foundations of the empire.

Islam has recognized the dangers of an inequitable distribution of wealth and has tried to do away with it by various means. The second caliph, in the last days of his caliphate, said that had he realized at the beginning the economic difficulties which people were facing, he would have taken the extra property of the wealthy people and redistributed it to the poor. Examples of such statements encouraging equitable distribution of wealth are many.

188

One of the main factors causing unequal distribution of wealth is excessive land holdings. Large land holdings which are not properly managed may represent a loss to the society in that not only is the land not well utilized,[175] but also the government revenue is decreased. Islam has taken care of such cases by allowing the state to take some effective measures to utilize the land. These measures range from financial facilities to compulsory sale of the land holdings. In this connection, the law and practice up to the first one hundred and fifty years of the Islamic period appears to be that if taxable agricultural land is not utilized by the owner, or if the land is mainly not irrigated, then, if improvement is possible, the government can still levy taxes on the land. In case the owner refrains from cultivating the land, the government can put another man in charge of the property so that it can get its taxes. What remains after the taxes are given to the owner. The government can also rent such lands or operate it on its own account. We have already cited the tradition of the Prophet that he who owns a farm must cultivate it or he should give it to his brother for cultivation. To encourage the utilization and expansion of land resources, Islamic law rules that whoever reclaims an unoccupied land and cultivates it, is recognized as the owner of that land.

Islam does not consider all natural and land resources as belonging to a particular class; it recognizes God as the real owner of all that exists in the heavens and on the earth, and according to a verse in the Quran, namely, "God has created all things on the earth for you (mankind)," the land resources are for the benefit of all. Of course, owing to various factors in history, the land distribution has become unequal. At any rate, this inequality should not go so far as to create social and economic problems. As far as land ownership is concerned, extreme inequalities may result in the misallocation and underutilization of resources. While in some regions there are big land holdings under-utilized, in other regions there are a great number of people without any land. To solve these problems, some economic systems have abolished private land ownership, while others have imposed limitations on it.

189

The Muslim jurists over the centuries have suggested two basic principles, namely, public expediency and prevention of mischief, to deal with mismanagement of land by those who own it. The basic purpose of this gift of nature is to produce, so agriculture has to be encouraged, even if it means changing ownership. A land without agriculture is of no use to the individual or to the community.

(1) According to the first principle, the government should always consider the interest of the public (or the general good) and work out programs and regulations within the context of Islam to promote and safeguard productive agriculture. According to this rule, the government is allowed to introduce changes in the prevailing policy of land revenue to increase the productivity of land thereby also increasing government revenues.

(2) According to the principle of prevention of mischief, if the prevailing conditions have been detrimental to the general welfare or the laws itself, in order to prevent further deterioration, the government is allowed to take the necessary steps.

These two general principles make the Islamic system flexible and allow the state to effectively intervene, if it so wishes, to ensure a healthy productivity of land.

It is, thus, the duty of the government to see that freedom of ownership is not misused, that is, the property is not used in such a way that it may impede the welfare of the society.

Though the practice of early Islam is entitled to the highest respect, the persistent doubts concerning the relationship between the landlord and the tenant do warrant a reexamination and fresh understanding of the undoubted injunction or advice of the Prophet on the subject.

The clear import of the Prophet's saying is that either a person cultivates the land himself or that he should part with it. In this case, the land will be owned by the person who cultivates it. Thus, the aim of Islamic law is to abolish absentee landlords and encourage landholdings which can be utilized by the persons who are actually the tillers of the soil. To avoid too much fragmentation, the law allows the state to come up with cooperative schemes or other devices based on a consideration of the community's desire to improve produce.

CHAPTER VIII

The Islamic State in the International Field

(A) Islamic State and International Affairs

Having examined the various essential ingredients of Islamic law and the philosophical and religious foundations of an Islamic state,[176] we can now turn finally to international affairs.

Respect for International Law Precepts

Here, the paramount aim before us is to discover the original attitude of the Islamic state towards international peace and its respect for international law.   Much has already been said, in one form or another, about the importance of peace in the religion of Islam.

The Muslim God is Peace (Quran 59:523).   He calls all to the Abode of Peace (Quran 10:25).   His Prophet is "a mercy to the world" (Quran 21:107).   His Book guides one to the "ways of peace" (Quran 5:18).   The very name of the religion is Islam, which means to submit to one's Maker and to be in peace with all creation (Quran 2:112).   A Muslim is one who makes this peace.   A Muslim's salutation on earth is the invocation of peace: "peace be to you" (as-salamu alaikum).   He gives the finishing touch to his prayers by invoking peace on all. He prays for peace with hands raised heavenwards.   In Heaven, he receives the greetings of peace from his Lord (Quran 36:58).

Thus, we find that one central theme in Islam is peace.   It is but a natural conclusion that non-violence in thought and action should form its essential code.   "And not alike are the good and the evil.   Repel evil by that which is the best;   then to he, between whom and thee was enmity would be as if he were a warm friend" (Quran 41:34).

The life of Mohammed is full of examples of patience and forgiveness.   According to one Hadith, in the second year of Hijra, once while returning from a battle, the Prophet was resting underneath a shady tree leaving his sword hanging in a branch.   He was suddenly awakened by a noise and found an enemy with a drawn sword.   He had taken the sword of the Prophet and was crying, "Who will save you from me?" "Allah, Allah, Allah," said the Prophet. The sword dropped from his hand. The Prophet instantly seized it, but he forgave the man ungrudgingly (Bukhari, Babal-Jihad). In the seventh year of Hijra, a woman poisoned the Prophet. According to Ameer Ali in "The Spirit of Islam," his life was saved, but the poison permeated his system, and subsequently he suffered severely from its effects and eventually died thereof. In spite of this act, Mohammed forgave the woman and she was allowed to remain among her people unharmed. After the conquest of Mecca, he proclaimed a general amnesty and forgave his bitterest personal enemies repeating the words of the Quran with tearful eyes: "There is no reproof against you today. May Allah forgive you and He is the most Merciful of the merciful" (Quran 12:92). We can, further, refer to the following prayer of the Prophet: "O Allah, Thou art Peace, and from Thee is Peace. Blessed art Thou, O Thou, Lord of Majesty and Honor!" (a hadith from Muslim).

Islam is, therefore, a religion of peace and forgiveness, and there should be goodwill towards all mankind. The moment, however, we say this, a question arises. Do Islamic states actually demonstrate and practice such ideas today? The answer, as in many similar questions, is that we have today a definite discord between the claimed teachings of Islam and in the actions of its twentieth century adherents. It is, therefore, incumbent on the present leaders of the Muslim states to comprehend and actually demonstrate their practice in their belief. Unquestionably, the one matter where Islamic precepts about international law have come under deep suspicion of many people is the hostage issue. It is submitted that it is basically an unfair charge since Islam or its laws have totally nothing to do with this event.

The taking of the American hostages in Tehran in November 1979, is essentially a bilateral matter between the U.S. and Iran. That the actual taking of the hostages has led and may lead to harmful consequences to international peace is possible. But the cause and its result in such an eventuality have to be seen in this context, i.e., they are political matters between states and not of religious context or content. Iran, by all accounts, even by the opponents of the Khomeini regime, is still in a state of revolution. The identification of Islam with every action of the revolutionaries is neither logical nor fair. Indeed, under Islamic International Law, the taking and such long detention of the hostages by the militants would appear to be illegal and morally wrong. It is illegal, for unquestionably an emissary, even of an enemy, is, under Islam, entitled to all kinds of protections. It is also morally indefensible; if once a point has been vindicated, Islam enjoins forgiveness. Law and morality were never lost sight of by Muslims in the early days of Islamic ascendancy. Some important Quranic verses on this point are later cited.

Islam promotes equality of mankind. God commands justice and forbids racial discrimination and oppression. Man is born with freedom and equal rights. The Quran says, "And people are but a single nation" (10:19), and "Surely the noblest of you with Allah is the most pious of you" (49:13). Prophet Mohammed says, "Allah will punish those who persecute others on the earth." The religion itself also shows this spirit of freedom and equality. "There is no compulsion in religion; truly the right way has become clearly distinct from error" (2:256). Thus, an Islamic state's relations with other nations have to be free of prejudice of race, religion, or fear. This is again the ideal, the proper realization of which should be pursued by Muslim States everywhere. It is sufficient to recount, that by and large, most Islamic States have attempted to conform to such aspirations.

Islam requires people to live peacefully with each other. Mankind should cooperate with and help each other in the cause of justice, as that is the sublime duty of Muslims. The Quran says, "Help one another in goodness and piety and do not help one another in sin and aggression" (5:2).

Islam stresses and emphasizes that human disputes should be solved by peaceful consultation. The first caliph, Abu Bakr, said in his inaugural address to the people: "I have been made a ruler over you, although I am in no way superior to you. If I do right, help me; if I go wrong, put me right." This righteous spirit of Caliph Abu Bakr suffices to explain the basic principle of Islamic polity. The Quran says, "Their affairs are decided by counsel among themselves" (42:38). Such is the Islamic tradition for solving disputes of mankind.

Islam promotes learning and considers the acquisition of knowledge transnationally as a duty of every Muslim. The Quran says, "My Lord, increase me in knowledge" (20:114). There is the famous saying of Prophet Mohammed who said, "The acquisition of knowledge is a duty incumbent on every Muslim male and female," and instructed man to "seek after knowledge though it be in China." As to the uses of knowledge, he said, "It enables the possessor to distinguish right from wrong, it lights the way to heaven." Undoubtedly, the purpose of seeking knowledge is to increase human welfare and establish world peace. It is also, therefore, submitted that there is no antipathy between Islam and modernization. It is a basic misconception to think so. It is, in fact, proper and desirable for an Islamic state to constantly acquire modern knowledge in all fields. This, indeed, may be an important reason for the early success of Islam. It was willing to acquire knowledge from all sources. Today, Muslims should try to acquire, whenever they can, the knowledge they lack. Knowledge is a heritage of mankind and not of a particular race, people, or religion.

In the international field, violence in religion has been expressly prohibited in the following verse of the Quran: "And if the Lord had willed, surely all those who are in the earth would have believed all of them; wilt thou therefore compel men till they become believers?" (10:99). About the occasion of the revelation of this verse, Ibn Jarir quotes a tradition to the effect that a Muslim had two sons who were Christian. He wanted to compel them to embrace Islam. But he was prohibited by the above verse revealed to the Prophet.[177] The Quran also forbids the use of violent words towards the objects of worship of other peoples. "And do not abuse those whom they call upon besides Allah, lest exceeding the limits they abuse Allah, out of ignorance. Thus have We made fair-seeming to every people their deeds; then to their Lord shall be their return, then He will inform them of what they did" (6:109).

But if there be religious persecution on a large scale, the Quran permits religious war.[178] "Permission (to fight) is given to those upon whom war is made, because they are oppressed; and most surely Allah is well able to assist them; those who have been expelled from their homes without a just cause except that they say: Our Lord is Allah. And had there not been Allah's repelling some people by others, certainly there would have been pulled down cloisters and churches and synagogues and mosques in which Allah's name is much remembered" (22:39, 40). A striking point in this permission is that the Muslims, the messengers of peace, are to put down religious persecution, no matter whether it is directed against the mosque, the cloister, the church, or the synagogue. "But fight them until there be no persecution and religion be unto Allah (alone); but if they desist, then let there be no hostility save against the unjust" (2:193).[179]

It can be seen from what has been said above that only in cases of political oppression or religious persecution in an organized form is it permissible to put down violence in a suitable manner. Lest there should be any doubt with regard to the treatment of those who are not political or religious opponents of the Muslims in general, the Quran distinctly says: "It may be that Allah will bring about love between you and those whom you hold to be your enemies among them; and Allah is Powerful; and Allah is Forgiving, Merciful. Allah does not forbid you respecting those who have not made war against you on account of (your) religion, and have not expelled you from your homes that you show them kindness and deal with them justly; surely Allah loves the just" (60:7, 8). "And let not the hatred of a people (to you) make you swerve to wrong and depart from justice. Be just as that is nearer to piety, and fear Allah. Allah is well-acquainted with what you do" (5:9).[180]

In view of what has been said, Islam's potential contribution to international peace is incalculable. Furthermore, Islam invites its followers to Dar-as-Salam, the Abode of Peace: "And Allah summoneth to the abode of Peace" (10:26) and ". . . their greetings therein will be Peace" (10:11). "There hear they no vain speaking for recrimination (naught) but the saying: Peace (and again) Peace" (56:25-26).

Some of the fundamental principles laid down by the Quran for the establishment of international peace may now be specifically seen. The Quran declares:

> "Mankind was one community and Allah sent (unto them) Prophets as bearers of good tidings and as warners" (2:213).

> "O mankind! Be careful of your duty to your Lord who created you from a single soul and from it created its mate and spread from these to many men and women" (4:1).

> "O mankind, Lo! We created you male and female, and have made you nations and tribes that you may know one another. Lo the noblest of you in the sight of Allah, is the best in conduct" (49:13).

From the above verses, it is clear that the whole of humanity, with its diverse races, is originally one. It derives its existence from one Creator, and that all barriers that separate humanity by sex, race, and color must vanish. The superiority of a person is to be judged by his conduct only. A Muslim, therefore, must succeed on the strength of his actions and convictions and not only by virtue of his belief in God. According to Islam, we are, therefore, brothers and sisters of one world family. In order to strengthen this brotherhood of mankind and guide people along the right path, God sent prophets and apostles to all nations in all ages. The Quran says:

> "Lo! We have sent thee with truth, a bearer of good tidings and a Warner: and there is not a nation but a Warner hath passed among them" (35:24).

> "Verily We sent messengers before thee, among them those of whom we have told thee, and some of whom we have not told thee" (40:78).

That the essential truth underlying the teachings of all the prophets is the same and that there must exist brotherly feeling among the followers of all prophets, may well be conceived from the following Quranic verses:

"Naught is said unto thee (Mohammed), save what was said unto the messengers before thee" (41:43).

"He hath ordained for you that religion which He commended unto Noah, and that which We inspired in thee (Mohammed), and that which We commended unto Abraham and Moses and Jesus, saying: Establish the religion, and be not divided therein" (42:13).

"Lo! religion with Allah is al-Islam" (the surrender to His will and guidance) (3:19).

"The messenger (Mohammed) believeth in that which hath been revealed unto him from his Lord and (so do) the believers. Each one believeth in Allah and His angels and His scriptures and His messengers. We make no distinction between any of His messengers" (2:285).

Thus, the Quran places the peoples of the Book, the Jews, Christians, and Muslims, in a close relationship.

The Doctrine of Tauhid

The Book of God asks a Muslim to keep a brotherly relationship with the followers of all the previous prophets. The Quran invites the followers of the revealed Books to come to an agreement by accepting the doctrine of Tauhid, the oneness of God, and strive jointly for international peace:

"Say : O people of the Scripture come to an agreement between us and you; that we shall worship none but Allah" (3:64).

The doctrine of Tauhid, according to Islamic conception, is one of the cornerstones of international peace. The formula "La ilaha illa Allah" signifies that there is nothing that deserves to be worshipped except Allah who is Rabb-ul-Alamin, the Creator, the Sustainer, and the Evolver of the destinies of mankind. Thus, Tauhid inspires us to surrender ourselves to God alone, consider all people to be equal, and live in peace and harmony under the direction of divine laws and statutes promulgated by His prophets. By the strength of Tauhid, the early Muslims effected a great moral change among the Arabs who believed in various gods and goddesses, lived a wild life, and fought day and night among themselves. It was Tauhid which brought peace and tranquility to Arabia and the adjoining countries.

The doctrine of Tauhid is capable of being accepted by the followers of all revealed Books, since all of them ultimately believe in one Almighty God and worship Him, because "unto Allah belongeth the Sovereignty of the heavens and the earth" (3:189).

Arbitration and mediation is directly encouraged by the Quran. Similar to various analogous principles in the law of the United Nations and international law, God commanded Muslims to solve disputes peacefully, amicably, and with the clear aim of achieving justice. Over fourteen hundred years ago, the Quran commended the Muslims to administer justice through witnesses and arbitration for the sake of God when it declared:

> "O ye who believe! Be ye staunch in justice, witness for Allah, even though it be against yourselves or (your) parents or (your) kindred, whether (the case be of) a rich man or a poor man, for Allah is nearer unto both (than ye are). So follow not passion lest ye lapse (from truth) and if ye lapse or fall away, then lo! Allah is ever informed of what ye do" (4:135).

> "And if two parties of Believers fall to fighting, then make peace between them, and if one party of them doeth wrong to the other, fight ye that which doeth wrong till it return unto the Ordinance of Allah; then if it return, make peace between them justly and act equitably. Lo! Allah loveth the equitable" (49:9).[181]

From the verse quoted above, it is clear that in fighting the aggressor there must not be any spirit of revenge against or favor to any party except the spirit of justice and equity. This is because "Allah loves those who judge equitably." The fighting does not always mean the use of armaments; any pressure backed by moral or social pressure amounts to such fighting.

In the pre-Islamic days, the Arabs buried their female children alive, on account of poverty, or for fear of suffering disgrace at the hands of enemies when vanquished. Having been addicted to obscene rites and superstitions, the Arabs were further engaged in fratricidal wars, and killed one another without compunction. At the advent of Islam, the Quran prohibited this practice in the following verse:

" . . . Whosoever killeth a human being for other than manslaughter or corruption in the earth, it shall be as if he had killed all mankind, and whosoever saveth the life of one, it shall be as if he had saved the life of all mankind" (5:32).

The meaning of the above verse is clear: that the State in its relations with others must avoid warfare. The emphasis on avoidance of killing demonstrates that principles such as those contained in Chapter VI of the U.N. Charter have to be encouraged for solving international disputes. Indeed, the philosophy of the Kellogg-Briand Pact of 1928, outlawing war with its emphasis on peaceful settlement of disputes, was laid down by Islam fourteen hundred years ago.

Toleration is another distinctive feature of Islam. The Prophet and his early Sahaba (Companions) faced tremendous opposition and hostility from the Arabs with extraordinary tolerance and patience. A mere reference to the terms of a treaty, the Charter granted by the Prophet to the monks of the monastery of St. Catherine near Mount Sinai and his treatment of the heathens of Quraish on the day of the victory of Mecca, bears ample testimony to the toleration in Islam.

Islam does not find fault with other revealed religions (e.g., Christianity) of the world. It even adopts an understanding attitude towards those religions which are diametrically opposed to it or encourage idol worship. The Quran says:

"And revile not those unto whom they pray besides Allah lest they wrongfully revile Allah through ignorance" (6:109).

Jihad

Jihad has erroneously been taken as synonymous with War. Jihad means striving in the way of Allah, and it may be of various types. To fight the enemies by way of defense is, of course, included in it. [182]

The accusation levelled against Islam, that it was spread by the sword, is untenable. If we look into the wars and battles undertaken by the Prophet and his early Caliphs during whose time numerous countries accepted Islam, we will see that these wars were political and not religious, and also at times defensive. The example already cited of forgiveness and generosity shown by the Prophet on the day of victory at Mecca is an early example of such a tradition. The ten thousand Muslims who invaded Mecca on that day could easily have crushed all the infidels who plotted against the life of the Prophet before his migration, but instead he chose to forgive them all.

The Quran does not recommend war for the propagation of Islam. Rather it declares, "unto you your religion, and unto me my religion" (109:6).

Unfortunately, the sword of Islam loomed large in the eyes of some European historians who equate Jihad with War. The only major kind of war, as already noted, is for the defense of the weak, against the aggressor in self-defense. A Muslim is only allowed to undertake a "just" war. In this sense, it is similar to the classical notion of international law enunciated by Grotius of just and unjust war. It is possible that the concept was borrowed by European writers in the sixteenth and seventeenth centuries from Islam. It is not, however, the cruel sword of the tyrant, but the merciful sword of a friend; it is not the sword of oppression, but the sword of protection; it is not the sword of war, but the sword of peace. "And what is the matter with you that you should not fight in the way of Allah and of the weak among men and women and children, who say: "Our Lord! Cause us to go forth from this town, whose people are oppressors and give us from Thee a guardian and give us from Thee a helper" (Quran 4:64).

As an example of a righteous war, or in the words of the Quran, "War in the way of Allah" (Jihad fi sabilillah), the Quran cites the case of the war of Saul and David against Goliath and the Philistines (2:246-251). There we find the Israelites saying, "What is the matter with us that we should not fight in the way of Allah and we have been expelled from our homes and our children?" It concludes the narration by observing, "And were it not for Allah's repelling some men with others, the earth would certainly be in a state of disorder; but Allah is generous to the worlds."

That Jihad is always for a righteous cause is clearly emphasized by the Quran: "And if two parties of the believers quarrel, make peace between them; but if one of them acts wrongfully towards the other, fight that which acts wrongfully, until it returns to the command of Allah; then if it returns, make peace between them with justice and act equitably; surely Allah loves those who act equitably" (Quran 49:9).

Even in warfare, Islam demands the minimum of violence. While sending an expedition against an aggressor tribe, the Prophet gave the following injunction to the leader, "Do not kill the very old nor the infants nor the minors nor the women folk. Do not cheat. Do not break trust. Do not mutilate and disfigure the bodies of your dead enemies (Hadith Abu Daud and Ahmad). Bokhari also records the following sayings and traditions of the Prophet. He prohibited in all cases the killing of any living creature by burning or drowning. "A true warrior," said the Prophet, "is he who fights his passions." In his instructions to the leaders of expeditions against marauding and hostile tribes and people, he invariably enjoined them in peremptory terms never to injure the weak. "In avenging the injuries inflicted upon us," he said to his troops, whom he dispatched against the Byzantines, "molest not the harmless inmates of domestic seclusion;[183] spare the weakness of the female sex; injure not the infant at the breasts or those who are ill in bed; abstain from demolishing the dwellings of the unresisting inhabitants; destroy not the means of their subsistence, nor their fruit trees; and touch not the palm trees." Abu Bakr following the Prophet, thus, enjoined his commander, "O Yezid, be

203

sure you do not oppress your own people nor make them uneasy, but consult them in all your affairs, and take care to do that which is right and just, for those who do otherwise shall not prosper. When you meet your enemies show yourselves like men and not turn your backs and if you gain victory, kill not little children, nor old people, nor women. Destroy no palm trees, nor burn any fields of corn. Cut down no fruit trees, nor do any mischief to cattle, only such as you kill for necessity of subsistence. When you make any covenant or article, stand to it, and be as good as your word. As you go on, you will find some religious persons that live retired in monasteries, who propose to themselves to serve God that way. Let them alone, and neither kill them nor destroy their monasteries."[184]

Jihad as an original theory has been represented by most of the non-Muslim scholars as an instrument that the Muslim state is bound to use eternally to compel the world to accept Islam. According to this view, it leaves for polytheists only one alternative to accepting Islam which is to fight.

It is not necessary to state and examine the arguments cited from Muslim law and history against this theory. That is all well-known. Besides, the reference to the famous Quranic verse, 2:256, against religious compulsion has already been made several times.

There is, however, another view which deserves some attention, not only from an academic angle, but also from the standpoint of its practical influence on the psychological and mental attitude of Muslim nations towards the non-Muslim world. According to this view, what Islam asks from a Muslim State is no different from that laid down by modern international law for all States. Consequently, Islam strives for peace rather than seeking war; it does not permit the killing of a human being merely because he or she fails to believe in Islam. Resort to war on the part of Muslims against non-Muslims, therefore, is not permitted on the basis of religious differences. Instead, Islam allows such measures only when non-Muslims force or attempt aggression on Muslims or interfere by force with the presentation of their message to the world. If there is no such aggression, then fighting with those who do not happen to believe in Islam is illegal and Muslims are permitted to undertake mutually profitable dealings with them. In brief, Jihad is not an offensive means for spreading Islam, rather it is permitted as a defensive measure to protect Muslims and their system of life.

We find a substantial body of literature advocating this point in volumes of works done by influential Muslim thinkers and scholars like Saiyyid Jamal al-Din, and Muhammad Abduhu. The two major arguments in this context may be summarized below.

(1) The verses concerning war in a number of Makki and Madani surahs (verses) of the Quran generally explain Jihad's raison d'etre which boils down to one of two things: (a) defense against an attack and (b) routing fitnah (persecution inspired by religious prejudices which eliminates the freedom of thought and belief), or, in other words, protection of the mission of God of Islam. Because the non-believers, polytheists, and even scriptuaries in the time of Mohammed directed their utmost efforts against Muslims by trying every possible means of clan and agnate to make them abandon their belief, and by threatening those who were inclined to accept the new faith with agonizing penalties, God laid an obligation on Muslims to fight these aggressors: "Fight in the way of Allah against those who fight against you, begin not hostilities, Lo Allah loves not aggressors."[185] "And fight them until persecution is no more and religion is all for Allah. But if they cease, then Lo, Allah is seer of what they do."[186] In support of this contention, the Quran further says:

"Sanction is given unto those who fight because they have been wronged . . . those who have been driven from their homes unjustly only because they said: 'our Lord is Allah . . .'"[187]

Again it is stated in the Quran:

"How should you not fight for the cause of Allah and of the feeble among men and of the women and the children who are crying: Our Lord! Bring us forth from out this town (Makka) of which the people are Oppressors. Oh, give us from Thy presence some

205

protecting friend! Oh, give us from Thy presence some defender."[188]

(2) Compulsory methods cannot be the means of inviting people to accept a faith or a mission. Belief is a matter of the heart and its foundation is love and devotion rather than the[189] sword . . . "There is no compulsion in religion;"[189] "And if the Lord willed, all who are in the earth would believe together. Would you (Mohammed) compel men until they are believers?"[190]

The supporters of this second view base the foreign policy of a Muslim state on the following principles.

(a) Preaching Islam and inviting the non-believers to this universal message of God is Fardh al-Kifayah (a collective obligation) on the Muslim community. If a group of them carry on the duty, others are free, but if none of them do so, the whole community is in sin. Hence, the first objective of the Muslim state would be to organize a peaceful campaign for Islam and to reveal the eternal truth of this divine system of living to the world.

(b) The basis of Islam's international conduct is peace unless and until force is used by non-Muslims to put into effect an aggression against Muslims or their system of life.

(c) Dar al-Isalm (abode of Islam) is the territory where the law of Islam prevails and Muslims can live in peace and security. Dar-al-Harb (abode of war), on the other hand, is the territory, whose inhabitants, by launching actual attacks on Muslims, or by threatening to do so, have replaced peaceful relations with war or a state of war. Hence, war can only result between a Muslim state and that or those non-Muslim state or states which have initiated aggression on Muslims or prevented them (by force) from preaching their doctrine. As a necessary consequence, the Muslims would defend themselves and would break relations with that other state, and trust would cease to exist between them. Therefore, if a non-Muslim state, which has not initiated any attack against Muslims, has not stopped by force the peaceful presentation of Islam and has not harmed any Muslims or threatened those so inclined, or there is no campaign for preaching Islam in that nation's territory, which can be attacked, it is not legal to fight such a non-Muslim state or break off peaceful relations with it. There exists an aman (safe conduct, peace) between this state and Muslims, not on the basis of any treaty or pledge, but because peace is the rule and nothing has happened which may, in law, allow a Muslim State to indulge in aggression.

Numerous other verses of the Quran and principles of Islam back this spirit of peace. It is unrealistic that Islam should lay the foundation of the relations of Muslims with others on the basis of continuous war and that Jihad should be obligatory fighting as a means of inviting people to Islam. God forbade compulsion in religion. Therefore, how can belief be brought about or go deep into the heart by sword? Ibn Taymiyyah Al Siyasat declares that he who neither fights with Muslims nor prevents them from presenting the word of God is not fought against because war is only valid against him who fights "us when we preach the word of God."[191]

Muhammad Abduhu (1842-1905) was one of the most prominent Muslim scholars of modern times. He insisted repeatedly on the defensive nature of Jihad. In his lectures at al-Azhar, he took every opportunity to emphasize the same view. These lectures are recorded by S.M. Rashid Ridha in Tafsir al-manar. (Reference should be made particularly to pages 208-16,[192] 312, 462 of the second volume of that valuable work.) Also, apart from doctrine in his writings with great insistence and enthusiasm. In this context, special reference should be made to his Al-Islam wa al-Nasraniyyah Maa al-ilm wa al-madaniyyah (Sec. II, pages 67-72)[193] and to Risalat al-Tawhid (pages 102-3).[194] We translate from Ridha only a paragraph which states Abduhu's view on this subject. "The wars of the Prophet were all for defending the truth and its followers, and protecting Islam . . . God has obligated war on us neither for the shedding of blood and taking away lives nor for material gains . . . The early wars fought by the Companions (of Mohammed) were for protecting the call of Islam and saving Muslims from being dominated by aggressors . . . The Islamic conquests which occurred later were a result of the nature of power and not all of them valid in Islam. So is the nature of

things: the strong attacks the weak, although, as some
Western scholars have testified,[195] there has never been a
nation more merciful in its conquests than the Arabs."[196]

Muhammad Abduhu's teacher, Saiyyid Jamal al-Din
(1839-1897), who for his modern approach to Islam as well
as his vigorous campaign against both imperialism and
political corruption in the East has been regarded as one
of the most influential figures in the modern history of
Islam, explained that in reality an offensive picture of
Jihad had been painted by Islam's enemies.

In the writings of a later writer, M.B. Makhzoomi, there is
much discussion on the subject of war, which he terms
"struggle for destruction." In answer to a question, he
hesitates to call the modern world "civilized" because, he
says, there are scenes of destruction caused by war and
demonstrations and preparation for it which bring the
human being of modern times much "below animals." A
country, he says, is part of the earth, and if peoples
were just, the earth would have room for them all . . .
how becoming it is for a human being to live with his
brother on earth in true brotherhood and prosperity till
death reaches all.[197] At the conclusion of Jamal al-Din's
renouncing comment on wars, Makhzoomi writes the story,
about which he (Jamal al-Din) was asked: "Then, what is
the meaning of the Quranic verse: And prepare for them
(enemies) as much power . . . as you can . . ." and of
the "verse of sword?" His answer, as recorded by
Makhzoomi, was to draw a distinction between bellum
justum and unjust war. He then explained that there was
no sanction and that the above verse was making it a first
degree obligation on Muslims to be strong in a defensive
way to meet any situation that arose should they have to
fight a just war. By being prepared for all possibilities
meant, according to Jamal al-Din, that they could stop any
power otherwise tempted by the weakness of Muslims to
aggress. In other words, the verse advised: If you want
peace, be prepared for war.[198]

Before leaving this point, reference must be made to the
view of Ali Abd Al-Raziq. In his much debated work,
al-Islam Wa Usul al Hukm, published just after the
abolition of the Khilafat in Turkey, he denies that the

message of Islam had any intention to bring about a universal Islamic government. It is sensible, he maintained, to bring the world in a unity of faith and ideology, but to compel the whole world to one government and bring it under one political unit is almost outside human nature, something which God does not intend.[199]

The above account was a brief presentation of the views of some leading writers who believed in Jihad as essentially a defensive instrument.

Before concluding this chapter, the views of a few earlier Muslim thinkers like Ibn Khaldun and other publicists must also be mentioned. To certain Muslim thinkers, writes an eminent modern writer, the realization of the concept of Jihad marked the change in the character of the nation from a warlike to a civilized stage. Thus, the change in the concept of Jihad was not merely an apologia for weakness and failure to live up to a doctrine, but a process of evolution dictated by Islam's interest and social conditions.[200] Al-Turtushi (died twelfth century) described "war crises" as social anomalies,[201] and al-Hasan ibn Abd Allah compared them to diseases of society.[202]

Anyone inclined to think of Jihad as, in theory at least, an instrument for compelling non-believers to accept Islam should pause to note these verses from the Quran: "Whoso obeyeth the messenger obeyeth Allah, and whoso turneth away: We have not sent you (O Muhammad) as a warder over them."[203] Or: "Say (O Muhammad): O mankind! now hath the Truth from your Lord come unto you. So whosoever is guided, is guided only for the good of his soul, and whosoever erreth, erreth only against it. And I am not a warder over you."[204] Or: "But if they are averse, we have not sent you as a warder over them. You are, only to convey (the message)."[205] Or: "We are best aware of what they say, and thou (O Muhammad) are in no way a compeller over them. But warn by the Quran him who fears My threat."[206] Or: "Remind them, for you are but a remembrance. You are not at all a warder over them."[207]

Furthermore, it should be remembered that in the Battle of Khaibar, Mohammed allowed Jews of Qainuqa to fight by his side. Similarly, Safwan ibn Wmmayyah, a polytheist, was fighting with Muslims headed by the Prophet against their enemies in the Ghazwah of Hunain. It is quite unreasonable for a group to be fighting against people to compel them to accept Islam, while it maintains non-Muslims on it own side.[208]

Conclusion

Those who like to point to some of the doctrines of the Muslim law of nations (especially that of Islamic fraternity) in their present status, as not fitted to modern conditions of international life, must bear in mind that even the modern law of nations in its formative period developed principles to govern the relations among Christian nations alone. Gentilies (1552-1608), who did not favor religious wars, made an exception in the case of Turkey.[209] He criticized Francis I for making an alliance with the Turks. An alliance between Christian and infidel princes, he stated, could not possibly be tolerated. Even Grotius, the father of modern international law, who emphasized the law of nature as its basis, advocated discriminatory treatment against non-Christian states.[210] Many people cherished the same notion even much later, and in 1889, Woolsey still insisted that international law was what Christian nations recognized as obligatory in their mutual relations only. According to a Papal Bull, the Christian nations were not bound by their pacts with Muslims.[211] Thus, one can see that the Muslim law of nations has more stable grounds for forming the basis of a modern law of nations than European international law had at its dawn, which was, admittedly, in the words of Grotius, for a few "civilized" European states.

One of the schemes for effectuating this cooperation would be to help secure through the advancement and development of international law, an Order and a Justice under Law for the community of nations. The Muslim Law of Nations is comprised of various realms of Peace, War, and Neutrality, as well as in the field of Conflict of Laws, maxims and theories which through further study in light of the experience of modern international law can be developed into elaborate theories to provide a moral basis of rules for controlling international behavior.

The words "develop" and "elaborate theories" are used with the qualification that the basic doctrines already exist; it is only that the Western or even the modern international lawyer is not familiar with them. In any case, they may be re-cast in modern terminology with which our generation is familiar and then understood and applied. The question of Jihad was examined in some depth, for this matter has been consistently misunderstood by non-Muslim scholars. After the crusades, it was particularly given a malicious connotation resulting in unnecessary complications and bitterness.

(B)   The Impact of the Islamic State on Western Nations

The previous chapters have indicated that, while building a vast empire, the Muslims also developed a sophisticated and advanced system of law, jurisprudence, and the art of statecraft. Did this system have any impact on the Western nations? The answer is in the affirmative. However, this effect has not always been recognized, mostly because of the prejudice which resulted from the Crusades and the Muslim conquest of various European countries. The impact of the Islamic state was felt; indeed it left an imperishable mark in its entirety. That is to say, the effect was not only in the field of law and political institutions but on other matters affecting the society, like language, art, architecture, science, mathematics, and philosophy.

We hear too much in history about wars and conflicts and too little about the cooperation and mutual influences between various peoples and their civilizations. This is particularly unfortunate in the sphere of religion, where the spirit of rivalry too often prevails over the spirit of good-will and understanding. The history of the relations between the two great faiths of Christianity and Islam has been so befogged by hostility that we are apt to forget how much they have in common, and how often in the past one has had a useful effect on the other.

Christians take pride in that their civilization is based on the civilizations of ancient Greece and Rome, combined with the religious heritage of Western Asia and the monotheistic Semitic traditions. But the same is true of Islamic civilization, perhaps even more so, since Western

211

civilization has been molded to suit the tastes and traditions of the Nordic and the Germanic races. Christianity, arose within the bounds of the Roman Empire, mostly in one of its easternmost provinces. For that reason, it tended to spread westward and never went far beyond the eastern bounds of the empire. Islam, however, arose just outside of those bounds and was, therefore, able to spread eastward as well as westward. The Prophet and his earliest followers were in close touch with what was by then left of the old Roman world, and, in spite of the Persian influences that it soon acquired, the spread of Islam actually caused less of a dislocation to the old ways of life than did the Nordic invasions further to the west. Istanbul (Constantinople), where the old Roman Empire lingered on (the Byzantine Empire, as we usually call it), was closer in culture to the Muslim caliphate than to the kingdoms of the West. It was in the Muslim world, as much as in Byzantium, that classical learning was still studied and maintained. Indeed, in the early Middle Ages, Islam and Byzantium were the joint heirs of Greco-Roman culture. Of the two, Byzantium was to prove the more isolated and less able to affect the stream of Western European cultural development.

It was only at the end of the eleventh century that Western Europe came into close contact with Muslim culture. Until then, the Westerners had been terrified of Islam, alarmed at its political power and suspicious of its civilization. The few Western scholars who penetrated Muslim schools in Spain, such as Gerbert of Aurillac, who later became Pope Sylvester II, came back suspect for their learning and were considered to have been corrupted by the Devil. But gradually relations grew closer. In Spain, which had been ruled by the Muslims for several centuries, the Christians reconquered their former territory, capturing various cities which were centers of Muslim learning such as Toledo, Granada, and Cordoba. Sicily, which had been Muslim for two and a half centuries, was conquered by Norman adventurers, coming from Europe by way of France. About the same time, thanks chiefly to the Byzantine navy, piracy was curbed in the Mediterranean Sea, and merchants from Italy began to trade with Muslim ports. At the end of the eleventh century, there occurred the movement known as the Crusades; the Western invasions of Syria and Palestine.

They were harmful because of the religious bitterness that they engendered. Nevertheless, they did create further contacts.

By this time, the Muslim world could offer a full store of ancient Greek learning, so enriched by Muslim additions that it was often hard to distinguish the original Greek from Muslim thought. In the process, it had been enriched further. In Spain, Muslim philosophy was not ended by the Christian advance. In the twelfth century, there were not only flourishing philosophers in the Muslim tradition, such as Maimonides (Musa Ibn Maimun), but, even more important, Ibn Rushd, whom the West called Averrhoes, a Muslim who actually had far more influence on Western religious thought than on his fellow Muslims. The Christian conquerors in Spain, thus, found an active school of Muslim philosophy which had not yet reached its greatest heights. King Alfonso VI of Castile, who conquered Toledo in 1085, was so impressed by the importance of his new Muslim subjects that he proclaimed himself the "Emperor of the Two Religions," to the disapproval of his bishops. Yet it was a Christian bishop, Raymond of Toledo, who really founded the first school of Oriental Studies in Europe in the middle of the twelfth century. He was so determined that the Christians should study the fruits of Muslim learning that he collected scholars from many countries and set them to learning Arabic and translating the Arabic works.

For the next century and a half, a number of distinguished Europeans worked at Toledo studying and translating Muslim authors. The most prominent and prolific was an Italian, Gerard of Cremona, who, by the time of his death in 1287, had translated eighty works. There were scholars from Britain amongst them, such as Adelard of Bath, one of the earliest who specialized in mathematical works and who frankly advised Western scholars to go to study with the Muslims. There was Robert Anglicus, perhaps the first European to try to translate the Quran. He produced a painstaking Latin translation. Even more distinguished was the Scotsman, Michael Scott, who was interested in philosophy, science, and music and who translated the works of Averrhoes during the great philosopher's own lifetime. Amongst the Spaniards was the monk Gundisalvus, whose philosophical system was directly based on Avicenna's; again in the thirteenth century, two remarkable scholars, Raymond Martin, whose knowledge of the Quran and the traditions has seldom been equalled, and Raymond Lull of Majorca, an eager Christian missionary, who realized that he ought to have an exhaustive knowledge of Islam for his work and wrote many books about Islamic learning.

The Spanish schools were mainly interested in philosophy and the more abstract sciences. In the Norman kingdom of Sicily, the emphasis was on the more practical sciences. The kings had many Muslim subjects and treated them well. A traveller, Ibn Jubayr, who visited Sicily in the middle of the twelfth century, was pleased to find that his co-religionists not only had complete religious freedom, but also a share in the government. Some Arabic was spoken at the Norman Court and Arabic poetry was encouraged there. Muslim architects were patronized. Norman Sicilian architecture is noted today as being a curious but very successful blend of French, Byzantine, and Muslim styles, its decorative work being almost entirely in the Muslim tradition. Medicine was chiefly studied in the Norman possessions on the Italian mainland. The town of Salerno had been a center for medical studies since Byzantine times. At the end of the eleventh century, a renegade Tunisian, known as Constantine the African, settled there and began, with the help of some disciples, to translate all the Arabic books on medicine that he could find. Constantine was an inaccurate translator, but he made accessible to Western doctors the works of the old Greek physicians, Galen and Hippocrates, together with ample comments added by Muslim doctors. The medical University of Salerno became, in consequence, one of the main schools of medicine in the West. Late, scholars made several better translations for use there.

In the thirteenth century, the Norman kingdom passed by inheritance to the Emperor Frederick II of Hohenstaufen, whose contemporaries surnamed him the Wonder of the World. He had a Muslim bodyguard and many Muslim friends. When crusading in the East, he shocked the Christians by his long and friendly conversations with Muslim ambassadors and scholars. He wrote a book on falconry, which is still amongst the best on the subject for which he drew on Muslim sources. He invited the scholar

214

Michael Scott to complete his translating work in Naples. His own eyesight was bad, and he took a great interest in optics and ophthalmic medicine. A Muslim author writing at that time in Cairo tells us that the Emperor sent there to ask the Muslim scholars the answers to three problems: why do oars look bent when they are put into the water, why do stars look bigger when they are close to the horizon, and why do men suffering from incipient cataract and other eye diseases see specks before them? He felt that he had to go to Muslim centers of learning to find the solution to such problems.

Even after the fall of Frederick's family, the Italian rulers kept up the tradition of encouraging Muslim scholarship, especially regarding medicine and mathematics. By now there were many translators working also in Northern Italy. Much of their knowledge was obtained from merchants who had visited Muslim ports, had subsequently fallen ill and had benefitted from the local doctors. They did much to popularize Muslim medicine and their knowledge of mathematics when they returned home.

Otherwise, the merchants' chief contribution was to raise the general standard of living in the West. They introduced useful and popular foods like refined granulated sugar. Many improvements for the comfort of the houses were imported; carpets began to appear on the floors and chairs replaced benches.[212] Clothing was revolutionized. Hitherto, wool had been the only material obtainable in the West, except for Byzantine silks, which only the rich could afford. Now cottons and linens came onto the market, as well as a far larger supply of silk. This merchantile intercourse did not do much to add to Western science and learning, but it added greatly to the material progress of the West. The merchants also seem to have helped in encouraging Arabic literary forms, with some effect on European literature.

The Crusading movement did not do much to help this progress, except insofar as Western soldiers and pilgrims adopted, like the merchants, the fashions and amenities of the Muslim East and tried to introduce them to Europe. It is probable that the pointed arch came into use in Western architecture as a result of such journeys. The earliest examples are found in the lands of a returned Crusader at the Court of Boulogne. Moreover, the Westerners who had settled in the East soon adopted the local ways of life. But there were very few scholars to be found in the Crusading states. The only one of note was William, Archbishop of Tyre, who was born in Palestine and learned Arabic there, though he went to France for his schooling. He became one of the greatest historians of the Middles Ages. Amongst his works was a history of the Arab Caliphate, based on Arabic sources, but now, unfortunately, lost. The children of the Crusaders born in the East knew Arabic well, such as Humphrey of Toron, who acted as interpreter for King Richard, Coeur de Lion, of England or Rainald of Sidon who, when he was captured by Saladin, so impressed the Muslims by his knowledge of the Quran that they spared his life, thinking that he would become a convert to their faith. On the whole, however, the Crusades by the bitter religious rivalry which they created did more harm than good. Nevertheless, when the movement had been a military failure and the politicians in the West sought to revive it, the Westerners began to realize that they should cultivate a better understanding of the East and of its ways of thought. There was, thus, by the time of the later Middle Ages a real desire on the part of Western merchants and wealthy men to enjoy the material benefits of the Muslim civilization and on the part of scholars and scientists to acquire its learning.

What was the total effect of it all on the European civilization? It is impossible to assess "civilizational impact" by a hard and fast standard. One can certainly say that the material way of life was greatly improved; and the words that passed from Arabic into European languages give illustrations of this. It is harder to be precise about the cultural outcome, but several examples can be seen which serve to show how widespread it was.

The Oriental art form which interested the West most was music, but in the long run, the effect produced was slight. Except in Spain and Sicily, countries where there had been a long Muslim domination, Western music moved in a different direction, though music theory was permanently enriched by the study of the Arabic writers and their comments on Greek theory. In architecture, the result is more clearly visible. As noted above, the pointed arch seems to have been copied from the East, though it was used in an entirely different manner in the West. The large Muslim contribution to Sicilian architecture was noted in the West, especially in Italy, while the Muslim buildings of Spain and those seen by Italian traders in the East had their effect on later Gothic and Renaissance buildings. For example, many of the elaborate arches erected in Tudor, England, are similar to earlier arches erected in Cairo, and are probably based on designs brought from Egypt by the Venetians. Similar likenesses can be seen in a great number of decorative motifs, including ornamental battlements. Italian architects, particularly in the seventeenth century, copied the domes which they saw in Muslim buildings in Spain, and were copied in turn by other European architects. Even more striking likenesses appear if we compare some of the towers built in Italy in the later Middle Ages and the Renaissance with towers in Cairo and further to the East. Here again the Italians spread the fashion to the rest of Europe. The great English architect, Sir Christopher Wren, working at the end of the seventeenth century, built towers for some of his churches in London whose designs can be traced back to those of the minarets of Muslim mosques. Similarly, later, when his works became known to Westerners, the great Turkish architect Sinan had his influence on Western styles.

In the lesser arts, the Venetian glass factories, through which the art of glassware spread through the West, were directly inspired by the factories of the East. Many branches of metal work, as the word "damascene" for metals shows, came to Europe from the East. Much European stitch work was guided by Persian and Turkish models, and from Persia and Turkey, too, came the main inspiration for European carpetmaking.

More unexpectedly, the Muslim influence was very great in the sphere of literature. We are apt to think of the European romantic literature of the later Middle Ages as a native product, but the deeper we probe, the more traces we find of an Oriental origin. The love story is, in fact, not so much a European as an Eastern invention. Many of the stories of King Arthur's roundtable have an Oriental origin. The medieval French romance, Hoire et Blanchefleur, is an Eastern story, while one of the most famous and lovely of all European romances, Aucassin et Nicolete, betrays its Muslim origin. The hero's name is really al-Qasim, while the heroine is stated to be a Muslim princess of Tunis. It seems, also, that the use of rhyme in medieval European verse was inspired by Arabic models, and many Arabic metres were copied. Arabic poems, presumably in translation, were so popular in thirteenth and fourteenth century Italy that the Italian poets complained that it was not fair to them. Long before Europe knew of the collection of stories which we call the Arabian Nights, Muslim romance and poetry were making a mark on European literature.

Many well-known writers like Dante felt Muslim influences. One of the most learned of medieval English scholars, Roger Bacon of Oxford, says in one of his works that philosophy must be learned from the Arabic writers and that no one should study the subject without taking the trouble to learn Oriental languages. He was not alone in his view. His contemporary and compatriot, John of Salisbury, continually reminds his readers of the debt owing to Muslim philosophers.

One must, however, not overstate these claims. In philosophy, a few of Aristotle's works and almost all of Plato's did, in fact, come to the West directly from the Greeks at Byzantium. But the philosophical works that affected Western thought more, perhaps, were those that came in translations from the Arabic, but were enriched by the comments made by Muslim thinkers, so much so that many Western scholars attributed to Aristotle theories which, in fact, were created and promulgated by such Muslim philosophers as Avicenna and Averrhoes. It was only later on, when the West began to be able to read the old Greek philosophers in the original language, that they realized how vastly they had been influenced by Muslim thought, much of which was by then fully integrated into Western Christian thought. The famous Christian theologian-philosopher of the Middle Ages was Thomas Aquinas, whose work is still the basis of the philosophical doctrine of the Catholic Church. He tried to disentangle Aristotelian philosophy from that of the Muslim philosophers, and he added to his system elements derived from a direct study of Plato. But in both his methods and in his theories, he continually shows Muslim influences.

In particular, his whole theory of the interplay between Faith and Reason seems to have been copied from that of Averrhoes, and his attitude to the Bible is paralled to that of Averrhoes to the Quran. Both believed that God's revealed Word was the supreme authority, but both believed that it could and should be explained in Aristotelian philosophical terms. Most Christian thinkers still today accept the relationship between theology and philosophy which was worked out by the Muslim philosophers. It is true that modern philosophical ideas have moved into a sphere which neither the Muslims nor the Christians of the Middle Ages would have understood. But it is interesting to note that the atomic theory put forward by many of the Muslim thinkers has some bearing on the scientific philosophy of today.

It would be a gigantic task to estimate in detail the contribution made by the Muslims to the world's store of scientific and mathematical learning. Their most important and fundamental contribution was to show that science was not incompatible with religion. In mathematics, we owe to the Muslims the whole science of algebra. The so-called Arabic numerals, the adoption of which entirely revolutionized European mathematics, were taken from the Muslims, though the actual figures were never those used by the Arabs. In geometry and trigonometry, the Muslims added enormously to old Greek learning. In astronomy, the Muslims made a large contribution, and a lasting one, in spite of all the knowledge that has been accumulated since the Middle Ages. The same is true of geography and such practical sciences as zoology and botany, metallurgy and chemistry. Their medical doctors revolutionized Western medicine by introducing old Greek methods and theories, along with their own additions and improvements. They taught men how to systematize diseases and how to attempt a proper diagnosis. It is true that most of their medical theories are now outmoded, but they marked an enormous advance at the time, and they represent a definite and valuable stage in the development of medical studies. In this connection, we may add that it was in a Muslim country, Turkey, that Western Europeans learned the practice of inoculation.

In order to see the extent of Muslim influence on Western Europe, we have only to think of the many words still in use in Western European languages which are of Muslim, mostly Arabic, origin. English provides numerous examples. Many describe goods and materials which Western merchants first brought from the East. Some of these are words such as sugar and syrup, orange and lemon, vegetables such as spinach and artichokes, spices such as saffron, and drinks such as coffee. All these are originally Arabic words and were adopted as and when the item they described was used. We can add words for furnishing, such as mat, mattress and sofa, or ottoman, whose names show their origin. Cotton is an Arabic word, and there are all the materials whose names are derived from cities in the East: muslin from Mosul, damask from Damascus, and so on. The word "tabby," which is English, is used to describe the common brindled cat as well as a patterned silk, comes from the Attaby Quarter of Baghdad. Such words describing articles of commerce could, of course, indicate commercial rather than cultural exchanges. More significant are all the commercial terms which we have taken from the East and which show that Western merchants learned the technique of business there. These terms include such common English words as traffic, tariff, check, (cheque), risk, magazine (in the sense of warehouse), or caliber. In shipping, the words "sloop" and "barque" show that both these kinds of ships were of Eastern design, and the word "cable" is also Eastern in origin. Even the Admiral's title is Eastern, though it originally had nothing to do with the sea. In the arts, the term "baroque" is Arabic in origin. Of musical instruments, the tambourine and the guitar are both Arabic. In the game of chess, we use Persian terms. Checkmate, a phrase that we often use metaphorically, is simply "shah mat," the king is dead. In astronomy, the names that we use for some of the brightest stars are Arabic. In mathematics, the term "cypher," is Arabic, as is the entire science of algebra, name and all.

It may be added that some of the derivations are incorrect. It is surprising to find among words of Muslim origin the word "alcohol," in view of the religious ban on drinking it. The derivation is due to the mistake of the Swiss Renaissance chemist, Paracelsus, who thought that liquid spirits had some connection with kohl--collyrium. A summary of the story is to be found in the word "alchemy." Alchemy, which was later regard as a half-magical practice, was in the Middle Ages, a serious study of chemistry, and the word is a combination of the Arabic article "al" with the Greek word "chimia" meaning chemistry, which itself seems to be derived from the ancient Egyptian word "khem," describing the black earth brought down by the Nile which the Egyptians used as the basis for their experiments.

This is the story of the sequence of events for just one word. Classical Greek learning, derived from the ancient East and systematized by the Greeks themselves, was further developed by the medieval Muslims and handed on by them to Western Europe.

The Muslims realized early in their history that it was worthwhile to study the Greek contributions to philosophy and science in all its branches. Already under the Ummayad caliphs, a number of Greek words of practical value for the government had been translated into Arabic. But the great era of translation began under the Abbasids, especially under al-Mamun, in the second quarter of the ninth century A.D. The chief translators were Nestorian Christians, but the caliph controlled their work. He sent them to collect manuscripts from all the libraries within his dominion, and when good editions were lacking, he would ask for manuscripts from the Byzantine Emperor or would try to persuade Byzantine scholars to settle at Baghdad. As a result of the patronage of the caliphs, by the end of the ninth century, translations had been made of nearly all the major works of Greek science, mathematics, logic, and medicine.[213] About the same time, the Muslim scholar al-Kindi set about translating the philosophical works of Aristotle, while some of his contemporaries translated the Neo-Platonic philosophers. In the following century, the learned al-Farabi completed the translation of Aristotle and added his own commentaries, and because of his work he was considered to be the chief philosopher of his time on the Islamic traditions. The Muslim world had the great advantage of being a cultural unit, across which scholars and their books could travel freely. As a result, the effect of these translations and commentaries was soon felt from India to Spain, and Muslim scholars began to add their own important contributions.

Some thirty years after al-Farabi's death there was born in Bokhara in the Turkish lands that then were the Eastern frontier of Islam, the most original and, perhaps, until then, the greatest of all Muslim philosophers, Ibn Sina, whom the West called Avicenna. His philosophical system, though not always orthodox, showed an immense power of individual thought and entitled him to rank amongst the greatest philosophers in world's history. It was not long before his works were read and studied in every Muslim country, especially in Spain.

Islam's contribution in the realm of philosophy and political theory are recorded by many modern historians such as Hitti. We need not, therefore, refer to them. But a word must be said about jurisprudence. We know today that the Greeks had dealt extensively with the conceptions of right and wrong, not only in the ethical, but also in the juristic sense. The classical Roman jurists, however, were greatly superior in their appreciation and treatment of the practical and substantive law. Perhaps better than any previous legal system, the Romans developed the principles of the law of contracts and legal rules of interpretation and those pertaining to presumptions. Though lacking in the legal philosophic refinement of the Greeks (or what we today call jurisprudence), in the realm of substantive law, the Romans did produce in their time the most comprehensive system of law ever known to mankind. The Muslim jurists, however, both in the realm of substantive law and jurisprudence, surpassed their predecessors. Indeed, it will not be hyperbolic to say that, before the rise of Europe, after the Dark Ages the Muslims had already produced for posterity the most complete system of law ever seen in any age before then. The most profound effect that this system left in Europe was the deductive and inductive system of argument. This is, undoubtedly, the hallmark of any sophisticated system of law. By developing this art to its highest form, the Muslim jurists left for the coming generations a glorious legacy. They also laid the basis of what later came to be known in Common Law of the seventeenth century as Equity. Especially while dealing with the doctrines of Istheslah and Istehsan, the Muslim jurists had strongly advocated that under various circumstances, the law had to yield. This "yielding" itself was subject to a body of laws and not left to the arbitrary whim or the personal opinion of a judge.

Finally, principles of far-reaching importance were laid down in the realm of constitutional and international law. Islam said more about these two fields of laws than had ever been said before. These principles found their way into European thought via Spain, Byzantium, and the region where today countries such as Bulgaria and Romania lie.

This is a summary of the debt that Western European civilization owes to the Muslims. A brief attempt has been made to portray how wide and important the Muslim influence has been. It did, in fact, affect the main stream of European erudition and thought. The moral to be learned from it is that none of the great faiths or the great civilizations of the world stand apart in isolation. It is not by religious or ideological wars that culture advances nor by creating barriers of nationalism. The followers of no faith and the citizens of no country are so perfect that they can afford to ignore or reject the rest of the world. It is by making friendly contacts and by attempting to effect an understanding that the various civilizations of the world can help each other. This was true in the Middle Ages; it is still true today.

CHAPTER IX

Islam and Other Religions

(A) The Attitude of Islam Towards Other Religions

Islam originated and was successfully preached in a complex society, in a place where the doctrines of almost all great religions were known. It was the force of its inherent philosophy which led to its ultimate victory over other creeds. The teaching was clear, the ideas were distinct yet not alien to human nature. There are certain obvious facts, which whosoever seeks the knowledge of the truth must discover.

It is not claimed that Islam tells us anything which has never been heard before, but rather that Islam is the confirmation and continuation of the same fundamental teaching which had been the guiding light of all those who achieved the highest enlightenment on spiritual matters. It is in reality a doctrine of love; love towards one object and one object alone, and, through Him, to all humanity and creatures. The Prophet himself (in the tradition of Abrahamic religions) was the embodiment of Love. Admittedly there are in the Quran rebukes and warnings to those who are evil doers. The idea is that a person deserves in the life hereafter what he earns in this life. Had this not been the case, there would have been no malice against anybody. Nor would there be any compulsion in the religion of Allah.

One peculiar feature of Islam is that its name is not based on an attachment with a person as we find in most other religions. The word Islam, which means "Peace" or "Submission" has always been explained to be a system aiming at peace between "Man and God" and "Man and Man," or a system of thought and action based on "Submission" to the overall Divine Plan of Life.

In order to ascertain the relation that Islam as a religion seeks to maintain with other religions, it is essential that the basic theory of life and its social responsibilities as enunciated by Islam should be first understood. Islam attaches very great importance to man. "Certainly we created man in the best make." (Quran 95:4). Man is the vice-regent of God in this world. ". . . the Lord said to the angels, I am going to appoint on earth a vice-regent" (Quran 2:30). Man has to deputize for the Almighty Lord in this world according to the plan of life and the plan of the working of the universe, as given by God himself. He has a goal and a destination definitely set before his eyes. He is duty-bound to move towards that destination with a clear intention and definite struggle.

"Blessed is He in whose hands is the Kingdom, and He is Possessor of power over all things. Who created death and life that He might try you; which of you is best in deeds." (Quran 67:1-2). The Quran again and again, affirms that life has not been created aimlessly. There is a definite purpose of life, and a very specific goal set before it.

"Do you then think that we created you in vain, and that you will not have to return to us" (Quran 23:115). Life has thus a plan behind it. Let us, therefore, study it from the point of view of Islam.

The Quran says:

"He is Allah, the Creator, the Maker, the Fashioner. His are the most beautiful names. Whatever is in the heavens and the earth declares His glory; and He is the Mighty, the Wise" (Quran 59:24).

Again:

"Our Lord is He Who gave to everything its creation (i.e., created it) and then guided it" (Quran 20:50).

"Glorify the name of the Lord, the most High, Who created, and perfected, and Who measured and guided (Everything)" (Quran 87:1-3).

God brought this Universe into existence from non-existence. All creation had its source and origin in the creative powers of the Supreme Being. All that we see and observe and all that exists whether we see it or not, has been brought about by God. This Unity of Creation is the fundamental belief about the relation of God and the Universe in Islam.

God created this Universe with which He continues His relations. He is maintaining and retaining it by providing facilities of progress and evolutionary development. This attribute of God is called "Rubuiyat." There is one Rabbul Alamin who is the maintainer of the Universes. This again leads to the conclusion that the Universe is the outcome of one creative power and is being maintained in development by the same Power. Islam, therefore, takes all existence as one Whole, and thus prepares itself to consider all problems regarding the Universe as pivoting around one central Power.

After the Unity of Creation, Islam invites attention to the Unity of Mankind. Man, as is already mentioned, has been described as the vice-regent of God, and the Masterpiece of His creative capacities.

> "Verily we have created man in the best make" (Quran 95: 4).

This masterpiece of creation, although found in various colors and shades in the expanse of this vast inhabited world, has had one origin. The Quran says:

> "O people of the world be mindful of your duties towards your Lord, Who created you from a single being, and created its mate from the same kind and spread from these two, many men and women. (Quran 4: 1).

This verse of the Quran definitely throws light on the common origin of mankind. The Prophet of Islam is reported to have said, "Mankind is the family of God." Just as there are no two gods, there could be no two families. Humanity is basically one. This is the Islamic basic message. The fundamental needs and urges of humanity are one. This message also throws light on the fact that man, while spreading out in the world acquired various habits and customs on account of the different geographical and anthropographical environments, but retains his status as "Man," the Supreme creation of God.

Human nature being one, the basis of internal demands of man always remains unswervingly one, but the immediate needs under pressure of circumstances and environments

227

continuously change. The way of life for man thus bears a stamp of permanent basic unity in addition to transitional environmental demands. Wherever man lived, his cravings and longings had these two aspects. His basic urges were similar everywhere, but besides those, there were cravings cropping up from the immediate local needs of his life. Islam says that the basic guidance was given by the Creator Himself.

"And the soul and its perfection! So He revealed to it, its way of evil and its way of good; he is indeed successful who keeps it pure, and he indeed fails who buries it" (Quran 91:7-10).

Mankind with this basic guidance spread out in the vast world. Whenever the basic guidance was ignored or lost sight of, the Creator sent reminders to revive the forgotten guidance.

"Surely there will be coming from Me guidance to you, then whoever follows My guidance, no fear shall come upon them, nor shall they grieve" (Quran 2:28).

This guidance was sent through those chosen ones whom we generally call Prophets. Prophets, according to Islam, were raised in all nations.

> "Verily We have sent thee with the Truth, a bearer of good tidings and a warner; and there hath not been a nation but a warner hath passed among them: (Quran 35:24).

> "And certainly We raised in every nation a messenger, saying: Serve Allah and shun the devil" (Quran 16:36).

> "And verily We sent messengers before thee of them are those We have mentioned to thee, and of them are those We have not mentioned to thee" (Quran 40:78 and 4:164).

> "And for every nation there has been a messenger" (Quran 10:47).

Thus Islam believes that Prophets were raised for the guidance of mankind wherever he lived. Further, it stresses that the main object in raising Prophets was also basically one, i.e., "Allah be worshipped and evil be shunned" (Quran 16:36).

This gives us the guidance of Islam's attitude toward other faiths; to respect the message of all Prophets and their disciples. The Creator being one, and nature being one, there could not be two guidances. This, according to Islam, is the basic guidance behind all true religions. "True" here means "revealed." Polytheism or idolatry is deprecated by Islam; but as a faith or religion it, too, is entitled to respect. Muslims are expressly forbidden to "abuse" the Gods of others so that they may not think ill of the Muslims' God. (Quran 6:109). Also, underlying the messages of all true Prophets was one. True religion in its essence is one and the same everywhere. The difference in form is either on account of the geographical environment or the immediate human circumstances. This would explain the variety of juristic and philosophic details in the theologies of various religions. In Islamic phraseology this is called Sharia or Minhaf. Hundreds of Sharias are found in history, but the basic religion behind all of them is one.

Attitude Towards Monotheistic Faiths

The present discussion would show that Islam has considerable inbuilt affinity with monotheistic faiths: for monotheism implies submission to one God, by whatever name to which He may be referred.

With the aforesaid fundamental principles, i.e., the Unity of Creation, the Unity of Mankind, respect for all prophets and their people, Islam puts a joint responsibility on man to realize and understand the plan of the Creator, and to help and serve His creation. What is Religion? It is respect for the Commandments of one God; as well as mercy, kindness, and sympathy for his Creation. Religion is the Code of selfless service to the whole of Divine creation, man or animal.

With this realization of joint and collective responsibility, a Muslim cannot disparage any system of life and guidance, and cannot hate any product of Divine Creation. Islam believes that true religion is one in origin. It is the emission of the one Eternal Light.

Fughani, the Persian mystic poet says:

> "There is one lamp in this Universe and from the light of that one lamp, wherever I see, I find assemblies illuminated."

Islam, therefore, inculcates an understanding and realization of the basic truth. A Muslim, if he understands what Islam is, can never talk of any religion disparagingly. He has to respect all religions, to respect the Prophets of all religions. He has to show respect to the leaders of religious orders. In respecting religions the question of true or untrue and good or bad does not arise. Man is respected in Islam as Man; a sound philosophical foundation for the modern contemporary philosophy of "Rights of Man." We have good men and bad men, and in spite of that fact the dignity of man does not lose its importance and respect. Similarly, there may be religions which retain their original intrinsic truth and there may be religious systems which unfortunately, through circumstances, have deviated from the original pattern. Nevertheless, as religions they have to be respected. This is the tradition of religious toleration and mutual understanding which was initiated by Mohammad.

This basic toleration of differences of opinion underlies the complete goal of life set by Islam. Mohammad and his immediate followers acted according to this spirit and the light of Islam spread out in the world. Islam spread through its teachings, which included basically the respect of Religion and the respect of Man. Compulsion in religion is prohibited in Islam. Several times we have quoted: "There is no compulsion in religion. The right way is indeed clearly distinct from error. So whoever disbelieves in the devil, and believes in Allah, he indeed lays hold on the firm handle which shall never break" (Quran 2:256).

Furthermore, it may be recalled that Islam asserts not to fight anyone because he is of a different faith. Mohammad never fought any battles against Judaism, Christianity or any other religion. He was always prepared to let them live, provided they let Islam and its followers also live. So the battles that we have in Islam's earliest period were not battles between religions. Rather, they were political battles between the followers of one religion and the followers of other religions.

Aggressive war is indeed expressly forbidden in Islam. "Permission (to fight) is given to those on whom war is made, because they are oppressed. And surely Allah is able to assist them those who are driven from their homes without a just cause except that they say: Our Lord is Allah" (Quran 22:39-40). "And fight in the way of Allah against those who fight against you, but be not aggressive. Surely Allah loves not the aggressors" (Quran 2:190). Thus when we do come across an agressive war waged by Muslims, it is by its very nature characteristically not Islamic.

As already explained, Islam teaches that revelation is a universal phenomenon and that divine guidance has never been and is not the monopoly of one particular people. The rays of the sun of revelation have been illuminating the paths of life of various nations in the world. Those whom Divine Mercy selected specially to guide others, and to whom the Divine message was given directly, are the real benefactors of Man, who taught morality, law and ethics. The Book of Islam mentions by name fewer than thirty such Prophets but has, at the same time, stated that there were other Prophets whose names have not been mentioned in the Quran.

> "And verily We sent messengers before thee, of them are those We have mentioned to thee and of them are those We have not mentioned to thee" (Quran 16:36).

The revelation given to the Prophet of Arabia seems to mention by name only those Prophets with whose names and fame the Arabs were fully conversant. There is a tradition of the Prophet which describes the number of Prophets in thousands. A Muslim has to believe in all these Prophets and to revere and respect their sacred memories. The Quran says: "They (the Muslims) believe in what has been revealed unto you, and also in that which was revealed before you" (Quran 2:4). There are other verses, too, which repeat the purport and substance of this verse. A Muslim cannot be a Muslim unless and until he respects the memory of all the Prophets, the great leaders of religious thought. "Say: We believe in Allah and (in) that which has been revealed to us, and (in) that which was revealed to Abraham, and Ismael and Isaac and Jacob and the tribes, and (in) that which was given to Moses and Jesus, and in that which was given to the Prophets from their Lord, we do not make any distinction between any of them and to Him do we submit" (Quran 2:136).

"The messenger, believes in what has been revealed to him from his Lord, and (so do) the believers. They all believe in Allah, and His angels and His Books and His messengers, (saying) we make no difference between any of His messengers: (Quran 2:285).

This teaching of accepting truth in its universal form, and of respecting the great teachers of truth provides an opportunity to the Muslims to extend the hand of goodwill and cooperation to religions other than their own. "Say: People of the Book, come to a word common between us and you, that we shall not worship anyone, but Allah and that we shall not associate aught with Him, and that some of us shall not take others for Lords besides Allah" (Quran 3:63).

Islam is a liberal religion and has a social equation with the followers of Moses and Jesus, two of its closest monotheistic sister faiths. The Quran says: "Those who believe in Islam, and the Jews, and the Christians, and the Sabians whoever believe in Allah and the last day and do good they shall have their reward from their Lord; and there is no fear for them, nor shall they grieve" (Quran 2:62).

Religions talk about salvation. The door of salvation is considered by Islam to be open for all people who have believed and acted rightly, irrespective of their faith. A question, naturally, arises here. If all religions are acceptable, what is the need for the Islam of Mohammad? We have already explained that Islam recognizes all religions in their true form to be Islam. Mohammad, according to Islam is one of the Prophets. However, he is the last Messenger of God, thereby also completing the

Religion of God. A Muslim's belief is thus wider than say that of a Christian or a Jew. Mohammed invited the followers of all religions to a common platform (Quran 3:63), reminding them that that was the real purpose of revealed religion. It is this universal invitation for cooperation in righteousness and piety that makes him a "Universal Teacher" (Quran 7:158) and a "Mercy for all nations" (Quran 22:107). The Muslim point of view is that without accepting this universal invitation, real understanding of religion is incomplete. It is this need which necessitates the acceptance of the teacher who stood for the final collaboration of the work of the great teachers before him. By accepting Mohammed, all Prophets are accepted and respected. To a Muslim, the belief in Islam, thus, is the culmination of monotheism, the most complete of all faiths. Moreover, saying categorically that Mohammed is the last Prophet, the door to future claims and calls was thus closed for good. This is the final message of Islam.

Having accepted the universality of Divine Revelation Islam respects the revelations given to other religions. Islam believes that before it, other religions had their scriptures, which were the records of divine relevation given to their respective founders, but these have not been properly preserved, and, in their present form, they are not without the impress of the vicissitudes of time. This statement, though very seldom properly appreciated by the followers of other religions, is historically and scientifically very true and correct. Islam thus respects Divine Guidance and revelation, but is cautious enough to discriminate between the authentic records and the less correct versions. But whatever form or contents religious scriptures may have taken, a Muslim is duty-bound to show respect to these books because they are respected by others.

Islam does not believe that one particular geographical spot is sacred, or that one particular direction is specifically the direction towards Allah. The Quran says, "To Allah belongs the East and the West" and therefore to whatever side you turn you will find God there (Quran 2:115). God is omnipresent, and because He is omnipresent, the sanctity of His presence makes the entire universe holy and sacred. Monopolies of sanctity and holiness are not acknowledged. There may be certain places which are sacred on account of their association with Prophets and holy personalities, but so far as Divine Presence is concerned, God does not particularly live or dwell in a particular place. The places of worship that men have raised for the worship of God and glory of His name all deserve people's respect, provided such places are not used for the glorification of beings other than the Supreme Being. Muslims are duty-bound to protect these places of worship, whether they are synagogues, churches, temples, or mosques, which are used for the glorification of the Divine Name of Allah. The Quran says: "And if Allah did not repel, some people by others, cloisters, and churches, and synagogues, and mosques in which Allah's name is much remembered, would have been pulled down. And surely Allah will help him who helps Him" (Quran 22:40).

Here protection of the places of worship to whatever religion they belong is described as helping God, i.e., serving the cause of God, the cause of Peace and general welfare of Humanity. Thus, Islam not only inculcates the spirit of tolerance towards temples of other religions, but also makes it a duty of the Muslims to protect them. The Muslims generally followed this policy during the days of their glory.

As for the Muslim places of worship, the Prophet of Islam is reported to have said that "the whole world has been made a mosque for him," meaning thereby that God can be worshiped anywhere and everywhere. But when particular places of worship are raised in the name of Allah, which are called masjids or mosques, they are to be used for His and only His worship (Quran 72:18). Mosques could be thrown open to members of other faiths for divine worship, provided that it did not create an awkward situation for any one of the two concerned faiths. It is a well-known fact that the Prophet of Islam permitted a deputation of Christians to hold a service in the Masjid-e-Nabwi at Madina which is one of the most sacred mosques of Islam. Accordingly, Muslims are required to respect all places of worship, whether they belong to their own religion or to other religions.

Islam does not allow interference with anyone else's faith or conviction even be it polytheism such as in Hindiusm.

It opens new vistas of religious understanding for believers of other faiths, for "there can be no compulsion in religions." A non-Muslim cannot, under any circumstances, be forcibly converted to Islam nor can he be victimized for his adherence to any other religion. Non-Muslims are free to believe in whatever they choose, and to practice whatever they deem fit. The difference of faith or creed does not hamper anyone's chances of progress or development in a country where Islam wields power. Islam strictly prohibits the disparagement of any faith whether true or false. Even idol gods cannot be abused. "And abuse not those whom they call upon besides Allah, lest exceeding the limits they abuse Allah through ignorance. Thus to every people we have made their deeds fair-seeming; then to their Lord is their return, so He will inform them of what they did" (Quran 6:109).

Attitude Towards Non-Monotheistic Faiths

The basic Quranic influence on this point has already been quoted. Islam's attitude towards non-monotheistic faiths is a subject frequently mentioned in the Quran and Hadiths, and about which much commentary has been written. One can find among Islamic scholars such widely differing interpretations as (1) keep away from them, (2) endure them, and (3) respect and cooperate with them. Succinctly put, Muslims cannot accept as truly revealed by God religious concepts which are at variance with the teachings of the Quran, especially concepts at variance with the doctrine of the unity of God. Muslims, as professors of a universal faith, must continue to strive for the defense of their faith among non-believers (mushrikun). But this is on the plane of the doctrine. In actual practice one can have perfectly good relations with believers of non-monotheistic faiths in matters other than that of the religion. The Quranic mandates which have already been quoted regarding peace would show that a Muslim is expected to have a friendly disposition toward all, regardless of difference of religion.

There have been wars during the period of ascendency of Islam, but, as in all ages, there has also been peace, friendship and cooperation with others who were non-monotheists. This is still true today. It is not necessary to go back in history. Today the Islamic states have generally very good relations with countries whose inhabitants are non-monotheists. There is no theological basis for criticizing the status quo in Muslim relations with non-monotheists. The Muslim protagonist of such relations would seem to have strong grounds on which to base his arguments. In Surah Al-Mumtahanah, it is said: "God forbiddeth you not those who warred not against you on account of religion and drove you not out from your homes, that ye should show them kindness and deal justly with them. Lo! God loveth the just dealers (60:8). Indeed, the same point is stated in a preceding verse: "It may be that God will ordain love between you and those of them with whom ye are at enmity. God is Mighty, and God is Forgiving, Merciful" (60:7). And in Surah Al-Maidah, it is said: "O ye who believe! Be steadfast witnesses for God in equity, and let not hatred of any people seduce you that he deal not justly. Deal justly, that is nearer to your duty . . ."(5:8).

There is also a hadith related by Bukhari and Muslim, "Love for men (mankind) what you love for yourself."

However, these pleasant contacts and mutually beneficial associations which Muslims enjoy with non-monotheists do not in any way imply Muslim acceptance of any non-monotheistic religion as a valid religion. More than one thousand verses of the Quran emphasize the unity of God. Polytheism (shirk) is denounced and warned against time and again. The idea that any religion is good and valid, that one religion is as good as another, is untenable for the Muslim. "There is no God but God, Mohammad is the Prophet of God," is as relevant in Muslim relations with non-monotheists today as in the time of Mohammad, and it must continue so as long as Islam exists. Since for Islam this is an eternal verity without possibility of compromise; certain concomitants of this truth necessarily follow, most particularly, the inevitableness of Muslim witness (shahada) to profess this fact.

> "Say: Unto God belong the East and the West. He guideth whom He will unto a straight path. Thus We have appointed you a middle nation (a people in the middle), that ye may be witnesses before mankind . . ." (Surah Al-Baqurah II: 142b, 143a).

236

As earlier observed, Islam is not basically a missionary religion in the generally accepted sense of that terminology. It has no organized priesthood. No one is entitled to be called Reverend or anything else of the kind. What seems clear, however, is that in different communities some people do help in spreading His truth and knowledge. But they are ordinary people. This was done by businessmen in Indonesia, or by trained religious leaders in parts of Africa, and has resulted in the acceptance of Islam by hundreds of millions of persons over the centuries. That Muslims will continue to witness for their faith this phenomenon, both today and in the future, is certain.

Accordingly, a Muslim in a non-monotheistic society serves and will continue to serve his faith, and there will be men converted from their former religions to Islam by this work, action and talk. The effect of this factor in the relationship of Islam with other faiths will vary from area to area, and from faith to faith. Changing times and technological advances encouraged clear the rise of new religious cults. Recognizing these facts, various Christian churches have undertaken large missionary activities in Africa over the past one hundred years. Until the beginning of the 20th century, it was generally presumed that Africa was a Muslim continent. This no longer appears to be true. As a result of European missionaries there are today several countries with a majority of Christian populations. A great many former pagan African tribes have accepted Christianity. Thus, we have witnessed the emergence of Christianity as one of the two principal faiths on that continent. Any serious challenge to this state of affairs seems now more likely to come from communism because of the expansionist designs of the Russians, than from Islam.[214]

In Asian countries where there are substantial Muslim minorities confronting non-monotheistic majorities, it is probable that the current trend of resurging interest in and emphasis on religion and nationalism, both by the Muslim and the non-Muslim, will result in a tenuous maintenance of the status quo in inter-religious and inter-community relationships.

237

The question of the Muslim attitude towards and relationships with those who profess the philosophy of atheistic materialism as a way of life, indeed, as a religion, must also be faced in this connection. Millions of Muslims live in countries where it is the policy of the government to discourage the practice of religion. There are conflicting accounts as to the extent of religious freedom enjoyed by Muslims in these countries. Official statistics, such as are available, would seem to indicate a decrease in believers among the population, perhaps running into tens of millions. A consensus of the views of objective observers who have travelled in these areas indicates that while most older people retain their faith, few of the younger generation are practicing Muslims. As indicated in another part of this book, the U.S.S.R. is the principal place where this has occurred and where government is attempting to wipe out Islam, as indeed other religions, from its territories.

How will Islam react to this attack in the future? Because of the political conditions of those countries (like in the U.S.S.R.) in which Islam is not dominant, Muslim have not been able to know what the situation is, much less come to grips with it. There is no Islamic Hierarchy to raise questions as Muslim politics have been subject to a strict government rule. Whatever remains of Islam in the Communist world is there because of the faithful witness of those who could not be seduced into unbelief, whose witness has impressed their children and instilled faith beyond the ability of a godless society to destroy it. Yet the evidence seems to be that slowly inroads are being made into the ranks of the faithful; that Islam, elsewhere resurgent with new vitality and strength, is losing ground in those countries where this new religion, protected and encouraged by the state, proclaims the absence of God. The Muslim world as well as the Christian world realize this, but the military might of the Soviet Union does not allow much room for interference. Israel appears to be the only state which has undertaken a massive effort to save the Jews from this state-run operation.

The duty of Muslims to understand these facts is clear. That those isolated and oppressed believers must be brought back into the mainstream of Muslim life and be protected by their Muslim brothers is mandatory on all

238

Muslims. The ways and means whereby this is to be accomplished do not as yet appear to exist. This remains an unconsidered item on Islam's agenda. Unless taken up soon by the Islamic states, the passing years may well make it an irrelevant item, considered too late to matter.

In conclusion, it may be stated that through its teachings regarding four fundamental unities (author's terminology), i.e., the unity of creation, the unity of mankind, the unity of divine guidance, and the unity of purpose of life, Islam initiated an era of interreligious, interfaith, and international toleration. The recognition of one Creator, and one cosmically well-knit and well-organized universe, one fraternity of mankind, one sisterhood of religions, and one purpose of life, means avoidance of considerable unnecessary controversy. Islam aims at being a society which would live with an open mind and open avenues of progress towards the goal of universal peace. The well-known prayer which is supposed to be recited by all Muslims five times during the day says: "O Lord you are Peace, from You comes Peace, and to You returns Peace, make us, O Lord, live in Peace and allow us to enter the house of Peace. O Lord of Glory and Grace thine is the Bliss and Elevation."

Thus Islamic attitude towards other faiths is determined by explicit Quranic teachings. The fundamental right of all faiths to exist in complete freedom is established unequivocally by the injunction quoted many times before: There shall be no compulsion in religion.

It is noteworthy that in Islam the defence of the places of worship of others is mentioned before the mosques. The defence of one's own place of worship is natural and is rooted in the psychology of groups; being self-evident, the concern for the mosque is expressed after the places of worship of the other creeds, which requires a total reorientation of the religious mind. It was on account of this concern for other creeds and their liberties that during the early battles of Islam, when its armies were ordered to march against the enemies they were ordered not to touch any non-combatant or old men, women and children and take special care that no priest of another creed was molested nor any place of worship desecrated.

When the Caliph Omar went personally to Palestine (taking with him no military escort but one camel to be ridden alternately by him and his accompanying servant), he was still negotiating with the bishop in the Church of Holy Sepulchre when the time for prayers arrived. He said to the bishop, "Let me go out and offer prayers." The bishop said, "This is also a house of prayer. You could pray here, there is no need of your going out." Omar replied, "You are right and we can pray anywhere on God's earth but my praying here is fraught with risk lest the Muslims later on assert that the Khalifa, by this act, converted the church into a mosque." Such was the original Islam demonstrating by practice that it stood for liberties of all creeds and not for self-aggrandizement. The Prophet did not debar the Christians from praying in his own mosque. A Christian deputation while conversing with him in his mosque said their time for prayer had arrived and proposed moving out. But the Prophet said, "Why don't you pray here?" The Christians said, "We hesitate because we use instrumental music with drums and other things in our religious service and it may be disliked in the mosque." The Prophet said, "Pray as you like in your own way." And so they prayed in the mosque beating their drums. The Quran has said that humanity shall never follow one single creed and so rituals and dogmas and modes of worship shall continue to differ, but notwithstanding this variety every creed in its own way should strive towards the maximum realization of the good; they should compete with each other only in this common effort (Quran 48:5).

It is on account of this belief in peaceful coexistence that large non-Muslim communities continued to flourish even in areas of Muslim political domination. The churches continued to toll their bells when actually constructed wall to wall with the mosques. Spain was under Muslims' rule for several centuries, and no effort was made to convert the population by violence or by pressure; as a result when their military power collapsed, they were decimated as a small minority by that very majority which had enjoyed unlimited religious liberty under the Muslims for long centuries and had jointly created a magnificent civilization far ahead of the rest of the then benighted Europe. The Turks ruled Eastern Europe for about four centuries, usually granting religious and cultural autonomy to communities of all denominations. They risked remaining in a minority with results that proved harmful for them. The case was similar in the Indian sub-continent. Without any political or practical pressure, the Hindu caste system brought converts to Islam. This continued even after the Muslims had lost all political power. Even during the stern Sikh regime, when the courtyard of the magnificent royal mosque of Lahore was used for the horses of Ranjit Singh's bodyguard, conversion to Islam under the very nose of the rulers continued because of its spiritual and ideological attraction. This has been happening in Africa and more recently in the United States. Islam has propagated itself by the momentum of its own ideology, simply and undogmatically, demonstrating the equality of man irrespective of the pigment of the skin. Islam spread in the Indonesian archipelago mostly under the Christian Dutch regime when the population was deprived of all political or economic power.

There is, therefore, the utmost toleration in Islam towards other faiths. It is clear that the people of the Book, that is, the Jews and Christians, occupy a special position. They are, philosophically, sister faiths of Islam, but even with those faiths which do not believe in one God, Islam has nothing but peace and goodwill to offer. Those who contend otherwise, do not understand the real message of Islam. The position, however, of Christianity in Islam is significant. Accordingly, we now turn to an examination of Islam's special relationship with Christianity.

(B) Islam and Christianity

The basic injunctions for the Muslims with respect to other religions have been dealt with in the last section. In these pages, we shall particularly focus on Islam's relations with Christianity. This is being done for two reasons. First, throughout the history of Man, only two monotheistic faiths have had universal impact at various times for prolonged periods. These two faiths have been Islam and Christianity. Second, today Christianity and Islam present two major monotheistic religions of the world. Their combined believers represent nearly half of mankind; for the future of monotheism, understanding between the followers of the two faiths is imperative.

The regard and respect which is to be shown to the Christians by Muslims is unique. One can never be a true Muslim unless one believes Jesus to be a great prophet like the Prophet of Islam himself. It is true that some of the fundamental dogmas of Christianity have been refuted by Islam. But here, too, the departure is constructive. It has been suggested that on these points Christian doctrines are difficult to reconcile with reality, the major difference being the Christian belief that Jesus was the Son of God, and the Muslims' conviction of Jesus being a human being. Jesus, according to Islam, was a Messenger of God and His word was communicated to Mary. The Spirit in him was as subservient to Allah as the spirit in Adam or any other Prophet. But the Quran accords the highest place to Jesus; he is even referred to as the "Spirit" of God. Islam, as we know, is a universal, or, as some Christian authors such as W. Wilson Cash would say, an eclectic religion.[215] Many prophets known to the Old Testament have been treated in the Quran by name with all reverence and sanctity. But among all those, Jesus occupies a specially privileged position. In Sura 4 he is called the Apostle of God, Word of God, and Spirit from God.

The classic Islamic commentators have advanced various explanations as to the meaning of these titles. Tabarsi, the well-known Shia commentator of the 12th century A.D., says that Word of God signifies that through Jesus the Truth of God is revealed to mankind, just as the spoken and written words reveal meanings. So Jesus is the living Word of God. In his exegesis of Christ being a Spirit from God, Tabarsi says that God, through His being, bestowed the Spirit from Himself to Mary's heart and the same was embodied in the person of Christ. Similar epithets exalting Jesus are repeated in the Quran. For instance, in Sura 2:87, 253 he is said to have been strengthened with the Holy Spirit and has been given clear signs. In Sura 3:45, he is described as exalted in this world and in the world to come, and one of the nearest to God. In Sura 19:30-31, he is called the blessed one, who got the Word of God while a child. In Sura 43:63 he is said to have come imbued with wisdom in order to guide mankind in their controversies. Christ's apostles and followers are described as helpers of God (3:45). The

242

Quran also says that his followers are qualified as being bestowed with kindness and charity in their hearts: (57:27).

In this manner the Quran speaks of Jesus, of his mission, of his teachings and of his followers. Dedicated to him are some 78 revealed in eighteen Suras, namely Suras 2,3, 4, 5, 6, 7, 9, 10, 19, 21, 33, 39, 42, 43, 57, 61, 72, 112.

As a result of this message, over one billion souls now believe in Jesus as an apostle of God, His Word and a Spirit from Him. He is guidance and light for humanity.

This understanding is a great asset for the Christendom as well as for the entire religious world. But this was not the way the old Christendom received Islam. The contact between the two faiths was usually hostile. The hostilities developed until they culminated in the Crusades. Of course, as time passed, the Christian students of comparative religion threw more light on the Islamic studies and more moderate and rather objective views emerged. Even a sort of self-criticism developed in the West, and modern Islamists tried to censure the prejudiced views of their fellow Christians about Islam. For instance, the Dutch Islamist, C. S. Hurgronje, in the introduction of his book on Islam, sums up the erroneous views of his predecessors and rejects them.[216] There are now well-known Christian authors, even missionaries, who at least concede that Mohammed was sincere in his mission. Men like Theodor Noeldeke, Gorges Sale, H.A.R. Gibb and W. Wilson Cash recognize this fact. Other thinkers like L. Bevan Jones and Kenneth Cragg, advise their fellow Christians to be of more friendly attitude and of a more receptive disposition towards the Muslims.

The controversy between Christianity and Islam can now be reduced to three main issues: the doctrine of the Divinity of Christ, the problem of Crucifixion, and the question of the Gospels. Jesus, according to Islam, is a Divine man, whereas, for the orthodox Christian he is Divinity Himself in the form of a man. In the first case he is a Godly man, in the second case, he is God as a man.[217] It is a fact that any idea of anthropomorphism and any form of incarnation is alien to Islam. Therefore, any relationship, even if it were only verbal, such as the doctrine of Trinity, is not compatible with the Islamic teachings. This Doctrine especially manifested itself with the Eastern Christians of the Prophet's time. Jones tells us that the Christians of Abyssinia in those days actually believed in a Trinity consisting of God, Mary, and Jesus.[218] But we need not go back to those times. Even at present the concept of the Father, the Son, and the Holy Ghost remains vital to Christian theology.

As for the crucifixion, the Muslim belief is that Jesus did not die on the cross but was "lifted" by God. The Christian belief is different in that it is said that he ascended after being crucified. The difference, though important, is slight. The Quran says that Jesus, being the embodiment of the Spirit from God, could not be killed or annihilated; he did not die because he possessed the ever-living spirit and so God raised him up unto Himself:(41:56).

Thirdly is the question of the Gospels. First of all, whatever we may say about it, Jesus did not leave a Gospel authorized by himself, or, if he did, we do not know about it. Secondly, the position of Islam relating to this matter is usually misunderstood. Muslims believe that the Bible and its message were revealed to Jesus. However, the testament we have is the work of several later saints, and therefore not word by word the Word of God. So the Bible we have is "altered" or "substituted" from God's work. By alteration in the Bible, spoken of in the Quran, it is not meant that the Christian believers sat down and willingly altered their scripture; all that is meant is that many, while quoting the scriptures, altered and substituted it according to their understanding. Another point is that, although the Gospels are not regarded to be the original genuine Gospel of Christ by the Muslims, they are at least supposed to contain the Truth of God and some teachings of Jesus. This is why an immense literature has developed in the Islamic world exhibiting Christ's teachings and sayings; such writings are in prose and poetry praising the message of Jesus. The Muslim attitude towards and relationships with Christians is a unique relation because it has existed, and continues to exist, between the two largest religions of

nankind. Suffice it to say that these two faiths hold much
nore in common with each other than do any other two
aiths.

"Thou wilt find the nearest of them in affection those
who say: Lo! We are Christians. That is because
there are among them priests and monks, and because
they are not proud" (Quran 5:82b).

This notwithstanding, the past connection of Muslims and
Christians has not always been a happy one. There have
been many periods in history where Muslims and Christians
have worked together especially in the courts of the
Muslim kings. Christians often served in positions of
responsibility and as scholars, and sometimes occupied
high places as advisors in matters of state. But in
general, the relationships of Muslims and Christians in the
entire Muslim world through the centuries, can be summed
up by the word ignorance; ignorance of each other with
resulting bitterness.

With this background it is hoped that a true understanding
between Christianity and Islam is possible. By this we do
not mean a fashionable peaceful coesistence, but a real and
very cordial reconciliation and even cooperation. There
are many reasons for holding this view:

1) Both religions believe in one God, an Eternal and
Supreme Being, the Creator of the Universe; both use
similar attributes, worship Him and offer prayers, although
they differ about His nature and personification.

2) Both believe in the immortality of the soul and the
responsibility of man.

3) Both believe in the spirit and the moral life, inviting
mankind to fight against the evil and live up to the higher
principles of love, service, sacrifice and other good deeds.

4) The guiding principles of both religions have more in
common alike than some of us realize. There are actually
passages in the Quran corresponding directly to passages
in the Scriptures. Compare for instance those illuminated
by Kenneth Cragg in "The Christian and Islam," namely

Sura 3:104 and Ephesians 2:13; Sura 3:104 and Romans 5:10; Sura 11:28 and 7:138 and I Corinthians 1:26; etc.

(5) After all, we have much in common as far as the Synoptic Gospels are concerned.

(6) Kinship and close connection in essential theological matters such as the proofs for the Existence of God are evident. Scholars like A. J. Wensinck have duly investigated the points of contact between the two faiths and similar attitudes regarding proofs for the existence of God, attributes of God, mission of the apostles to different peoples, difference between apostles and prophets, doctrine of peccatum mortale and peccatum veniale, relation between faith and work, relation between essence and existence, etc.[219]

The unity of God, the text of prayer, the mission of angels, the doctrine of fall and atonement, the story of creation, Adam and Eve, Cain and Abel, Noah and the Ark, the Flood, etc., all symbolize a common background. Also, linguistic studies carried out by scholars like Arthur Jeffery and others point to a common Jesuit heritage.

The time is appropriate to have the followers of both religions, which together comprise almost one half of the population of the world, think of a reconciliation. Perhaps more than that, they should attempt a cooperation. By this we do not mean any concession or attempt for compromise in the two religions. We have already enough in common to try to safeguard our spiritual values. The age of bigotry is expiring and the time is calling us for mutual understanding. There was a time when Pope Innocent IV and King Louis resorted to an alliance in order to fight the Muslims, but now it is time to declare a crusade against common enemies, especially the godlessness of communism. In order to attain such an aim the following suggestions are offered:

(1) Let us first realize that we are not required to make undue concession for that is not feasible in matters of faith. But let us hold together to safeguard the religion as a whole.

246

(2) The scholars of both faiths should make genuine efforts to study each other's faith with earnest desire to get at the truth. The aim should be to understand and not to refute it. For a purpose such as this, besides fair-mindedness and objectivity, a thorough survey of historical and psychological background of each faith is indispensable.

(3) Both religions summon their followers to take their message to the rest of the world and guide mankind to the right path. This is different from finding faults with each other. The Muslim missionary, instead of attacking the doctrine of the Trinity, should try to study the Sermon on the Mount, the story of the woman of Samaria in St. John, the wonderful teaching on faith, hope, and charity in Corinthians. The Christian missionary, instead of attacking the practice of Polygamy, or the questions of the Holy War, should emphasize the genuine moral and social teachings of the Quran, such as the opening verses of Sura 23 called "The Believers." Faith in the Eternal God who is the Eternal Truth, Supreme Being, Creator and Sustainer of the Universe, the source of life, light and all goodness, and the doctrine of man's moral responsibility are the cardinal teachings of Islam. Let us make good use of these immense spiritual assets at a time when both communism and materialism, institutionalized, are politically destroying the fundamentals of decent religion.

So, therefore, a thorough revision of the traditional method of missionary activity is indispensable. We should follow the teaching of the Quran that orders us to ask all the peoples of the Book to join us in the name of God, and say to them, "O People of the Book! come to common terms as between us and you, that we worship none but God (3:64), our God and your God is the same (Quran 29:46). We should act according to this unique universal message: "O mankind: We created you male or female, and made you into nations and tribes, that you may know each other. Verily the most honored of you in the sight of God is the most righteous of you" (Quran 49:13). Political events of far-reaching significance now taking place in the Middle East make it imperative for this kind of approach by both Christian and Muslim scholars so that monotheism and belief may survive an age frought with the dangers of nuclear holocaust.

CHAPTER X
The Islamic State in the 1980's

The previous narrative, would have, hopefully, clearly established the leading questions, if not their possible answers, regarding an "Islamic State." Our predominant inquiry was concerned with the conceptual understanding of what is precisely meant by this term today. In that context we analyzed various characteristics which Islam requires for a state which bears the title of an "Islamic Republic." Although this text is not really concerned with an analysis of politics or international affairs, a brief survey of important contemporary events was undertaken in Chapters I and VI, since it is clear to the author that the future of such states which profess Islam has become inextricably bound with a number of foreign policy considerations of the super powers. Events, such as that in Afghanistan, indeed stress that a super power may be bent on destroying the deep convictions of a people, when they constitute an obstacle in its path. In countries, and there are only a few of them, which fall into the category of "unimportant" from this foreign policy perspective, economic realities seem to be more pressing than a zealous pursuit of an ideal. Indeed, this economic element is present even in most of those states which are, unfortunately, caught in the conflicting ambitions of super powers.

Accordingly, some assessment of contemporary political affairs is necessary for a meaningful understanding of the subject. This point assumes more importance when we look into the future. With this significance of predictions in mind, we approach the observations which follow. A caveat may be mentioned: evaluation of future events in any case is difficult; it becomes more so when the subject revolves around an ideological ideal and constantly changing international priorities of many nations, particularly of the major ones. It would not be indulgence in hyperbole to say that as we start the decade of the eighties, the "revival" of Islam, both in religious and political terms, constitutes a topic of the highest interest in the thoughts of people all over the world. Events in Iran and Afghanistan, with the corresponding involvement of the U. S and U.S.S.R., have combined to ensure this fact. This set of facts needs some attention for the kind of exercise now contemplated.

An analysis of the present situation requires that we restate, briefly, the basic points which have been enunciated thus far. A clear understanding of the following issues is necessary for future assessment. Four such issues are sufficient for this purpose.

1. First, the Muslims the world over long to recapture their past historical glory. History, in this sense, is crucial to a Muslim's identity.

2. Second, while so hoping, they believe that only if they can recreate the kind of values they once had will they regain their erstwhile status. The goal of creating an "Islamic State" is the cornerstone of this endeavor. In this endeavor scholars and jurists have, broadly speaking, taken two views. The orthodox view supports a complete return to the eighth century structure of the Islamic State. The reformists maintain that this is not possible. Accordingly, the Islamic State of today must incorporate, mutatis mutandis, changes which have occurred since those days of Islamic glory.

3. Third, without exception, none of the contemporary Islamic states is politically stable. This lack of continuity in political institutions, or, worse, the preservation of a government by authoritarianism, has created all sorts of problems; the predominant one being that there has been an absence of a total calm which is needed for the nourishment of any system of government, including, of course, an Islamic one. Domestic political squabbles have resulted in weak governments with consequential disorders followed by military takeovers. Coupled with this is an additional fact--the disunity and discord, even hostility between several of the Islamic countries.

4. Along with these internal struggles, conflicts and turmoil, we find a fluid, volatile and rapidly changing international scenario. Within this larger and complex conflict, Islam and the goal to create an "Islamic State" have become deeply involved. Events of great

significance during the last three or four years show that an Islamic society, even if it so wishes, cannot simply proceed to embrace and create an Islamic State assuming, of course, such a thing in either the orthodox or reformist sense, is possible. Such a wish or desire, for a variety of reasons, might not be allowed by the super powers, directly or indirectly.

In view of the immense complications which the last of the above points contains, let us proceed to deal with it more deeply. Once that is done, we shall return to deal with the preceding three issues.

Events in Afghanistan and Iran, two contemporary matters, emphasize in simple terms the dependence of the Islamic revival movements on the whims and policies of the U.S. and the U.S.S.R. If the U.S., hypothetically speaking, were not interested in the Shah, we may never have seen the rise of Khomeini, his movement, and what it has come to signify. Similarly, if the geo-political aims of the Soviet Union were other than what they now appear to be, the freedom fighters of Afghanistan may not have had to fight to safeguard Islam. Conversely, the movement for the establishment of an Islamic Republic in Iran, now or before, cannot, in practice, succeed until we also have no interference from the U.S. or the U.S.S.R. Mutatis mutandis, the same applies to the case of Afghanistan.

The view which the U.S. takes, or at least should take, towards an Islamic State may be different from the one taken by the Soviet Union; again, in this case, because of the ideological conflict with the goals of Islamic States.

This requires an ideological and a historical overview of the positions of some Islamic states and the super powers.

The ideological questions are easily disposed of. Whereas, to the Communists all religion, per se, is an obstacle, there is no such difficulty for the U.S. Because of various factors previously articulated (e.g. large Muslim populations in the U.S.S.R. and the rise of Islam in political terms) the Russians are particularly concerned about the revival or even the threat of revival of Islamic fundamentalism. An example stressing this point is provided by Iran. Despite that country's troubles with the U.S., internal turmoil, and a rapidly dwindling economy, it has spoken out vociferously against the Russians since the Afghanistan invasion. Khomeini perceives clearly the ideological danger of the U.S.S.R. to his neighboring Islamic state. Equally, the Russians do not want Khomeini's philosophy taking root in their Islamic community across the borders of Iran. This antipathy between Islam and Communism is bound to keep, doctrinally at least, the Islamic States more inclined towards the Western states, which would generally include the U.S. On important issues, however, Western Europe and the U.S. do not always have the same views. An important recent example of such differing attitudes is provided by the independent approaches of the European Community regarding the Palestinian issue. In June, 1980, the European Community took up its own initiative in opposition to the American-Israeli stands which desired the peaceful settlement within the Camp David formula of 1978.

With this preliminary understanding of the ideological point, we can move on to examine the historical implications of this matter.

The Russian invasion of Afghanistan raises two questions, one relating to motives and the other involving the consequences. Regarding motive, we must ask, why did it happen? With respect to consequences, we are eager to find out what will happen as a result of this fait accompli. What major political results will emerge as a consequence of the Russian troops and weaponry in an area predominantly of Muslims? How will they exploit the existing factionalism in these regions in their favor? What will the U.S. do when the Russians are barely two hundred miles from an age-old dream of getting to the Indian Ocean? Can Islamic Fundamentalism be of greater help or hindrance to the global interests of the Western nations, particularly that of the U.S.?

It is evident, therefore, that the examination of consequences raises more complex questions than an inquiry into Russian motivations. The Russian foreign policy, like that of every major power, is a mixture of ideology and Realpolitick. Expansionism, it is submitted, is necessary for both its ideological and political success.

For at least the last three hundred years, the Soviet Union and its predecessor, the Czarist Russia, did not have the best of ties with the Muslim states which lay to the south of its borders. In the seventeenth century, Peter the Great was very conscious of and deeply concerned with finding an outlet to the warm southern seas in the Arabian Ocean. However, that was no easy task, for to his south lay the Turkish Empire, and the Turks were no easy prey. Despite a number of military encounters in what is today northwest Iran and northern Turkey, the Russians were unable to make any headway in their drive toward the south. Meanwhile in India, the British were able to control not only the south of India from where they started,[220] but gradually they expanded in all directions; they reached in the north, the Himalayan Mountains and Hindu Kush in the northwest. In this march they were able to replace the gradually disappearing Mogul Dynasty and so control most of the sub-continent. The British in their far-sightedness[221] considered it necessary to leave Afghanistan alone. Afghanistan, therefore, became a traditional buffer state between the British in the south and the Russians in the north. Apart from providing a useful buffer, there was nothing of much use in Afghanistan which could attract the British from the south to overtake it. It was a large, rugged, mountainous terrain, without even a navigable river; the control of such a region would have provided more political headache than benefit. So the British expanded as far north as it was geographically and militarily feasible; that is, up to Peshawar, which is just south of the historic Khyber Pass. Afghanistan, therefore, remained uncolonized. In the year 1855, which was the last year of the reign of Czar Nicholas, it seemed probable that the British might face the Russians and fight them over the control of Afghanistan. This war looked inevitable, since at the same time nearly two thousand miles to the west, the British were already fighting the Russians in the Crimean War. However, the Indian mutiny of 1857, and the ending of the Crimean War prevented hostilities between the British and the Russians over Afghanistan. And so Afghanistan continued unconquered. After 1917, following the Russian Revolution, the relationship between Afghanistan and the Soviet Union continued cordial. The Kremlin, under both Lenin and Stalin, kept good relations with the Afghan government, which at that time was ruled

253

by King Amanullah. Since he was deeply anti-British, it served the Russian interests to have a hostile Afghan king against the British. After World War II, Afghanistan generally remained on very friendly terms with its powerful northern neighbor. For its part, the U.S.S.R. provided support in development programs. During the fifties and early sixties, Afghanistan in more and more political matters sided with the Kremlin. Its status as a client state of the Soviet Union was then undisputed.

The Afghan Monarchy ended in 1973, when the last king, Zahir Shah, was removed by Mohammed Daoud. The Soviet Union hailed this as a triumph of the proletariat, and within a month more than thirty-eight agreements were signed with the new Afghan regime. This, in fact, is paradoxical, since the Soviet Union had also always praised the monarchy of the previous ruler. The Daoud regime, as long as it stayed, was not a communist government, although it continued, like the previous Afghan regime, to be a close friend of the Soviet Union. It is now clear the the U.S.S.R. wanted more than just friendship; it wanted a communist regime in Aghanistan. They succeeded in April, 1978, when one Nur Mohammed Taraki, in a coup d'etat, grabbed power from Daoud with the material help of the Soviet Union. Taraki's gain of power was the first signal of the communist party actually gaining control in Afghanistan. Indeed, it was the first takeover by a communist power in any Islamic country. Just like Daoud (when he overthrew the king in 1973), Taraki, on his coming to power, received both rhetorical and military support from the Soviet Union. However, barely a month had passed before the fierce and devout Muslim population of Afghanistan started to become hostile to his regime. They saw that he was being supported by the communists, who were not only the oppressors of various Muslim nations within the Soviet Union, but were also supposed to be anti-God. Hostility soon became insurgency. During the course of this insurgency, several hundred thousand refugees began to arrive in Pakistan and some in Iran. The success of Khomeini in Iran gave a further impetus to the Afghan rebellion. In September, 1979, one Hafizula Amin, the Prime Minister of Taraki, overthrew him. As soon as Amin came to power, he, like his predecessors, immediately received both verbal and material support from the Soviet Union. However, Amin's stay in power was very short-lived. On the twenty-seventh of December, 1979, partly by taking advantage of the hostage situation in Iran (the focus of the world's attention) and the Christmas holidays falling on the twenty-fifth and twenty-sixth of December, the Soviet Union moved nearly twenty thousand troops into Afghanistan ostensibly to save the government of Amin. Their first act on the second day was to overthrow his government, execute him, and install one Babrak Karmal, who had been living in exile in Czechoslovakia. In 1978 Karmal had been appointed by Takaki as an ambassador, but because of differences, had been dismissed. However, he did not return to Afghanistan, and is believed to have lived in Czechoslovakia and in Moscow before returning to Kabul on or around the twenty-seventh of December to become the new President.

This continuous interest of the Russians in this region must be kept in mind. Whatever is opposed to their domination plans must be treated by the Soviets in an appropriate manner. This practical assertion of Soviet control is, in theory, contrary to both the Constitution of the U.S.S.R. and Lenin's repeated assurances that "self-determination" was so sacred to the Marxists that even the non-Russian nationalities in the U.S.S.R. could separate to become independent. Indeed, Lenin himself and later Stalin ruthlessly crushed such attempts, particularly in the Muslim regions of the Soviet Union, first in Azerbaijan (annexed from Persia in the nineteenth century), and later in Kazakstan, Uzbekistan and Tadjikistan.

In global terms the Russians suffered a major setback in the Cuban missile crisis of 1962. Thereafter, the Russians methodically set their goal: first of all, military superiority vis-a-vis the U. S. in nuclear and conventional capability. Krushchev simultaneously went ahead with a policy of detente with the U.S. It thus insured its continued military development, avoided the risk of accidental nuclear war, and most of all allowed its hold to become more secure in Europe. After all, its European gains were most valuable and prestigious to it as a result of World War II, e.g., permanent division of Germany.

Its Middle East policy seemed to be temporarily halted on account of a failure to secure a foothold in Turkey, Iran or Pakistan, though it was not for lack of trying. Its main technique or modus operandi was to exploit the ethnic diversity of the peoples of these regions. In addition, its client Arab states were unable to militarily gain an advantage in their confrontation with Israel. With the ouster of Russians from Egypt in 1973, it appeared that, at least for some time, the Soviet Union had suffered a most decisive setback in the Middle East and Southwest Asia. But this fact was considerably "balanced" by the American defeat in Vietnam and Watergate.

Apart from the above "balance" the American and Western position in international terms of political conflicts, was weakened by two basic errors. (1) A total miscalculation of the Russian arms build-up since the early sixties, and (2) the magnitude of the Sino-Soviet rift. For example, the Americans were convinced that it was China which was behind North Vietnam, and that within the canopy of detente, Russia could be persuaded to help the U.S., as it were, behind the scenes!

In addition to an overall policy regarding extending the Soviet sphere of influence, Russia has not overlooked the constant American efforts to encircle it from the early fifties by military alliances. The rise of China made the Middle East region the only area where her efforts for breaking through this encirclement promised some success. The basic realities of this area, i.e., the Arab-Israeli conflict, the constantly rising spate of hatred against the former Shah, and the simultaneous event of the revival of Islamic Fundamentalism in Pakistan and Iran, made the Russians all the more eager to act decisively and promptly. Thus, she began her international comeback as a matter of urgency. Angola, in 1975, was her first breakthrough. That success demonstrated its use of proxy Cuban troops and her capacity to transport over long distances military hardware and manpower. Furthermore it won a psychological battle in Angola against the U. S., which had previously succeeded in ousting her from the Middle East negotiations. It also apparently outmaneuvered the U.S., since both in Angola and Ethiopia the Soviets backed the "legitimate" governments. That is, the governments considered "recognized" by the O.A.U. This was, in part, due to the miscalculation of Dr. Kissinger.

It is with these facts in mind that we must evaluate the Afghanistan and Iranian crises. The Soviet action was, primarily, it is submitted, prompted by defensive considerations. Russia wanted to preserve what had been gained since the 1978 coup. Combined with such defensive considerations were far-reaching goals, e.g., oil, access to the Indian Ocean becoming closer, and laying the foundations for eventual Soviet hegemony by Balkanizing the entire region. Initially, this region would include the countries immediately to the south of the Soviet Union (all Muslim). Of all such countries, Pakistan appears to be the first target of the Red Army. Its internal factional and regional conflicts in the shape of armed rebellions, first in East Pakistan, followed by insurrection in Baluchistan, were attractive signs for Soviet expansionism. By encouraging Baluchi dissidents, a none too difficult task, an easy corridor to the sea and thus to the Gulf area could be obtained.

In taking this step, however, the U.S.S.R. definitely lost a great deal in political terms. But that is not necessarily an American or a Western gain. In the wake of the Russian invasion the Conference of Islamic Foreign Ministers was called in Islamabad in January, 1980. It condemned the Soviet Union comprehensively. During the same month, on January 14, the General Assembly of the U.N. passed a resolution condemning the Russian action by a vote of 104 to 18.[222] A breakdown of the votes would show that the only countries not to vote against the Russians were those in the Communist Block. It is, therefore, easy to see what the Soviets have lost in the context of international propaganda and in the eyes of the Muslim nations. Of course, the Russian hope is to see this hostility against them soon becoming past history.

In the motives of the Russian invasion discussed above, it was mentioned that, apart from short and long-term goals, the Soviet Union is bound to act negatively to any aspirations in the nature of Islamic revival or Islamic Fundamentalism because of the possible repercussions in its own territories. Coincidental with the Iranian revolution, in which one has often heard of Islamic goals, considerable indications have come from Soviet Azerbiajan of increasing Islamic activity. This could hardly be ignored by the Kremlin. But of equal concern was the psychological

257

impact of a replacement in Kabul of a staunch pro-Islamic and anti-Soviet government on the Russian image domestically and abroad. So in their calculations, the Russians reasoned that more was likely to be lost than gained by not acting as they did.

A number of points have already emerged to show that if the Muslims are not happy with the Russians, they don't feel too comfortable with the Americans either. For the sake of convenience, three points regarding the U.S. must again be mentioned: (i) American policy in the Arab-Israeli conflict, (ii) American support of unpopular ruling governments, and (iii) American efforts to stop any Islamic country from acquiring nuclear capability. As a qualification to the point (i) above, it might be added that there appears to be a shift in the U.S. policy since the advent of the Carter Administration. Now it seems that, although the U.S. commitment to Israel's security is unchanged, yet this does not imply a blanket endorsement of every action of the government of Israel. For example, in August, 1980, when the Security Council took up the matter of the "shifting" of the Israeli capital to Jerusalem, the vote in the chamber was 14 to 0 with the U.S. abstaining and not using its veto. Further, we find several references to acknowledging the rights of the Palestinians and an oppostion to the settlements on the West Bank.

The present narrative has stressed, then, the point that, at the moment, in the beginning of the 1980 decade, Islamic States are at odds with both the Soviet Union and the United States. Ironically, the best index of this feeling is once again provided by Iran. On hearing the news of the Russian invasion of Afghanistan, some Iranians, along with some Afghan refugees living in Tehran, marched on the Russian Embassy on the last two days of 1979. They would have, but for the strong help of the revolutionary guards, taken over the embassy almost in the same fashion as the American Embassy had been taken over some weeks earlier. The mob attack in Tehran on both the embassies, though with varied consequences, is the truest index of what the public presently feels in many Islamic states towards both the United States and the Soviet Union. Non-alignment is thus gaining ground.

But in the ultimate analysis, the Islamic States, because of ideological reasons, will have more reason to look to the Western nations in friendly terms than to the U.S.S.R. The fact that in the future, the Islamic States, on important issues, might have a common cause with the Western countries (and not the U.S.S.R.) is borne out by the fact that on January 3, 1980, forty-three states petitioned for the calling of the Security Council to discuss the Afghanistan crisis. This large number of countries represented both Islamic and Western nations. The call for this session, as far as Islamic countries were concerned, was spearheaded, by Pakistan which, needless to say, had more than an Islamic interest in mind, being the immediate physical recipient of the events in Afghanistan. On the fourth of January, when the Security Council was actually to start the discussion, seven more countries joined, six of them being Islamic. Therefore, the session was called by fifty states, namely a third of the membership of the United Nations. About one-fifth of the nations which sponsored this resolution were Islamic countries. The fact that all Islamic countries did not join in this resolution does not signify that they are against the thrust of such a resolution.[223] The diversity of the states which petitioned for the calling of this resolution shows the extent of resentment against the Soviet Union's invasion of Afghanistan. From the Far East, the Philippines was a sponsor; as was Indonesia, then Bangladesh, and Pakistan. Also joining in this call were several countries from the Gulf region and a number of countries from Africa. This clearly shows that Islamic countries in general feel that their ultimate aspirations for remaining free in an environment where Islamic precepts can flourish, are threatened directly by the communist countries led by the Soviet Union. This is also the first time in about two generations that so much of the Third World, which includes the Islamic States, is siding with the Western states in preference to the U.S.S.R. This evidence is important for future developments.

The revival and the renaissance of the Islamic State has, therefore, now become dependent on and heavily involved in the global geopolitical strategies of the United States and the Soviet Union, particularly in the Middle East. This is an area which has produced the present intellectual thrust of the movement, as well as most of the thinkers of the past. Since the aspirations of the Islamic states in these regions and the future long-range strategic interests of the Western nations are identical, i.e. to be safe from Russian expansions, mutual trust and new cooperation is necessary. A threat at this time to crush the Islamic revival would be a bad thing, not only for the Muslims, but also for the interests of the Western nations. The Western nations (for their benefit) have, in the Islamic ideology, perhaps the greatest psychological and political bulwark against the expansionism of the Communist ideology.

This chapter has so far been concerned with the Middle East and West Asia, since it is from these regions that the immediate future controversies will surface. But in parentheses a word may be said about Africa. As earlier noticed, in Africa, despite a number of states with Islamic populations, the idea of the establishment of an Islamic state along the same lines as in Pakistan or Iran, has not really come up, with the exception of Libya. Libya, however, is a small country. Nevertheless, it has enormous financial resources. Its leader, the youthful Colonel Mohammar Gaddafi, has been doing what, perhaps in a different form, has been done by Khomeini in Iran. The Libyan state is, indeed, called an "Islamic Republic." In terms of the implementation of the Islamic directives, Libya, like Iran and Pakistan, has many Islamic laws in its statute book. But apart from this factor, Africa does not appear presently to be the focus of the attention of either the forces of an "Islamic state" or of any significant regional or international controversy dealing with this phenomenon.

We started this chapter by channeling our thoughts on four specific issues. The last one involved some of the foreign policy and international geopolitical matters analyzed above. It is hoped that this basic understanding of important contemporary matters will make us aware of where the Islamic states and this "revival" of Islam in reality stands today. Finally, therefore, we turn to a brief examination of the other three points. The first two basically concern ideology or doctrinal aspects of importance to the Muslims in the coming years; the third issue is merely a factual assessment of the political situation of the Islamic countries. This last point may now

260

be taken up. It deals with the political situation of Islamic countries and will serve as an appendix to the international survey just completed.

The most striking things we notice when we look at the Islamic countries are (1) despite apparent unity and calls for Islamic solidarity, there are many elements which show the actual reality to be otherwise, and (2) there is domestic instability within most of these countries. The troubles are of two kinds and, in a way, have led to grave problems for many such countries.

The first kind of trouble is exemplified by major international conflicts between Islamic countries. The more important of these may be noted: the political expulsion of Egypt from, at least the Arab League, as a result of the Camp David Accord, the Iraqi-Iranian border disputes, the disputes of Iran with some of its small Gulf neighbors concerning territorial claims over various islands, the Afghanistan-Pakistan controversy over the "Pakhtoonistan" issue, and the frequent Libyan-Egyptian hostilities. But equally pressing is a disunity of another kind, i.e., factionalism within the Islamic countries. The most serious, undoubtedly, was the civil war in Pakistan in 1971 leading to the creation of Bangladesh. In 1973 in Pakistan again there was a Baluch insurgency. Similarly there has been the trouble of the Kurdish people in both Turkey and Iran, the controversy between different tribes in the Sudan, and the conflict between the Azerbijan province in western Iran and the rest of the country since, particularly, Khomeini took over. Indeed the Ayatollah Shriat Madari expressly refused to accept the assumption of the title of the Fagahi (a trustee) by Khomeini. There are also many other smaller controversies of this type in the Gulf states. Fortunately for Islamic states, the principal division in Islam between the Sunnis and Shiaties, has been less important during the last few years, but it still does produce conflicts from time to time in various countries of the Gulf area, and in Iraq, Iran and Pakistan. Now a look at the domestic misfortunes.

Partly because of such factional disturbances and partly on account of lack of conventional and traditional institutions of self government, in actuality we have few instances of political stability in Islamic countries. This lack of maturity of successful institutions of a political nature is largely the result of the long colonial domination of most lands where Muslims now live. This factor has led to two direct consequences. First, the government in power, in most cases, is led to assume dictatorial powers. Second, because the people are denied any voice in governmental affairs and are usually also without many civil and political rights, they attempt to fall back on religious fervor to fight for their liberty and rights. Such events have occurred in exactly this manner on more than one occasion. In this sense, Islam is the force of acquiring a better status in life. It is in this manner that Islam's potential as a political and sociological cleanser is important. It is because of this fact that we speak of Islamic "revival" or the rise of Islamic Fundamentalism as people are falling back on their ancient faith to come to grips with their current maladies. It is, thus, as earlier observed at one point, a classical use of a religion: to make the people arise from their present misfortunes by a change in their outlook on life. This point of political instability is important to remember in view of recent history.

Finally, we come to a brief discussion of the first two points. They deal with the ideological foundations of a Muslim's aspirations and hopes today. That is to say that in his desire to regain his past distinguished status, the Muslim wishes to create this "Islamic State." He feels that neither the industrialized West nor the Communist East can fulfill his innermost ideals for the here and hereafter; the ultimate panacea for his ills is his meeting with his historical identity.

The memory of Islam's past glory for a Muslim is more than mere nostalgia. For him it is imperative to find his true self, his proper identification, his real place in this earthly existence. His faith is his history; his history is his religion. This all-embracing impact of Islam is a phenomenon which distinguishes it from all other religions and groups. This assertion is not merely platitudinous for an examination of the substantive parts of this text clearly shows the comprehensive impact of Islam on not only a Muslim, but on a community which calls itself Islamic or a nation which is of Muslim orientation.

Comparatively speaking, no other religion even claims such total impact. No political system even tries to regulate the lives of its subscribers in every department of their existence. The closest that any ideology comes to having the same type of characteristics is Marxism. On the secular plane this particular movement presents the most organized attempt to control a person's life. However, Marxism is not a religion and only deals with the secular and the mundane. There is nothing in it to supply the spiritual vaccuum. But there remains another more important and fundamental difference between the two. Marxism, over the span of nearly half a century, has consistently required and depended on force to keep it alive, to keep it going. On the psychological plane, it has done little for its adherents. Islam, on the other hand has lived through fourteen hundred years and is still a world faith despite the lack of political power for a long time. Indeed, in distress, its adherents turn to it for improving their present lot. The cosmic nature of human dignity to be found in Islam is the exact opposite in Marxism in which neither the individual nor his dignity has any doctrinal value.

The ideal of the Islamic State thus has in front of it a highly unpredictable future, but abundant enthusiasm and will. To what extent the Islamic countries can transform themselves into Islamic States will depend, it is submitted, on the outcome of various matters analyzed above. However, if history is any guide and if an intellectualized attempt and not a bigoted one is made to create a system of living, of governance, like it once possessed, the Islamic community, the Umma, can play a vital and a vigorous role in the cause of human freedom and dignity in the times we now approach.

Important Reference Bibliography

It is impossible in a text of this kind to even list the major works of reference, since there are so many of them. The two best known translations of the Quran are by A. Yusuf Ali and by Marmaduke Picthall, with the former enjoying the highest respect for accuracy and learning. The two leading compilations of the Hadith (Traditions of the Prophet) are by Bokhari and Muslim. Each of these works contains three volumes. In presenting the original conceptions the author consulted these sources. In addition to these texts in which the major sources of the Shariah and Islamic Jurisprudence are to be found, there are several monumental Commentaries on the Quran (Tafsirs). These Commentaries are not the sources; they are the interpretations of the various schools of Islamic Jurisprudence. A few well known works of such character are: Muhammad Ibn Jarir, Tabri (A Tafsir), Husain Ragib's Mufradat (a dictionary of difficult Quranic phrases and words), Abul Qasim Mahmud's Kashaf (explanations of idioms in the Quran), Fakhr-ud-din Razi's Tafsir Kabir (an analysis of the Quran from the Sufi point of view), and Jalal-ud-din Suyuti's Itqan fi ulum il Quran (a review of the Quranic Sciences).

NOTES

(Most of the bibliography cited herein is very well-known; various works have, therefore, appeared in numerous editions and have been published by many institutions. In such cases, the year of publication or the publisher's name has not been given. The year of publication or the publisher's name only appears if there is only one publisher of a work, or if it has not appeared in a number of editions.)

1. Secretary General of the United Nations, Kurt Waldheim's opinion, while calling the Security Council meeting November, 1979, to discuss the question of American hostages.

2. The White Paper published by the government of President Zia and the various judgments of superior courts of Pakistan appearing during 1978 fully underscore his point.

3. See, e.g., Chicago Sun Times, December 2, 1979, p. 36.

4. Op. cit., p.36.

5. At the moment of writing this narrative there has taken place a tragedy of grave magnitude. On November 4, 1979, a number of Iranian students stormed the United States Embassy in Tehran and took captive over 60 American hostages. The drama which has followed since then is contemporary history. It is not the purpose of this narrative to examine that controversy. However, one thing which has come out of this controversy is that both the Iranians as well as the press have played up the element of religion. One argument is that this is the result of the fanaticism of Islam. As a result of the continued detention of the hostages, those responsible have, therefore, brought a stigma on Islam. In any case, as discussed in the text, it is improper to involve religion in this matter.

6. Baladhuri, Futah al-Buldan, 471-2; Ibn Abd Rabbihi, al-Iqd al-Farid, I, 34, 41 III. 48.

7. Hamidullah, City State of Mecca, 40, 42; Ibn Hisham, Sirat 251; Ibn Sad, Tabaqat, II, 25; Ibn Khaldun, Tarikh I, 28.

8. Baladhuri, op. cit., 63, 64; Hamidullah, op. cit. 43; Ibn Khaludn, op. cit., 28-9.

9. Ibn Hisham, op. cit. (English tr.), 35 ff.; Ibn Khaldun, op. cit., 29 ff.

10. Cf. Wallullah, Hujjat Allah al-Balighah, I, 326; Hamidullah, op. cit., 24; Quran, 2:198; 9:36; Ibn Sad, I, 41; Yaqubi, Tavikh, III, 122; Ibn Hisham, op. cit., 561; Ibn Abd Rabbihi, op. cit., II, 45.

11. Islam contains much of what is believed by the Jews and Christians.

12. Mahmasani, Philosophy, 15

13. Ibn Sad, op. cit., I, 41; Ibn Abd Rabbihi, op. cit., II, 45; Yaqubi, I, 275-6; Ibn Hisham, op. cit., 72; Ibn Duraid, Kitab al-Ishtiqaq, 171-2; Arzaqi, Akhbar al-Makkah, 106-7; Quran, 7:31; This practice is still in vogue today at the time of Hajj.

14. Ibn Abi Dawud, Kitab al-Masahif, 4-5; Baladhuri, op. cit., 471; Hamidullah, Le Prophete de l-Islam, 400.

15. Ibn Abd Rabbihi, op. cit., 45-6; Ibn Sad, op. cit., II, i, 27; cf. Quran, 2: 130; 3: 45; 4: 125.

16. Ibn Hisham, op. cit., passim; Ibn Abd Rabbihi, op. cit. II, 45; Hamidullah, Ahd-i-Nabawi, 30ff.

17. Ibn Abd Rabbihi, op. cit. II, 46; Masudi, al-Tanbih wal-Ashraf, 268-80; Ibn Duraid, op. cit. 64, 145, 318. The people mentioned herein were of great significance at Islam's infancy. See generally: History of the Arabs, Hitti, McMillan, who specifically projects the Arabism in Islam.

18. Yaqubi, op. cit., I, 300; Ibn Sad, op. cit., I,i,42; Musnad by Imam Hanbal, 1, 190.

19.   Qastallani, VI, 176; Tafsir-i-Ahmadi, 57; Kashf al-Ghummah, II, 195 ff. This explains some elements of Islamic criminal law, which were originally borrowed from Jewish practice.

20.   Smith, Kinship, 116; Ibn Abd Rabbihi, op. cit., III, 290; Razi, Mafatih III, 153; Zamakhsahri, Tafsir, I, 249; Fath-ul-Quadir, III, 151. Similar was the case in other parts of the world at the time. See for details Vinogradoff, Historical Jurisprudence, I, passim; Mulla, Principles of Hindu Law, passim.

21.   Tafsir-I-Ahmadi, 130, 610; Razi, Tafsir al-Kabir, II, 357.

22.   Ibn Khaldun, Muqaddimah, I, 250, 347, 441.

23.   There are other enumerations; see the Latin version of Maracci's Refutatio Alcorani (1698); Rodwell (1861) arranges the surahs chronologically; Palmer (1880) produced a translation in the semitic tradition; Marmaduke Pickthall's (1930) translation is very successful. Richard Bell (1937-39) attempts a critical rearrangement of the verses. The earliest Arabic printing of the Quran was done between 1485 and 1499 in Venice by Alessandro de Paganini. Maraccio's work did great damage, since it was produced with the sole intention of refuting Islam in Europe.

24.   Ibn Hisham, Sirah, p. 125; Yaqubi, vol. ii, p. 18; Masudi, vol. iv, p. 127.

25.   G. Gurvitch, L'Experience Juridique, 213. Lon L. Fuller compares analytical jurisprudence with its theories of law, the State, and the sovereign to theology with its doctrine of the Trinity: The Law in Quest of Itself, 41; R. Pound, 57 Harv.L.R. (1944), 1193.

26.   Jurisprudence, Lect. VI. It is difficult to say precisely what is the smallest community which could be rightfully regarded as a state. In practice, the doctrines of international law are usually invoked to determine whether a particular society is a state or not.

27. J. Austin, Jurisprudence, i. 267.

28. For the philosophic issues that lie behind the Hegelian theory of the State, see B. Bosanquet, Philosophical Theory of State; F. Hallis, Corporate Personality, 61 et seq. But as W. Friedmann shows, Legal Theory (4th ed.), Stevens, 345, finally the Nazis turn to Nietzsche rather than Hegal.

29. F. Hallis, Corporate Personality, 68.

30. Hegel, Philosophic des Rechts, 349.

31. F. Pollock and F. W. Maitland, History of English Law, i. 160.

32. Such an approach really strengthens H. Kelsen's argument that the problem should be looked at not as a conflict between law and government, but on the basis of the postulates of the legal order.

33. Law of the Constitution (8th ed.), ch. iv.

34. W. I. Jennings, The Law and the Constitution, Appendix II.

35. Note the interesting argument of Dixon J. (as he then was) in 51 L.Q.R. (1935), 590. In English legal history mainly two conceptions have been struggling for mastery - the supremacy of the Crown symbolized in the Divine Right of Kings, and secondly, the supremacy of Parliament established by the revolution settlement.

36. See the many publications of the International Commission of Jurists, and in particular the Declaration of Delhi on the Rule of Law.

37. See e.g., Lon L. Fuller, Positivism and Fidelity to Law - A Reply to Professor Hart, 71 Harv. L.R. (1958), 630.

38. "It can be said that the state creates the law, but this means only that the law regulates its own creation": H. Kelsen, 55 Harv. L.R. (1941), 65.

39. See generally E. Bodenheimer, Jurisprudence.

40. See J. W. Salmond, Jurisprudence; in order to take this point, he argues that only a 'just war' can be regarded as an essential form of state activity. Salmond's own view is seen in the 9th ed., p. 165. This discussion does not appear in later editions. This concept of 'just' and 'unjust' war finds a parallel in the Islamic concept of 'Jihad' or what is loosely referred to as 'holy' war.

41. Cited by many authors e.g. 'Not the Whole Truth', M. R. Kiayani, Lahore, p. 48.

42. The greatest spiritual landmark against communist ideologies.

43. e. g. Maudoodi.

44. Somewhat like the framework of the U. S. Constitution.

45. This is, perhaps, a unique feature of the Islamic theory of State. The resentment of people in Iran under the Shah showed a facet of this underlying assumption.

46. The Kharijites, indeed, maintained the duty of insurrection against an impious imam, but they remained a minority outside the main stream of Sunni tradition.

47. See Sir Hamilton Gibb, views on al-Mawardi's Theory of the khilafat in Islamic Culture, XI, 3.

48. See L. Binder, al-Ghazali and Islamic Government in the Muslim World, July, 1955.

49. See A. von Kremer, Geschichte der herrschenden Ideen des Islams (Leipzig, 1868), p. 416; Gulturgeschichte des Orients (Vienna, 1875), i, 403; and G. E. von Grunebaum, Medieval Islam (Chicago, 1946), p. 169.

50. See a Bombay ed., 1923

51. Mirsad al-ibad min al-mabda ila l-maad (ed. Husayn al-Husayni an-Nimatullahi, Tehran, 1933-34), p. 256.

52. Dhakhirat ul-Muluk B.M., f. 996b.

53. The same theory was used in late 1978 to stage demonstrations against the Shah in Iran.

54. Muhammad Hussain Heykel, Al-Siddiq, Cairo, p.67.

55. Quran, 4: 58.

56. ibid., 49: 13.

57. ibid., 18: 28.

58. Quoted by Bukhari.

59. Quoted by Bukhari and Muslim.

60. Quoted by Abu Daud.

61. See Dicey, Law of the Constitution and Maitland, English Constitutional History.

62. e.g., Pakistan to-date has had three "Islamic Constitutions" and Iran one since Khomeini took over control in 1979.

63. In most Muslim countries, women are elected to the Parliament, e.g., Pakistan, Turkey. The difference between the rights of men and women pertain to the law of divorce and inheritance, particularly in the Sunni Schools of jurisprudence.

64. Pakistan is the only country, in a sense, where this problem has received extended legal attention for about twenty-five years. Iran recently, in December 1979, produced an Islamic constitution, but we have to see how it operates. Saudi Arabia and Gulf States apply more substantive civil and criminal Islamic law; however, as regards having a developed legal system, these latter states are not in the same category of countries such as Pakistan or Turkey, which possess advanced systems of administration of justice similar to the ones in Europe and North America.

270

65. Even the principles of social solidarity were not unknown to Islam for the Quran itself declares that the "believers men and women are protectors one of another". Indeed, the essence of Islam is that the whole mankind has a common purpose and each one should so conduct himself as if he were a shepherd unto the other. This, in my opinion, is the quintessence of the concept of social solidarity.

66. The preamble to the Constitution of Pakistan, 1973.

67. Bilal, originally a black slave, was one of the close associates of the Prophet and he also had the privilege of giving the call for prayers from the main mosque at Medina.

68. Bracton said, "Rex non debit esse, sub homine, sed sub Deo et lege." Before him Ulpian had said, "Quod principi placuit legis habet vigorem."

69. Quran, 24: 55

70. Quran, 2: 229.

71. Quran, 4: 59.

72. See Tibrani, also Muslim.

73. Sharh al-Sunnah: Mishkat No. 3515.

74. Quran, 33: 36.

75. ibid., 5: 44.

76. After the fall of Bhutto the government ushered in some Islamic law, 1977-80. In Iran during 1979 several Islamic laws have been enacted.

77. See M. Khadduri, Law in the Middle East (Washington, D.C., 1955), p. 27.

78. This is mainly on account of the Quran being indisputably the foremost and the only source of guidance.

79. See Shah Walliullah, op. cit., I, 215-26, 303 ff.

80. Cf. Quran, 5:46-50; 7:172.

81. Cf. Sherwani, Studies in Muslim Political Thought and Administration, 22 ff; Ibn Khaldun, Muqaddimah.

82. Cf. Surah Al-i-Imran verses 137-141.

83. See Waliullah, op. cit., I, 215-325; Quran, 112: 1-4.

84. See Ibn Manzur, Lisan al-Arab, XV, 184 ff.; Zabidi, Taj al-Urus, VII, 337: Firuzabadi, Qamusal-Huhit, IV, 129.

85. Cf. Quran, 3: 110, which says: "Ye are the best of peoples, evolved for mankind, enjoining what is right, forbidding what is wrong, and believing in God . . . "

86. See A. Yusuf Ali, Commentary on the Quran, I, n. 434, II, nn. 4547, 4937.

87. For more details, the reader should consult Razi, Tafsir al-Kabir; works of Suyuti, Tafsir al-Abdul Qadir, Tafsir Muwadih-ul-Quran; Naimuddin, Khasain al-Quran; Baidawi, Answear-ut-Tanzil; Abdul Haqq, Tafsir Haqqani.

88. See Quran, 2:177, Miskhat, I, i, 5-16.

89. On concrete provisions, see the Quran, 2:216; 4:59 (peace and obedience); 2:283; 4:58; 5:8, 24:4 (law and justice); 2: 5; 22:27; 33:72; 59:24; 60:12 (social reform and counsel); 2:256; 2:118; 5:82; 7:86; 14:115; 20:44 (toleration); 2:194; 4:74; 6:65; 6:166; 8:62; 2:1-12; 2:123; 17:21; 17:39; 47:5; 47:139; 49:13; 60:8 (international principles).

90. See general comments on Sadrat-ush-Shariah, by Taftaza Talwih. As opposed to the intellectual (aqliyyah) sciences which are acquired through the exercise of intellect or perception, the general science of ulum mudawwanah, and the traditional (naqliyyah) sciences are acquired by way of tradition. Traditional sciences (also historical sciences) are generally the instrumental (aliyyah or lisaniyyah) basis of the Shariah sciences. These

Shariah sciences are called, firstly, asliyyah when they relate to the reading of the Quran, or its interpretation (Tafsir) and Hadith (Traditions). Secondly, the Shariah science is called mustanbatah or deduced when it is comprised of dogmatics or itiqadiyyah, i.e., the science of unity and attributes of God; thirdly, it is called amaliyyah or fiqh science when it is practical as opposed to merely academic, i.e., the self knowledge of what is to one's advantage and what is to one's disadvantage in matters of conduct (amaliyyah), or belief (i'tiqadiyyah) and transactions (muamalat).

Though the scope and operation of the science of self's knowledge or Ilm-ul-Fiqh originally included all the sciences in the Shariah, later its meaning was restricted only to practical matters and problems. Nevertheless, the science of Fiqh still contains a wide area of operation and thus, primarily, its main divisions are Tahdhib-ul-Akhlaq, Tadbir-ul-Manzil and Siyasat-ul-Mudun. The branch Tahdhib-ul-Akhlaq is related to Ibadat (the Creator), to oneself and piety (Taqwa), and to humanity in general (Ibad). The branches Tadbir-ul-Mauzil and Siyasat-i-Mudun relate to Munakihat (marriages), Muamalat (transactions), Hudud and Tazirat (penal matters), Janayat (torts), Siyar (international relations), Ahkam-i-Sultaniyyah (administration), Adab al-Qadi (procedure and practice in judicial matters), qada (justice) and other relations contemplated in law and jurisprudence.

91. For authorities, see the Quran, 4: 79-80; 15: 9; 59: 7; and for their discussion of what is Shariah, see Mulla Jiwan, Ntir-ul-Anwur, 3, 4, 383.

92. See "Al-Fiqh fi al-Quran, Voice of Islam, SVI, No. 4, 293-305 (reproduced in the Islamic Literature, XIV, no. 27-39).

93. No other system of law has such categories of what is legally allowed.

94. Man has been termed Ashraf-ul-Makhluqat. The Quran says: "Lo! I am about to place a viceroy (i.e. Adam) in the earth" (2:30). It may be reminded that the conception of Din in Islam is not entirely a private affair between man and God. Though the privacy is there, it

never means to establish any kind of sanctity in a man or a class of men. The individual is ruled by the Shariah which is binding on all mankind.

95. Echo of Greek philosophy--particularly Aristotle.

96. For modern expositions of similar ideas, see the writings of Kant.

97. Article I of Majallah, 1877.

98. For this reason there are many fundamental laws in Islam dealing with economic matters. These laws, indirectly, also deal with some aspects of human rights.

99. For the Shariah discussions, see Hifz-ur-Rahman, Islam ka Iqtisadi Nizam; Ibd Hazm, Mahalla, VI, 158, 725. Social Security and Monopoly Control Laws have only recently been made in the Western Countries, a striking example of the vision in Shariah.

100. For details, see an-Nasafi, al-Manar, I, 87; Ibn Kathir, Tafsir, I, 203; Waliullah, op. cit., II, 202; Bukhari, Sahih; Mishkat.

101. One of the basic landmarks against communism, where the individual has no place.

102. On the question of relationship, the individual and the society, compare Maine's famous statement that law has moved from status to contract and the current trend of a movement back from contract to status.

103. On the theory of covenant: Mithaq-i-azali, also Taftazani.

104. See Hidayah; Kitab-ul-Qadi.

105. This position contrasts fundamentally with the common law notion of 'legal personality' granted by law to "units" recognized by law as having rights and duties. See F. Hallis, "Corporate Personality; Duff, Personality in Roman Private Law, and Hart, 5 & 6 Aust. Jour. of Pol. History, 246.

106. See e.g., W. Friedman, Legal Theory, in which classical views of Aristotle, Hegel, Kant and modern jurists are discussed.

107. See Friedmann, supra, chapter XXVII; Pound in 57 Harv. L.R., 1193; generally see Sieghart, Government by Decree.

108. See Mawardi, op. cit.,; Ghazali, Ihya Ulum-al-Din; Farabi, Madinat-ul-Fadilah. Iba Khaldun, Muqaddimah; Tusi, Siyasat Namah and Dastur-ul-Wuzara.

109. The concept of "Natural Law" has had a variable content. In the domain of philosophy and political science it has no settled meaning. The Greeks, Romans, Christian missionaries, medieval thinkers of the 17th century, and even modern theories judged it with limitations of national, religious, or regional and racial fervor.

110. For more details, see Bukhari, and Muslim.

111. See Muslim.

112. The U.N. Declaration of Human Rights, 1948, has no such provision, although technically it is not a "fundamental right."

113. Ibn Taimiyyah is explicit with other jurists; see on the point, Laoust, Essai sur les doctrine Sociales et Politiques de Taki-d-Din Ahmad b. Taimiya (1939), 407; Abu Yusuf, op. cit., 34.

114. See Abu Zahrah, Hanifa, 350. Historically, only the school of law based on the philosphy of Hegel even admits of this sociological or anthropological phenomenon, but still does not grant an authority to a jurist to trace law by this method.

115. For historical cases of justice and equality, see A. Qadri, Justice in Historical Islam.

116. For details, see Mawardi, op. cit. and Chapter IV.

117. It remains to be seen how the courts in Pakistan or Iran will deal with such matters in the future in view of the contemporary religious fervor in these lands.

118.   Analogous to the modern notion of a referendum.

119.   (Von Grunebaum, Islam: Essays in the Nature and Growth of a Cultural Tradition, p. 20)

120.   S. Hurgronje: Mohammadanism, p. 44.

121.   Countries like Egypt, Libya, Syria or Iraq are omitted since the points which the author wishes to raise can be discerned through an examination of the three countries selected. In a later discussion references will be made, generally, to some other Islamic states; Iran is omitted here since reference has been made to the events therein at several places in this book.

122.   Also exemplified by the present struggle between President Bani Sadr and the orthodox clergy in Iran. Very often this orthodox clergy has little else to offer except dogma and a bigoted picture of Islam. They realize that the illiterate population very seldom, if at all, question what in fact is Islamic.

123.   The constitutional status of India was, however, different from the other three countries mentioned here which were, legally speaking, Dominions. As a mere "possession," India was not self-governing.

124.   Sir Mohammed Iqbal, The Reconstruction of Religious Thought in Islam, 1944 Edition, Lahore, p. 159.

125.   In 1971, East Pakistan, as a result of a civil war and an attack by Indian Armed Forces, became Bangladesh.

126.   With, perhaps, the exception of the present government headed by General Zia, which has introduced certain Islamic measures, like Zakat, in the country.

127.   At times e.g. at the passing of the 1956 Constitution, it was the government in power which used the name of religion to quiet the discontent, or to confuse the important political controversies of the day by putting up an Islamic facade for its actions.

128. The so-called "Munir Report," 1954. The issue of Qadianis was finally settled, nevertheless, a quarter of a century later, when the Bhutto government declared in accordance with the wishes of the majority--the Quadianis as non-Muslims.

129. The two concrete political effects were 1) the introduction of martial law in the political scene of Pakistan and 2) the fall of the civilian government in the province of Punjab.

130. Private land would directly come from the rich, who also had a controlling share in the industrial sector: excess means the maximum allowed to be kept in private ownership.

131. Along with the local Mullahs (who were physically on the streets), the legal community played a decisive role in maintaining the continuity of the movement against Bhutto.

133. See generally W. C. Smith, Islam in Modern History, Mentor Books, 1957.

134. In the Austinian sense.

135. The Khilafat movement is particularly astonishing for non-muslims for it is not easy to comprehend the desires, e.g., of an Indian Muslim for Pan-Islamic values and glory.

136. For example, the present Article 4 of the Turkish Constitution is contrary to the undisputed Islamic theory of sovereignty; it reads Sovereignty: Article 4 - Sovereignty is vested in the Turkish Nation without reservation and condition."

137. Throughout 1979-80, Turkey has been almost continuously in a state of domestic terrorism. To subdue some dissent, the right wing government of Demeril granted some "concessions" to the so-called Islamic fundamentalists. In this unrest, since January, 1980, an average of ten persons have been killed every day.

138. Afghanistan had maintained off and on that the boundary between Pakistan and Afghanistan, formerly

between Afghanistan and British India drawn by the British, was arbitrary and without regard to the ethnic nature of the people who lived there. It was contended on many occasions that some of the tribes which lived in the northwest of Pakistan, like the Pathans, were basically of the same ethnic type as those living in Afghanistan; therefore, the land where they lived should have been given to Afghanistan when the boundary was drawn by the British. However, the same argument could have been used by Pakistan, although it has not been used, that the territory on which Pathan tribes live in Afghanistan should have come to the south within Pakistan rather than to have remained within Afghanistan.

139. Thus in the last few years the institution of monarchy has ended in two important Muslim states, Afghanistan and Iran.

140. As a country, Afghanistan has few cities; most people live in its rugged countryside and invariably belong to one of the several tribes.

141. Five out of fifteen republics in the Soviet Union are Muslims, i.e., one-third. In terms of population, Muslims constitute about one-fourth of the Russian population.

142. See particularly Y. G. Wheeler, Racial Problems in Soviet Muslim Asia, 1973 Oxford University Press.

143. Christian Science Monitor, December 28, 1979, p. 5. It is ironical since this becomes a threat to the Communist Party which, under Tito, has allowed the Muslims an environment of relative liberty.

144. In the wake of the Afghanistan-Iran crisis, note the description by President Carter of the Persian Gulf as constituting America's vital interest area.

145. An important consequence of Egypt-Israeli accord, the Camp David Agreement, 1978, was the isolation of Egypt by, particularly, the Arab countries, including a state like Saudi Arabia. See e.g. Strategic Survey, 1979, 80, London.

146. "Considered" for this is how America is generally perceived, but their perceptions are incorrect since, apart from the various aspects of the American foreign policy discussed here, the U. S. has always extended a friendly hand to the Islamic peoples.

147. His statement before the Supreme Court of Pakistan, 1979.

148. However, in the last one hundred years, the work of the Christian missionaries has been very successful. In terms of population, the ratio between Muslims and Christians could be 58% to 42% for the entire continent.

149. And also for propaganda purposes in the United States.

150. In the south of the Phillippines.

151. e.g., Amnesty.

152. e.g., Conference of Islamic Foreign Ministers.

153. The latest being in July-August, 1980, leading to the imposition of curfew and emergency proclaimed by the government of Indira Ghandi in several cities e.g., Muradabad, Delhi, etc.

154. See the excellent analysis of Wilfred Cantwell Smith about the Indian Muslim in his leading book, Islam: In Modern History, Mentor Books.

155. Pakistan and Libya have been examining this matter through officially approved commissions of experts in 1978-79.

156. See generally Buckland, Roman Law, and Gibbon, Decline and Fall of the Roman Empire.

157. Cf. Quran, 87: 14; "He is successful who groweth."

158. For detailed explanations, see Hidayah, I, 1-70; II, 222, 329; Minhaj, 80 f.; Fatawa-i-Kubra, II, 32; Mawardi, op. cit., 192 f.

159.   Cf. Farishta G. de Zayas, The Law and Philosophy of Zakat (Damascus, 1960), I, 4 f.; Aghnides, Mohammedan Theories of Finance, Pt. II, 203, 207 ff.

160.   Reference be made for details to Hidayah; also Shafi, Mawardi, op. cit.; The supremacy of spiritual values over man's property and possession is the most precise criterion of purity and for this reason Zakat has been linked with prayer in eighty-two injunctions of the Quran. See Yusuf, op. cit.

161.   See the present author's article on this point in Law and Society's East-West Center, Honolulu, Hawaii, 1977, p. 23.

162.   Begging for alms was strongly deprecated by Prophet Mohammad.

163.   Likewise, the teaching of Islam prohibits a person from spending extravagantly, the prodigals being prevented by Islamic law from frittering away their wealth.

164.   Last sermon.

165.   The confiscation by the Second Caliph Omar of lands held idle by Bilal, and of half the property of those governors of the Provinces who were making unlawful use of their official position are cases in point.

166.   The law of primogeniture prevailing in some other contemporary societies contrasts drastically with the Islamic system.

167.   Old age pensions were also granted to old Christian and Jewish citizens from the Baitul-Mal, who were exempt from payment of any tax.

168.   Futuhal-Buldan by Baladhuri p. 456.

169.   Ibid. p. 456.

170.   Ibid. p. 457.

171.   Zakat being part of a whole system, can only be fully effective when combined, for instance, with a non-interest

banking system. See also, Shareef Al-Mujahid Muslim Finance: Islamic Review, August, 1953. In Pakistan, since July, 1977, General Zia has specially instructed a council to examine the possibility of implementing the Zakat system in place of Income Tax; it was, in fact, implemented partly though not as a substitute for income tax, in June, 1980.

172. This example and argument has been utilized by several writers on land tenure, kharaj and ushr. Also see: Abdul-Fadl, Aen-i-Akbari, ii, Calcutta, 1872, p. 293 and other books cited therein. See Imam Abu Yusuf, Kitab-ul-kharaj, Cairo, 1302 A.H., pp. 35-38.

173. See Moreland, The Agrarian System of Muslim India; Cambridge, 1929, p. 56 et. seq.

174. See Bukhari (Mujtabai Press, Delhi, ed.) Vol. I, pp. 313-315, for the background of the material discussed above.

175. Compare the famous Permanent Settlement of Bengal in 1793. Thornton, History of British India, ii, London, 1842, p. 524. It was against government interest to have non-utilized land . . . Ibid. Thornton says "...it is certain that the Permanent Settlement of Lord Cornwallis was concluded under the influence of an extraordinary degree of ignorance." For a fuller discussion of the topic, see the Revenue Appendix to the Report of the Committee of the House of Commons, 1832, minutes by Marquis of Hastings.

176. Also see Chapters VI and X.

177. See Margin of Tafsir Jalalyn, Vol. I, p. 70, Egyptian Edn.

178. Analogous to the doctrine of intervention on humanitarian grounds in modern international law.

179. It is, therefore, possible for the Muslim States to combine to oppose the Russian invasion of Afghanistan of 1980.

180.   For the sake of Islam, the author wishes that these verses had guided the present regime in Iran.

181.   In light of such verses, trials and punishments in a summary fashion are totally un-Islamic.

182.   In this sense, it is analogous to the right of self-defense of modern international law, contained in Art. 51 of the U.N. Charter.

183.   Perhaps the juridical genesis of modern laws of war and of humanitarian law, e.g., Geneva Conventions of 1949 and their modern improvements.

184.   See Ameer Ali, Spirit of Islam p. 85.

185.   Quran 2: 190, 192.

186.   Quran 8: 39.

187.   Quran 22: 39, 40.

188.   Quran 4: 75.

189.   Quran 2: 256.

190.   Quran 10: 100.

191.   T. Ibn Taymiyyah, al-Siyasat al-Sharaiyyah, 3rd ed., Cairo, (1955) pp. 123-4.

192.   Rashid Ridha, Tafsir al-manar, 1st ed. Cairo, 1346 A.H. (1927).

193.   Published in Cairo, 1349 A.H. (1930).

194.   Published in Cairo, 1343 A.H. (1924).

195.   M. Abduhu refers to the statement made to his effect by Gostave le Bon (1841-1931).

196.   Rashid Ridha, op. cit. pp. 215-16.

197.   Mohammad Bash al-Makhzoomi, Khairat al Saiyyed Jamal al-Din al-Afghani al-Husaini, pp. 147-54, Beirut (1931)

198.   Makhzoomi, op. cit., pp. 155-61.

199.   Ali Abd al-Raziq, al-Islam Wa Usul al-Hukm, 2nd ed. Cairo, 1925, ch. 3 pp. 64-80.

200.   Khadduri, War and Peace in the Law of Islam,Baltimore, 1955, pp. 65-6.

201.   Siraj al-muluk, pp. 150-153, cited by Khadduri, op. cit. p. 70.

202.   Hasan ibn Abd Allah, Athar al-uwal Fi Tartib al-Duwal, pp. 167-8, cited by Khadduri, op. cit., p. 70; For Ibn Khaldun's view see his al-Muqaddimah, Cairo, 1311 (1892) ch. 38, pp. 160-1.

203.   Quran 4: 80.

204.   Quran 10: 109.

205.   Quran 41: 48.

206.   Quran 50: 45.

207.   Quran 88: 21-22.

208.   Abu Yosuf, Al-Rad Ala Siyar al-Awzaai, Cairo, IV, pp. 34-40.

209.   Gentilies. De Jure Billi, 1588.

210.   See Khadduri, op. cit., pp. 275-6. Important Islamic treatises on international law appeared at least 800 years before Grotius wrote.

211.   See Woolsey, International Law, 4th ed., New York, 1889.

212.   Whereas benches were common in the furniture of Europe following the Byzantine traditions, the sofa-like chair came from the Muslims.

213.   Similar to the practice of Justinian, when he compiled the Corpus Juris of the Roman Law in the Sixth Century A.D.

214. Also see: The Black Muslims in America, E. Lincoln, 1970, Chicago.

215. W. Wilson Cash, Christendom and Islam, New York and London, 1937.

216. C. Snouck Hurgronje: Mohammadanism, New York and London, 1916.

217. L. Bevan Jones, The People of the Mosque, London, 1932; Kenneth Cragg, The Christian and Islam, Mimeographed 1957

218. L. Beven Jones, op. cit.

219. A. J. Wensinck, The Muslim Creed, Cambridge, 1932.

220. The East India Company got its initial foothold in South India (along with the French).

221. For a brief period in the nineteenth century they controlled its foreign policy.

222. G. A. Res. ES/6/2, January 14, 1980.

223. Official Iraqi papers condemned Russian invasion; only Syria, because of its total dependence on the U.S.S.R. in its confrontation with Israel, has been silent.

See note on Transliteration p. IV. as such, several words of Arabic origin may not always follow consistent English alphabetical construction. The reader may, therefore, find the same word spelled differently at different places.

Abbasids, 221
Abdullah b. Umar, 116
Abdullah b. Uthman, 23
Abode of Islam, 206;
  see Dar al-Islam
Abode of Peace, 193, 197;
  see Dar-As-Salam
Abode of War, 206;
  see Dar-al-Harb
Abraham, 100, 232
Abrahamic religions, 225
Abu Bakr, 23, 28, 35, 121,
  195, 203
Abu Hanifa, 39, 119
Abu-Talib, 27
Abu Yusuf, 54, 91;
  see Gibb
Adam, 242
Adam and Eve, 246
Adam Harj, 102
Adelard of Bath, 213
Adil, 102
Adilat al-Shariah, 101;
  see also Quran, Sunnah,
  Ijma, or Qiyas
Adl, 53
Administration and Justice,
  in Arabian Tribal
  Society: generally, 22-
  25; language, 23; admin-
  istration in Mecca, 23;
  law, the Hakam, 24;
  punishment of tribe as
  a whole, 24; family
  structure, 24; female
  status, 25; pride, 26;
  attitude difference
  between Islam and other
  religions, 26; Funda-

mental source of Islamic
  law, Quran, 26
Admiral's title, 220
Afghan: border, 158;
  crisis, 155, 259;
  monarchy, 254; refugees,
  154; tribesman, 153
Afghanistan: generally,
  152-156; historical
  review, 153; Daud and
  the monarchial system,
  153; civil war origins,
  154; Soviet invasion,
  154-155
Afghanistan-Pakistan
  controversy, 261
Africa, 84, 132, 165, 166,
  241, 259, 260
African peoples, 165
African population, 88
Aggressive war prohibited,
  231
Ahkam, 101, 121, 124
Ahl al-hal waal-aqd, 75
Ajami, 20
Ajamiyyah, 24
A. J. Wensinck, 246
al-Azhar, 207
Albania, 61, 131
alchemy, 220
Alexandria, 19
al-Farabi, 221
Algeria, 61, 77, 131, 165
al-Hakim, 124
al-Hasan ibn Abd Allah, 209
Ali, 28, 35, 104
Ali Abd Al-Raziq, 208; see
  al-Islam Wa Usul al
  Hukm

Al-Islam wa al-Nasraniyyah
  Maa al-ilm wa al
  madaniyyah, 207
al-Islam Wa Usul al Hukum,
  208; see also Ali Abd
  Al-Raziq
al-Kindi, 221; see Muslim
  Scholar
Allah, 21, 38, 56, 57,
  72, 74, 97, 117, 169,
  170, 174, 194, 195,
  196, 197, 198, 199,
  200, 201, 202, 205,
  225, 226, 229, 230,
  231, 232, 233, 234,
  235, 242
Allies, 146
All Powerful Sovereign,
  99; see God
al-Mamun, 221
Almighty, 96, 99, 169;
  see Allah
Almighty Allah, 69
Almighty God, 200
Almighty Lord, 226
al Sirat-ul-Mustaqim, 100
Al-Turtushi, 209
al-Uzza, 21
Ameer Ali, 194; see
  Spirit of Islam
America, 163
American, 258; Bill of
  Rights, 69, Declaration
  of Independence of 1776,
  114; Embassy, 258; for-
  eign policy, 163, 165;
  hostages, 164, 194;
  President, 56
Americas, 84
Amir, 47, 48, 55
Amnesty International,
  11, 12
Amwal-ul-Mahajjarah, 23
Angola, 256
Ansari, 41

Antioch, 19
Anwar Sadat, 141, 166
Apostle of God, 242
Arab: Caliphate, 216;
  country, 144; heritage,
  83; Israeli Conflict, 164,
  258; League, 261; nations,
  163; states, 256
Arabia, 2, 19, 22, 200
Arabian: economic system,
  22; ocean, 253; nights,
  218, taxation system,
  22; tribal system, 21
Arabic, 5, 213, 214, 215,
  216, 218, 219, 220;
  alphabet, 149; literary
  forms, 215; models, 218;
  numerals, 219; poems, 218;
  poetry, 214; writers, 127,
  216, 218; works, 213
Arabism, 38
Arabs, 19, 20, 22, 25, 145,
  163, 165, 201, 208,
Arabs at the Jahiliyyah,
  the time of ignorance, 19
Arafat, 70
Aristotle, 113, 218, 221
Aristotelian Philosophy,
  218
Arthur Jeffrey, 246
Asia, 84, 85
Asian Countries, 237;
  population, 87
Aslama, 96
Attaby quarter of Bagdad, 220
Aucassin et Nicolete, 218
Aushirwan the Great, 19
Averrhoes, 213, 218
Aus, 82
Austin, 29, 30
Austinian: school, 31;
  sense, 80; tradition, 44
Australia, 132, 165
Avars, 19
Avicenna, 214, 222; see

also Ibn Sina
Ayatollah Khomeini, 9, 11,
14, 15, 16, 154, 156,
159, 166; see Khomeini
Ayatollah Shriat Madari,
261
Azerbaijan Province, 255,
261

Babrak Karmal, 255
Babur, 146
Baghdad, 221
Bahrain, 61, 131
Baitul-Mal, 48, 184
Balkanizing, 257
Bangladesh, 61, 131, 167,
259, 261; see East
Pakistan
Bangladesh Crisis of 1971,
141
Baluch insurgency, 261
Bani Ismail, 21
Bani Israil, 105
Bani Sadr, 12, 13
Baqarah (177), 105
Bar Association of
Pakistan, 55
Bashkiria, 158
Batan, 20
Belgian review "la Nouvelle
Ciio" (Bruxelles, 1952-
IV, pp. 171-198), 176
Bengali Origin, 167
Bentham, 29
Bhutto, 10, 14, 15, 55,
140, 141, 142, 142,
145, 160
Bible, 219, 244; see Injil
Bilal, 175
Bokhara, 156, 222
Bokhari, 37, 203; (Sahih,
I 34), 97; see Bukhari
Book, 21, 241
Book of God, 74, 138, 199
Book of Islam, 231

Bracton, 31, 71
Britain, 213
British, 10, 253; Consti-
tutional Law, 47; Govern-
ment, 132, 135; Imperial-
ism, 133; Monarch, 56;
Parliament, 135; Posses-
sions, 132; Prime Minister,
56
Bukhari, 94, 174, 194, 236;
see Bokhari
Bulgaria, 159, 223
Bulgars, 19
Burma, 61
Byzantine: architecture,
214; navy, 212; scholars,
221; silks, 215
Byzantines, 202, 214
Byzantium, 146, 212, 223
Byzantium Empire, 147, 212;
see Roman Empire

C. S. Hurgronje, 243
Cabinet in England, 51
Caesarea, 19
Cain and Abel, 246
Cairo, 215, 217
Caliph, 28, 35, 44, 56,
67, 72, 221
caliphate, 52, 53, 120, 176
Caliph of the Ottoman
Empire, 147
Caliph Omar, 175, 240
Cameroon, 61
Camp David Accord, 261;
formula of 1978; 252
Canada, 132
Canon Law, 84
capitalism, 49
Carter administration, 258
Catholic, beliefs, 150;
Church, 218
Central: Asia, 83, 146;
African Empire, 61;
Intelligence Agency, 14;

Baitul-Mal, 48, see
Legislative Assembly,
48; Treasury, 48
Chad, 61, 131
Chancellor, 110
China, 131, 158, 256
Chinese: Government, 159;
Islam, 85; Muslims, 158
Christendom, 243
Christian, 97, 211, 233;
belief of automatic
salvation, 83; bishop,
213; calendar, 52;
community, 84, 88; Duth
regime, 241; era, 35;
faith, 20, 79; nations,
210; princes, 210;
students, 243; thinkers,
219; theology, 244;
world, 238
Christianity, 1, 25, 79,
83, 88, 128, 133, 211,
230, 237, 243, 245
Christians of Abyssinia,
244
Christians of the Middle
Ages, 219
Church of Holy Sepulchre,
240
Classical Greek learning,
221
Code: Familiale Ottomane,
77; Morand, 77; Qudri
Pasha, 77; Santillana, 77
Colonel Mohammar Gaddafi,
260
Commandments, 229
Common Law, 68, 222
Communism, 49, 50, 154,
252
Communist: Block, 257;
China, 158; East, 262;
Ideology, 260; Party 153
Communist World - effect
of Islam: generally
156-161; disfavor of

Islam among Soviet rulers,
157; irreconcilable nat-
ure of Islam and commu-
nism, 157; Muslim
Clergy, 157; Communist
China, 158; Yugoslavia,
159; Bulgaria, 159
Community: generally, 83-
92; Umma, 83, ties by
religion, 83; Germanic
tribes, 83; reconstitu-
tion of Europe, 84;
Muslim self-identifi-
cation, 84; Turks and
the Turkish nation, 89;
Development of Western-
Christian countries, 90;
unity among individuals,
90; supremacy of Umma,
91; consistency of
Muslim thinking in the
area, 91
Companions, 101
Conference of Islamic
Foreign Ministers, 257
Constantine the African,
214
Constituent Assembly, 135
Constituent Assembly in
Karachi, 137
Constitution: generally,
58-70; birth of Pakistan,
59; statutes, 60;
countries which could
develop constitutions,
61; Quran, 61; Lack of
dichotomy of church
and state, 62; sovereignty
of God alone, 63;
equality of mankind,
63; method of
deliberation, 64; rights
as to inheritances, 64;
freedom to profess any
faith, 64; mutual
rights of men and

women, 64; independence
of judiciary, 65; modern
welfare state, 65; family
life, 65; treaties and
covenants, 65; wealth in
the hands of few, 66;
Sunnah, 67; precedents
of Khulf-a-Rashdin, 67;
rulings of great jurists,
68; despotism, 69; Sermon
of Prophet at Arafat, 70
Constitution of United
States of America, 59
Constitution of USSR, 255
Constitution of Iran, 73
Constitution of Pakistan:
generally, 138-140;
sovereignty as vesting
in God, 138; directives
of public policy, 139
Corinthians, 247
Coronation Charter of
Henry I, 59
Corpus Juris of Justinian,
19
Craftsman Covenant, 177;
see also Belgian Review
Creator, 96, 101, 199, 226,
228, 229, 247
Creator of the Universe,
245
Crime, 44
Crimean War, 253
Crucifixion, 244
Crusader at the Court of
Boulogne, 215, 216
Crusader states, 215
Crusaders, 216
Crusades, 146
Cuban missile crisis, 255
Cuban troups, 256
Czar Nicholas, 253
Czarist Russia, 253
Czechoslovakia, 255

Dahomey, 61, 131

Damascus, 19
Dante, 218
Daoud regime, 254, 255
Dar-al-Harb, 206; see
abode of war
Dar al-Islam, 206; see
abode of Islam
Dam-As-Salam, 197; see
Abode of peace
Dark Ages, 1, 222
Dar-un-Nadway, 23
David, 203
Day of Reckoning, 70
Declaration of Human
Rights, Article 3, 117
Devlin, 44
Dhimmis, 45, 46, 49
Dicey, 32, 51
Dician Notion of Omni-
potence, 70
Din, 102
Din qayyim, 97
Dissolution of Muslim
Marriages Act of 1939,
77
Divine: Creation, 230;
Mercy, 231; name of
Allah, 233; Plan of
life, 225; Revelation, 2
Divinity of Christ, 243
Diyat, 23
Door of Ijtihad, 77
Dutch Islamist, 243; see
also C.S. Hurgronje

East, 146, 214, 215, 216,
217
East Pakistan, 137, 167;
see Bangladesh
Eastern Europe, 240
Eastern Roman Provinces,
178
Ecclesiastical authorities,
46
Economic Structure: gen-
erally, 169-191; Quran

as guide for, 169;
Social Order influence,
170; necessities of life
assured, 170; interest,
171; taxation, Zakat,
172; concentration of
wealth in a few individ-
uals disallowed, 172;
free enterprise, 172;
women as an economic
entity, 173; hoarding,
173; dispersal of wealth,
174; profiteering, 174;
employee treatment, 174;
slavery and wages, 174;
private property, 174;
acquisition of private
property, 175; national-
ization of land, 175;
position of labor and
workmen, 176, Futuwwa
craftsmen covenant, 177;
Zakat, the principal
tax, 178-185; Zakat as
an obligatory social
tax, 179; tax as a duty,
wajib, 179; year of pos-
session of property
(Haul-ul haul), 180;
Zakat placed in Public
Treasury, 180; Zakat
as giving poor a quasi-
right in wealth of others,
181; stress on earned
livelihood, 182;
connection of Zakat to
religion, elimination
of hoarding, 183; inher-
itances, 183; interest-
free loans, 183; histor-
ical review of economic
system, 184-185; agri-
culture and land tenure
system, 185-186; prac-
tice of letting, 187-
189; safeguarding of
productive agriculture,
190; state intervention
to safeguard production,
190

Egypt, 61, 77, 80, 95,
131, 147, 166, 217,
256, 261
Egyptian Islam, 85
Egyptians, 20, 22
elements of state, 34
Emirates (UAE), 61
Emperor Akbar, 133
Emperor Fredrick II of
Hohenstaufen, 214
Emperor of Iran, 10
Emperor of the two
Religions, 213
England, 68, 110, 112
134, 147
English Architect, 217
Ephesians (2:13), 246
equality, 41
Equity, 222
Eternal and Supreme
Being, 245
Eternal God, 247
Eternal Law, the evolu-
tion of: generally,
123-129; the role of
Ijtihad, the exercise
of judgment, 123-129;
fiqh, science of dis-
covering the legal
system, 124; juris-
prudence, 125; Nass,
basic principle of
legislation, 125; Ijtihad
and the Nass, 125-126;
comparison with Western
Christian nations, 127;
necessity of Ijtihad,
129
Eternal Light, 230
Eternal Truth, 247
Ethiopia, 61, 131, 256
Europe, 94, 215, 217, 218,

240, 255

European: architects, 217; Christian States, 88; carpetmaking, 217; Community, 252; Continent, 29; coutries, 211; literature, 215, 218; mathematics, 219; missionaries, 237; reconstitution thereof, 83; romantic literature, 217; states, 210; stitch work, 217

Evolver, 199; see Allah

Existence of God, 246

Expansionism, 252

Faculty of Theology, 151

Fagahi, 73, 261

faith, 218, 222

family structure, Arabs, 24

Fard, 102; see Wajib

Fardh al-Kifayah, 206

Fascist, 31

Fashioner, 226

Father, 244

Fatwa, 44

Faizieh, Madresa, 14

feudalism, 35

Field Marshall Mohammed Ayub, 140, 141

Fiji, 61

Fiqh, 2, 75, 101, 124, 179

fitnah, 205

Flood, 246

France, 147, 212, 216

Francis I, 210

Fraternity, 40

Fredrick's family 215

French: architecture, 214; President, 56; Revolution, 35, 114

Fughani, 230

Fuller, 44

Fundamentalists, 39

Galin, 214

General Mohammed Zia, 142, 142, 144; see President Zia

Gerard of Cremona, 213

Gerbert of Aurillac, 212; see Pope Sylvester II

Germanic race, 212

Germanic peoples, 83

Germanic tribes, 83

Germany, 10

Guinea, 166

Ghazali, 52

Gazwah of Hunain, 210

Gheznevi tribe 146

Gibb, 91

God, 2, 4, 27, 28, 35, 41, 44, 45, 54, 55, 63, 83, 96, 98, 100, 109, 111, 112, 113, 124, 154, 170, 181, 182, 194, 198, 206, 207, 209, 219, 226, 229, 234, 241, 244, 245, 246, 247; see Allah

God Almighty, 43

Godless Society, 238

Goliath, 203

G. Sale, 243

Gospels, 243, 244

Gospels of Christ, 244

Gothic Buildings, 217

Governor of Yemen, 38

Great Britain, 59

Great Messengers, 50

Greece, 90, 211

Greeks, 221, 222; of Byzantium, 218

Greek, 20; learning, 219; logic, 221; mathematics, 221; medicine, 221; philosphers, 218; science, 221; theory, 216

Grotius, 114, 202, 210

Gulf region, 259
Gulf states, 261
Gundisalvus, 213

Hadith, 36, 125, 127, 193,
    203, 235
Hadith Abu Daud,
    203
Hadith of Tirmidhi (12:4),
    173
hafiz, 27
Hafiz-Ullah Amin, 155,
    254
Haqin, 24
Hajj, 21, 22, 96, 152;
    see pilgrimage
Hakam, 24
Hakim, 101; see also
    Supreme Sovereign
Hambal, 39
Hanafite School, 77
Haram, 103, 119
H.A.R. Gibb, 243
Harim, 22
Harun al-Rashid, 91; see
    also Gibb
Hart, 44. 111, 122
Haul-ul-haul, 180
Head of State, 63
Head of the Islamic State,
    43, 56
Hebrew, 27
Hegel, 29, 66
Hegelianism, 31
Hidayah, 100
High Court at Lahore, 74,
    144
Hijadah, 23
Hijra, 38, 193, 194
Hijrat, 40, 52
hikmah, 98
Himalayan Mountains, 253
Hindu, caste system, 241
Hindu community, 133
Hinduism, 133, 234
Hindu Kush, 253

Hippocrites, 214
Hirah, 22
His Messenger, 74
Hitti, 26, 222
Hobbes, 113
Hoire et Blanchefleur, 217
Holy Book, 62, 193; Ghost,
    244; Prophet--last
    sermon, 174; War, 247
hostages, 194
Hudud, 65
Hukam, 101; see Ahkam
Humanity, 227, 234
Human Rights: generally,
    114, 115; Magna Carta,
    114; Petition of Rights
    of 1628, 114; Bill of
    Rights of 1689, 114;
    Virginian Declaration
    of Human Rights, 114;
    United Nations Univer-
    sal Declaration of
    Human Rights, 114;
    American Declaration of
    Independence, 114; pro-
    tection of, 116; com-
    parison of Islamic and
    Universal Declaration of
    Human Rights, 117;
    justicibility of, 142
Humphrey of Toron, 216
Huquq Allah, 101; see
    Ibdat
Huquq-ul-ibad, 101
Husayn Vaiz, 57
Husn, 96
Hydrabad, 142

Ibddat, 101; see Huquq
    Allah
ibadat, 96, 103, 117
Ibn Jamaa, 53
Ibn Jarir, 196
Ibn Khaldun, 209
Ibn Rushd, 213
Ibn Sina, 221; see Avicenna

Ibn Taymiyyah Al Siyasat, 207
Idafah, 23
Ideal of the Islamic State, 263
ideological state, 46
Ihering, 32
Ijma, 38, 67, 101, 108, 123, 125
Ijtihad, 6, 37, 38, 39, 50, 62, 123, 124, 125, 126, 127, 129
Ilm-ul-Faru, 102
Ilm-ul-Fiqh, 101
Inam, 105
India, 61, 132, 133, 146
Indian: Congress, 133; Independence Act of 1947, 135; Meeting of 1857, 253; Ocean, 252, 257; Subcontinent, 77, 146, 241
Indochinese social background, 167
Indonesia, 61, 131, 167, 237, 259
Indonesian archipelago, 241
initial premise, 30
Injil, 21; see Bible
Intellectual Mullah, 4
interest, on investments, 171
International geopolitical matters, 260
International law and Affairs: generally, 193-211; respect for international law as derived from the Quran, 193; central idea of peace, 193; peace and forgiveness, 194; taking of American hostages, 194; promotion of equality of mankind, 195;

Islam advocates democracy, 195; promotion of learning and knowledge, 196; Quran prohibition on violence, 196; criteria for use of violence, 197; invitation to Dar-As-Salam, Abode of Peace, 197; humanity as a unit, 198; doctrine of Tauhid, oneness of God, 199; Arbitration and mediation, 200; mandation of lack of revenge in retaliation, 200; avoid killings, 201; toleration, 201; Jihad, the concept of war, 202; war only for the defense of the weak or self-defense, 202; war in the way of Allah, 203; warfare injunctions of non-violence, Prophetic instructions, 203; war not be used to compel acceptance of Islam, 204; defense against attack, 205; protection of mission of God of Islam, routing fitnah, 205; foreign policy of Islamic state, 206-210
Iqbal, 63 (see below)
Iqbal, Sir Mohammed, 134, 150
Iran, 9, 12, 14, 61, 80, 95, 131, 133, 156, 167, 194, 249, 251, 252, 254, 256, 258, 260, 261
Iranian crisis, 5
Iranian Revolution, 257
Iraq, 14, 61, 95, 131, 175, 261
Iraqi-Iranian Border Disputes, 261

Isaac, 232
Isharah, 23
Ishmael, 20, 232
Islam: Africa, 260;
  Christianity, 241;
  Monotheistic Faiths,
  229; Non-monotheism,
  235; other religions,
  225; Republic and Crisis,
  5; the 1980's, 249; and
  priesthood, 4
Islamabad, 257
Islamic: civilization,
  146; community, 8; con-
  stitution, 60; constitutional organization, 91,
  see Gibb; democratic
  principles, 96; economic
  system, 181; Empire, 146,
  147; Empire of Turkey,
  147; fundamentalism, 9,
  252; hierarchy, 238;
  jurisprudence, 3, 4, 55,
  81, see Sariah, Fiqh,
  Nass and Ijtihad; law,
  2, 34, 35, 93, 94, 123;
  polity, 42; renaissance,
  259, 260; Republic, 5,
  73, 260; Republic of
  Pakistan, 135; revival,
  144
Islamic State, impact on
  Western Nations:
  generally, 211-223;
  prejudice from Crusades
  as to acceptance of
  Islamic law, juris-
  prudence and state-
  craft, 211; thirteenth
  century contacts, translation of Greek learning,
  213; Emperor Frederick
  II of Hohenstaufen and
  unusual Muslim contacts,
  214; Italian encourage-
  ment of Muslim scholar-

ship, 215; Muslim
  merchants contribution
  to West, 215; Oriental
  art, Arabic writers, and
  Arabic Architecture, 216;
  Venetian glass factories,
  217; Muslim literary
  influence, 217; enrich-
  ment of Greek philosophy
  via Muslim scholar translations, 218; Muslim
  influence in western
  science and mathematics,
  219; Muslim influence in
  Western languages, 219;
  Muslim study of Greek
  science and mathematics,
  221; Avicenna, 221
Islamisization, 13
Israel, 238, 256
Israilites, 203
Istanbul, 212; see
  Constantinople
Istehsan, 126, 222
Italian: architects,
  217; poets, 217; traders,
  217
Italians, 217
Italy, 217, 218
ius naturale, 31
Ivory Coast, 61, 131

Jabal Muadh Bin, 38
Jacob, 232
Jahad, 37
Jahiliyyah, time of
  ignorance, 19, 94
Jaiz, 103
Jamat-a-Islami, 143, 145
Jannat, 171
Jerusalem, 19, 146
Jesuit heritage, 246
Jesus, 72, 83, 100, 232,
  242, 243, 244
Jesus, titles in Quran,
  242, 243

Jew, 1, 24, 45, 97, 209, 233, 238, 241
Jewish faith, 20
Jewish people 95
Jews of Quainuqa, 209
Jihad, (also Jehad), 37, 183, 202, 204, 207, 209; see International Law and Affairs
Jihad fi sabilillah, 203
Jihad's raison d'etre, 205
Jizia, 46
Jizyah, 178; see also poll-tax
John of Salisbury, 218
Jordan, 61, 131
Judaism, 1, 25, 230
Jumah, 105
Jurisprudence, 3; see also Ijtihad, Nass, Fiqh, and Islamic Jurisprudence
Jurists, 39
Justice: generally, 42, 109-110; under Islamic law, 109; under the Common law, 109

Kabah, 22, 23
Kabul, 255, 258
Kalima, 41
Kant, 37
Kalam, 101
Kanz-ul-Amal, volume 2, 173
Karachi, 134, 142
Karmal, Babrak, 255
Kazakstan, 255
Kellog--Briand Pact of 1928, 201
Kemal Ata Turk, 134, 141 147
Kennedy Edward, 12
Kenya, 165
Khaiber, 175
Khair-ul-Hakimin, 99; see God, 107

Khalid b. Walid, 23
Khalifa (also Khalifah), 28, 72
Khatibs, 151
Khazars, 19
Khazraj, 82
Khilafat, 71, 72, 208
Khomeini, 73, 145, 160, 160, 166, 251, 252, 254, 260; see Ayatollah Khomeini
Khomeini, brotherhood, 160
Khomeini socialism, 160
Khulafa-i-Rashidin, 66
Khyber Pass, 133, 253
King Alfonso VI of Castile, 213
King Richard, Coeur de Lion, of England, 216
Kissinger, 256
Kremlin, 157, 253, 254, 258
Kufah, 22
Kurdish people 261
Kuwait, 61, 131

labor, 176
Lahore, 137, 142, 176
Lahore High Court, 143
land tenance, controversy over, 186-187
Last Day, 74
Latin Alphabet, 149
Law: generally, 110-123; Western examination of the concept, 111; Shariah, 112; origin and relationship of law and state, 112; comparison of Islam and Western political thought, 113; peace for mankind, 113; human rights, 114-123; aims and essence of the law, 115; Shariah and human rights, 116-117;

protection of life, 117;
concept of freedom, 118;
property rights, 119;
protection of rights,
120-121; system of
Shariah--recognition of
ideals of life, 122; see
also sources of law
Lawgiver, 101
laylat al-qadr, 27
Leadership: generally, 51-
58; righteous and unrighteous rulers, 51; Sunni,
52; Mawardi, historical
development of caliphate,
52; Mirrors of Princes,
53; removal of ruler by
people, 55; righteous,
55; oaths of office, 56;
qualifications and
characteristics of
rulers, 56; oppression
of subjects, 58; doctrine
of consultation, 58
League of Nations, 114
Lebanon, 61, 131
Legal Concepts:
generally, 93-130;
Shariah, law and
jurisprudence, 93; nature
of the Shariah, 93;
information, amalgamation
of church and state,
93-94; modification in
Islamic religion, 94;
historical examples of
use in Quran, 95; unity
of God, one religion,
96; definition of Islam,
96; the Quran and Islam,
97-103; Islamic state
not a theocracy, 103-
104; economic system of
the Shariah, 104-106;
political science and
the Shariah, 106-110

Legislation: generally,
70-83; major problems,
70; position of the
Caliph, 71; viceregent
71-72; limits on legis-
lations, 73-75; functions
of the legislature, 75-
76; legislation on
existing law, 76-80;
composition of the
legislature, 81
Libya, 61, 80, 131, 165,
260
Libyan-Egyptian hostil-
ities, 261
Libyan State, 260
Liwa, 23
Locke, 51, 113
Lyallpur, 142

M.B. Makhzoomi, 208
Madina, 234, 235; see
also Masjid-e-Nabwi
Madani surahs, 205
Madresa Faizieh, 14
Magian, 97
Magna Charta (Carta), 114
Mahkum Alaihi, 102
Maimonides, 213; see Musa
Ibn Maimun
Majlis-i-Shura, 47
Majran, 234
Maker, 226
Makki surahs, 205
Malaysia, 61, 131
Mali, 61, 131, 166
Malik, 39
Maliki, 180
Malik-ul-Mulk, 99, 102,
106; see God
Malik-ul-Quddus, 106
Malik-un-Nas, 106
Marxism, 263
Marxists, 255
Mary, 242, 244
Masjid-e-Nabwi, 234; see

also Medina
Maudoodi, 145
Mauritania, 61, 131
Mawardi, 52
Maylasia, 167
Mecca, 19, 20, 22, 23, 27, 52, 82, 201
medieval English Scholars, 218
medieval European verse, 217
Medieval Western Theocracy, 46
Medina, 27, 52, 53, 81, 82, 175, 234
Mejielle, (also Majalla), 77
Memluks, 147
Messenger of God, 232, 242
Michael Scott, 213, 215
Middle Ages, 216, 217, 219, 221, 223
Middle East, 247, 259
Middle East Countries, 164
Milla, 47
Millet, 126
Minhaf, 229
Mirrors of Princes, 53, 54
missionary activity, 247
modernization, of Islam, 15; of Christianity, 128
Mogul Dynasty, 133, 146, 253
Mohammed, (also Muhammad), 27, 86, 98, 100, 194, 205, 232, 233, 236, 243; see Prophet Mohammed
Mohammed Ali Jinnah, 134
Mohammed Daoud, 254
Mohammed Daud Kahn, 152
Mohammed Iqbal, Sir, 134, 150
Mohammed Reza Pahlai, 9, 10, 11, 58
Monarchy, 35
Mongols, 19

Mongul Devastation, 147
Montenegrans, 160
Moors, 1
Morocco, 61, 131, 166, 176
Moscow, 255
Moses, 100, 232
Mosul 220
Mount Arafat, 116
Mount Sinai, 201
Muadh Bin Jabal, 38
Mubah, 103
Mufti, 44, 121
Mufti of Belgrade, 160
Mughal Sultans, 91
Muhajir, 40
Muhammed Abuhu, 207
Mujlis (also Majlis), 16
Mujtahids, 38, 126, 127
Mukruh, 103
Mullah, 4, 39, 143, 145, 158
Mullah, fanaticism of, 4
Multan, 142
Muminin, 105
Musa Ibn Maimun, 213; see Maimonides
Mushrikun, 235
Musketeers, 176
Muslim: generally, 10, 12, 13, 16, 26, 27, 28, 37, 40, 41, 42, 45, 46, 50, 53, 118, 123, 132, 145, 151, 158, 159, 178, 219, 229; Architects, 214, author, 214, brotherhood, 166; buildings, 216; calendar, 52; civilization, 216; clergy, 158, community, 58, 63, 84, 85, 87; domination, 216; east, 215; God, 193; influence on Western Europe, 219; jurists, 38; law, 59; Law of Nations, 210; learning, 213; League, 133; medicine, 215;

middle ages, 83; mosques, 217; philosophers,218, philosophy, 213; poetry, 218; Princess of Tunis, 217; romance, 218; rule, 240; rulers, 58; scholars, 214, 215, 221, see also al-Kindi; theologians, 51; thinkers, 218; world, 218
Mussalman Wakf Validating Act of 1930, 77
Mustahab, 103
Mutazilah, 124
Mujtahid, 126, 127

Nadwah, 23
Nahl, 105
Najm ud-Din Razi, 54
Nasara, 100
Nass, 125-127
Nasser, 141
National Assembly, 139, 141
nationalism, 17
Nationalization in Islam, 175
Natural Law, 29
Neo-Platonic philosphers, 221
Nestorian Christians, 221
New Zealand, 132
Niger, 61, 131, 166
Nigeria, 61, 131, 166
Nile, 221
nisab, 180
Noah and the Ark, 246
Nordic invasion, 212
Nordic race, 212
Norman: adventurers, 212; Court, 214; kingdom of Sicily, 214; Sicilian architecture, 214
North Africa, 85; see also Grand Mosque
North America, 69, 88

North Vietnam, 256
Northern Italy, 215
Nur Mohammed Taraki, 153

Objectives Resolution of 1949, 135
Old Testament, 242
Oman, 131
Omar, 35, 104
Oppenheim, 34
Ordinance of Allah, 200
Oriental: art form, 216; languages, 218; origin, 217; studies in Europe, 213
Ottoman Empire, 147
Ottoman sultans, 91

Paine, 114
Pakhtoonistan, 261
Pakistan: generally, 132-146; modern state, 132; as part of India under British control, 132-133; constitution of, 137-140; Bhutto, 140; Field Marshall Ayub, 140; reign of Bhutto, 141-143; National Alliance, 143; General Zia, 144; Islamic, Zia, 144; Islamic revival, 144-146
Pakistan People's Party, 140
Palestine, 216, 240
Palestinians, 258
Papacy, 71
Papal Bull, 210
Paracelsus, 220; see Swiss Renaissance Chemist
Parliament, 112
Peace, 193, 225, 234, 239
People of the Book, 232
Persia, 1, 19, 53, 217, 255
Persian, 134
Persian Gulf, 161, 167

Persian influence, 212
Peshawar, 142
Peter, 72
Peter the Great, 253
Philippines, 61, 85, 259;
  see also Grand Mosque,
  167, 168
Philistines, 203
Pilgrimage, 20
place of worship, 234
plan of the Creator, 229
Plato, 218
Poland, 90
Political philosophy of
  Islam, 3
poll-tax, 178; see also
  Jizyah
Polygamy, 247
Polytheism, 229
Pope Innocent IV, 246
Pope Sylvester II, 212;
  see Gilbert of Aurillac
powers of government, 59
Precedents of Khulf-a-
  Rashdin, 67
President of the State, 56
President Tito, 159
President Zia, 154; see
  General Zia
Pre-Socratic thought, 88
Prime Minister of Pakistan,
  141
Private property, insti-
  tution of, 182
Proleteriat, 112
Prophet, 6, 23, 35, 38,
  40, 56, 57, 64, 67, 72,
  81, 82, 86, 93, 94, 101,
  111, 116, 121, 173, 182,
  193, 194, 196, 201, 202,
  203, 210, 212, 225, 228,
  229, 230, 231, 232, 233,
  234, 240, 242, 244
Prophet of Arabia, 231
Prophet of God, 236
Prophet of Islam, 21, 96,

100, 227, 234, 242
Prophet Mohammed, 19, 35,
  83, 108, 137, 196; see
  Mohammed
Prophetic Sunnah, 115
Protestant communities, 88
Protestant faith, 150
provincial treasures, 48
Public Treasury, 188, 184;
  see Baitul-Mal

Qadi, 48, 109, 121
Qadianis, 137
Qadis, 43, 44
Qatar, 61, 131
Qiyadah, 23
Qiyas, 101, 123, 126
Qurayash, 27
Quarish tribes, 20
Quraish, 23
Quasi-socialist, 160
Queen Elizabeth I, 133
Qum, 14
Quran, composition of,
  26, 101
Quranic chapters: Buqarah
  (164), 118; Yunus(191),
  118; Tariq (5-7), 118;
  Imran (7), 118; Hajj
  (46), 118
Quran: see special tab-
  ulation at end of index
Quranic: injunctions, 36,
  43, 50; Laws, 2; princi-
  ples, 48, 115; revela-
  tions, 115; Social Order,
  170
Qusayy, 22, 23

Rabbihi, 23
Rabb-ul Alamin, 99, 199,
  227; see God, Allah
Rafadah, 23
Rahim, 102; see Rahman
Rahman, 102; see Rahim
Ranjit Singh's bodyguard, 241

Raymond Lull of Marjoca,
214; see Christian
Bishop
Raymond Martin, 214
Raymond of Toledo, 213
Reason, 219
Rebwah, 137
Reconstruction of
Religious Thought
in Islam, 134; see
also, Iqbal, Sir
Reformation of Islam, 150
Religion, Islamic view
of others: generally,
225-248; name of Islam
is not based on a
personlity, 225;
importance of men and
social responsibilities,
225-226; Unity of
Creation, 226; Unity
of Mankind, 227;
permanent basic unity
versus transitional
environmental demand,
228; Prophets raised
for benefit of all
mankind, 229; inbuilt
empathy for monotheistic
faiths, 229; religion
defined, 229; basic
truth of Islam, Divine
Creation, 230; toleration
of differences required
by fundamentals of Islam,
230;aggressive war for-
bidden, 231; revelation
as universal phenomenon
not monopolized by one
people, 231; Muslim
goodwill to other
religions, 232; door of
salvation open for all
of mankind, 232; divine
revelation of other
religions impressed by
scholars with vissitudes
of the time, 233; no
particular geographic
spot as sacred, 233;
places of worship of all
religions protected, 234;
prohibition on inter-
ference with another's
faith, 234-235; attitudes
towards Non-Monotheistic
faiths, 235; Islam with
no organized priesthood,
237; maintenance of
Islam in Non-Monotheistic
faith countries, 237;
Islam and atheism, 238;
Unity of creation, Unity
of mankind, Unity of
divine guidance, Unity
of purpose of life, 239;
Islamic practice of
allowing non-Islamic
religious worship in the
Mosque, 240; utmost
toleration in Islam of
other faiths, 241; Islam
and Christianity, 241;
belief of Jesus as a
great prophet, 242;
Islamic commentators
on the titles used for
Christ, 242; Divinity of
Christ, 243; problem of
Crucifixion, 244;
Gospels, 244; cooperation
between Islam and Christ-
ianity, 245; cooperation
not requiring undue
concessions, 246; thorough
survey of Islam and
Christianity advocated,
247; Islam and Christ-
ianity to unite and
enlighten all mankind,
247
Religion and Communist

300

education, 157
Religion of God, 233
Renaissance, 217
Renaissance building, 217
Respect for International
Law, 193
Revelation, 3
Riba, 172
Rifadah, 23
Righteous Caliphs, 76
Risalat al-Tawhid, 207;
see S.M. Rashid Ridha
Robert Anglius, 213
Roger Bacon of Oxford, 218
Rome, 19, 211
Romans, 19, 20, 222
Romans (5:10), 240; see
also Sura (3:104)
Roman Empire, 95, 146,212
Rousseau, 113
Rubuiyat, 227
rule of law, 32
Russell, 1
Russia, 58, 257
Russian, 234, 251-256, 258;
Afghan Relations, 253;
Embassy, 258; expansion,
260; invasion of Afghan-
istan, 252

S. M. Rashid Ridha, 207
Sabians, 232
Sacred Law, 100
Safwan ibn Wammayyah, 209
Sahih (I 34), 97, 118, 221
Saint Catherine, 201
Saladin, 216
Salam, 97; see also
Quran 19:62
Salat, 96
Salerno, University of, 214
Salmond, 34
Samarkand, 156
Saudia Arabia, 61, 80, 131,
166

Saul, 203
Savak, 12
Saiyyid Jamal al-Din, 205,
208
Schools of Muslim Thought,
125
Science and Islam, 15
Scriptures, 245
Secularization attempts,
149
Security Council, 258, 259
Semitic, 19
Semitic traditions, 211
Senegal, 61, 311
Separations of Powers,
48
Serbs, 160
Sermon of the Prophet, 70
Sermon on the Mount, 247
Shadow of God, 53
Shafi, 180
Shah, 12, 14, 16, 162, 251,
256, see Shah of Iran
Shah of Iran, 9
Shahada, 236
Sharia, 229
Shariah, 41, 47, 52, 55,
56, 76, 91, 93, 99-102,
105, 106, 108-111, 115-
122, 179
Shariah evidences, 101
Shariah Law, 43
Shariat benches, 144
Shariat law of Turkey, 147
Shia commentator, 242;
see Tabarsi
Shiaties, 261
Shihab un-Din Ali b.
Muhammad al-Hamadani,
54
Sicilian architecture,
217
Sicily, 212, 216
Sierra Leone, 61
Sikh regime, 241

Sinan, 217
Sino-Soviet rift, 256
Sir Christopher Wren, 217
Sir Mohammed Iqbal, 134,
    150; (see Iqbal)
Sir Sayyed Ahmed Khan, 13
siyasat, 53
Sick Man of Europe, 147
Slovaks, 160
Snouck Hurgronje, 79, 129
Social Order, Quranic, 170
Somolia, 165
Son, 244
Son of God, 242
Sophia, 159
sources of law; Quran, 36;
    Sunna or Hadith, 36;
    Ijtihad, 37; Ijma 38;
    see also, Law
Southeastern Europe, 147
Southwest Asia, 256
Sovereignty: generally,
    112; of Parliament, 112;
    of Congress, 112
Soviet Azerbiajan, 257
Soviet Union, 153-158, 251-
    254, 257-259
Soviets, 256, 257
Spain, 147, 212, 213, 216,
    217, 221, 222, 240
Spaniards, 213
Spanish schools, 214
Spirit from God, 242
Spirit of Islam, 194
Spiritualism of Law, 127
Stalin, 253, 255
State: concept of state
    generally, 29-51; three
    juristic theories, 29-34;
    the Islamic concept, 34-
    51; historically, 35;
    ending of monarchies, 35;
    the role of God, 35; the
    role of the Quran, 36;
    Quranic verses, 36; four
    sources of law, 36-38;

restricted right of
    legislation, 40;
    paternity, 40; equality,
    41; liberty, 41;
    justice, 42; Head of
    Islamic State, 43;
    difference between sin
    and crime, 44-45;
    toleration, 45;
    religious and temporal
    nature, 46-47; admin-
    istration and govern-
    ment, 47; separation
    of powers, 48; economic
    policy, 49
State and Law, relation-
    ships of, 33
State Department, 163
Submission, 225
Sudan, 61, 131
Sudan tribes, 261
Sudaqah, 179
Sufiism, 147
Sunna (also Sunnah), 36,
    37, 38, 47, 50, 67, 75,
    76, 101, 108, 123, 124,
    135
Sunnah of the Prophet,
    74, 97, 107
Sunni form of Islamic
    Law, 77
Sunnis, 261
Supreme Being, 226, 234,
    247
Supreme Court, 144
Supreme Court of U.S., 112
Supreme Sovereign, 101
Suras: (24:54), 63; (2-7,
    9, 10, 19, 21, 23, 39, 42,
    43, 57, 61, 72 and 112)
    243; (3:104), 246, (see
    Ephesians 2:13); (3:104),
    246, (see Romans 5:10);
    (11:28), 246, (see I Cor-
    inthians 1:26); (7:138),
    246, (I Corinthians 1:26);

302

(23), 247
Sura al-Baqara, 65
Surah Al-Baqurah II:
    (142b, 143a); 236
Surah Al-Maidah, (5:8),
    236
Surah Hashr, verse 7, 105,
    185
Surah Hujurat, 117
Surahs, 105
Sustainer, 199
Sustainer of Universe, 247
Swiss Renaissance Chemist,
    220
Synoptic Gospels, 246
Syria, 19, 61, 131

Tabarsi, 242
tadbir-i-manzil, 21
Tadjikstan, 255
Tadrij, 102
Tafsir al-manar, 207
Tanzania, 61, 131
taqwa, 40, 75, 107, 126
Taraki, 154, 155, 254
taxation, Zakat, 178-185;
    see also Economic
    structure
Tauhid, concept of, 63,
    199, 200; see Inter-
    national Law and Affairs
Tehran, 194, 258
Tehranian Upheavel, 15
tenancy of land, controversy
    over, 188
Thailand, 61, 167
Thamud, 95
Theo-Democracy, 47
Theodor Noeldeke, 243
Third World, 158, 163, 175
Third World heads of govern-
    ments, 142
Thomas Aquinas, 218
time of ignorance, 19;
    see Jahilyyah
Togo, 61, 131

Toledo, 212, 213
Torah, 21, 24
Teachers' Gazette, 157;
    see Uchitelskaia Gazeta
tribal set-up, 21
Trinity, 244, 247
True Believers, 86
Truth, 228
Truth of God, 242, 244
Tudor England, 216
Tunisia, 61, 77, 131, 166
Turk, 89, 90
Turks, 146, 210, 240, 253
Turkey: generally, 146-
    152; historical review,
    148-149; Kemal Ata Turk,
    changes in Republic,
    149; as an example of
    and Islamic community,
    149; secularization
    attempts, 149-152
Turkish: Architect, 217;
    border, 158; call for
    prayer, 149; constitu-
    tion, article 2 of 1924,
    148; empire, 147, 158,
    159, 253; government,
    151; republic, 149
Turkistan, 157
Turkish Empire, 1

Uchitelskaia Gazeta, 157;
    see Teachers' Gazette
Uganda, 131
ulama, 124
Ul-il-Amr, 69
Umar, son of Khattab, 27,
    28
Umma (also Ummah), 23, 28,
    47, 51, 83, 87, 89, 102,
    107, 164
Ummayad caliphs, 221
Union of Arab Emirates, 131
United Kingdom, 5, 58
United Nations, 114, 166,
    259

United Nations Charter,
Chapter VI, 201
United Nations Secretary
General, 12; see Kurt
Waldheim
United States, 11, 112,
161, 162, 164, 194, 241,
249, 251, 252, 256, 258,
259
United States and Islam:
generally, 161-169;
misconception of Muslim
World, 161-162; support
of rulers as opposed to
populace in general, 162-
163; Corrections neces-
sary for U.S. to establish
friendly ties with Muslim
populace, 163-164; mis-
handling of foreign
policy, 164; evidence
of Muslim feelings,
hostages, 164; Islamic
countries and nuclear
capability, 165; other
Islamic areas; the Muslim
crescent, 165; Islam
faith as a means to
independence, 167; the
case of India, 168
United States foreign
policy, 258
United States-Russian
global policies, 255
Unity: of creation, 226,
227, 229, 239; of God,
199; of guidance, 239;
of Mankind, 227, 229, 239;
of purpose of life, 239
Universal Declaration of
Human Rights, 114, 120
Universal teacher, 233
Universe, 226, 227, 230
Universe in Islam, 226
University of Ankara, 151
University of Salerno, 214

untouchables, 133
Upper Volta, 61, 131
Uqab, 23
ushr, 22
Usman, 35; see Uthman
U.S.S.R., 61, 131, 158,
238, 257
Usul-ul-Fiqh, 101, 124
Uthman, 28; see Usman
Uzbekistan, 255

Venetians, 217
Venetian glass factories,
217
Viceregent, 71
Vietnam, 256
Vietnam, North, 256
Vittoria, 66
Von Grunebaum, 128

Wahhabi, 85
wajib, 102; see Fard
Waldheim, Kurt, 12
War of Hunain, 204
Watergate, 256
West, 134, 166, 212,
213, 215, 216, 218,
243; as compared to
Islamic World; as to
diversity of traditions,
84
West Bank, 258
Western: Architecture, 215;
Asia, 211, 260; Asian
Religious traditions, 211
215; Christian thought,
213, 218; -Christian
countries, 90; westerners,
in general, 212, 216;
ethos, 89; Europe, 69,
88, 219, 252; European
cultural development,
212; European languages,
220; learning, 215; man,
88; medicine, 219;
merchants, 219; Middle

Ages, 83; music, 216;
  scholars, 218; science,
  215; unity, 89
western theories of state,
  29
Wilfred Cantwell Smith,
  134, 147
Willed Justice, 86
woman of Samaria in
  St. John, 247
Wonder of the World, 214;
  see Emperor Fredrick II
  of Hohenstauffen
Word of God, 242
Workment, 176
World War I, 133, 136
World War II years, 132,
  151, 254, 255
W. Wilson Cash, 242, 243

Yemen, 19, 61, 131
Yezid, 203
Yugoslavia, 159, 160

Zahir Shah, 152, 254
Zakat, 6, 36, 48, 49, 50,
  105, 144, 172, 177–183;
  see Economic structure
Zalim, 55
Zul-Hajj, 70
Zulm, cruelty of
  unrighteous ruler, 54

QURAN
Chronological Tabulation of Citations

Citations	Arabic Equivalent of Roman Numeral Citations
(i. 1, 3), 102;	
(i. 5-6), 107;	
(2:4), 231;	
(2:28), 228;	
(II:29), 182;	(2:29), 182
(2:30), 226;	
(2:62), 232;	
(2:87), 242;	
(2:112), 193;	
(2:115), 233;	
(ii. 124), 121;	(2:124), 121
(2:136), 232;	
(ii. 137), 93;	(2:137), 93
(ii. 143), 107;	(2:143), 107
(ii. 185), 102;	(2:185), 102
(ii. 188), 118;	(2:188), 118
(2:190), 231;	
(2:193), 197;	
(ii. 213), 94, 115;	(2:213), 94, 115
(2:213), 198;	
(ii. 219), 179;	(2:219), 179
(2:253), 242;	
(ii. 256), 98, 117;	(2:256), 98, 117
(2:256), 195, 204, 230;	
(II:257), 45;	(2:257), 45
(2:285), 199, 232;	
(III:19), 97;	(3:19), 97
(3:19), 199;	
(3:45), 242;	
(3:63), 232, 233;	
(3:64), 199, 247;	
(iii. 110), 105;	(3:110), 105
(III:153), 47;	(3:153), 47
(iii. 159), 120;	(3:159), 120
(iii. 164), 98;	(3:164), 98
(3:189), 200;	
(iv. 1), 94;	(4:1), 94
(4:1), 198, 227;	
(4:32), 173;	
(iv. 36), 120;	(4:36), 120
(iv. 58), 119, 120;	(4:58), 119, 120

Citations	Arabic Equivalent of Roman Numeral Citations
(iv. 59), 118;	.(4:59), 118
(4:64), 202;	
(iv. 65), 120;	.(4:65), 120
(iv. 105), 120;	.(4:105), 120
(IV:134), 42;	.(4:134), 42
(iv. 135), 120;	.(4:135), 120
(4:135), 200;	
(iv. 148), 118;	.(4:148), 118
(4:164), 228;	
(iv. 170), 98	.(4:170), 98
(v. 1), 119;	.(5:1), 119
(5:2), 195;	
(v. 3), 117;	.(5:3), 117
(5:8), 236;	
(5:9), 197;	
(5:18), 193;	
(5:32), 201;	
(V:46), 42;	.(5:46), 42
(v. 47), 100;	.(5:47), 100
(vi. 108), 117;	.(6:108), 117
(6:109), 196, 201, 229, 235	
(vi. 165), 115;	.(6:165), 115
(vii. 29), 120;	.(7:29), 120
(7:158), 233;	
(vii. 199), 117;	.(7:199), 117
(viii. 61), 98;	.(8:61), 98
(ix. 11), 179;	.(9:11), 179
(9:34,35), 173;	
(9:60), 172;	
(ix. 60), 180;	.(9:60), 180
(ix. 61), 98;	.(9:61), 98
(ix. 104), 179;	.(9:104), 179
(10:11), 197;	
(x. 14), 95;	.(10:14), 95
(x. 19), 115;	.(10:19), 115
(10:19), 195;	
(10:25), 193;	
(10:26), 197;	
(10:47), 228;	
(x. 50), 95	.(10:50), 95
(x. 64), 109;	.(10:64), 109
(x. 99), 115;	.(10:99), 115
(10:99), 196;	

Citations	Arabic Equivalent of Roman Numeral Citations
(xi. 6), 104;	(11:6), 104
(12:4), 173;	
(12:92), 194;	
(14:24), 126;	
(xiv. 31-34), 95;	(14:31-34), 95
(xv. 29), 113;	(15:29), 113
(xv. 88), 115;	(15:88), 115
(16:36), 228, 229, 231;	
(xvi. 71), 104;	(16:71), 104
(xvi. 90), 116, 120;	(16:90), 116, 120
(xvii. 11), 106;	(17:11), 106
(xvii. 24), 116;	(17:24), 116
(17:31), 169;	
(xvii. 39), 117;	(17:39), 117
(xvii. 91), 102;	(17:91), 102
(xviii. 11), 95;	(18:11), 95
(xviii. 110), 103;	(18:110), 103
(19:30-31), 242;	
(xix. 62), 97;	(19:62), 97
(xix. 95), 120;	(19:95), 120
(20:7), 172;	
(20:50), 226;	
(20:114), 196;	
(20:118), 170;	
(xxi. 22), 106;	(21:22), 106
(xxi. 47), 108;	(21:47), 108
(xxi. 107), 98	(21:107), 98
(21:107), 193	
(22:39-40), 197, 231;	
(22:40), 234;	
(22:107), 233;	
(xxiii. 52), 113;	(23:52), 113
(23:115), 226;	
(xxvi. 215), 115;	(26:215), 115
(29:46), 247;	
(xxx. 30), 97, 98;	(30:30), 97, 98
(xxxiii. 40), 98;	(33:40), 98
(xxxiv. 28), 98;	(34:28), 98
(35:24), 198, 228;	
(36:47), 170;	
(36:58), 193;	
(40:78), 198, 228;	
(41:34), 193;	

	Citations	Arabic Equivalent of Roman Numeral Citations

(41:43), 199;
(41:56), 244;
(42:13), 199;
(xlii. 15), 100; . . . . (42:15), 100
(xlii. 38), 107, 120; . . . . (42:38), 107, 120
(42:38), 196;
(43:63), 242;
(xlv. 18), 100; . . . . (45:18), 100
(48:5), 240;
(49:9), 200, 203;
(XLIX:10), 40; . . . . (49:10), 40
(xlix. 12), 117; . . . . (49:12), 117
(XLIX:13), 40; . . . . (49:13), 40
(49:13), 195, 247;
(1i. 21), 104; . . . . (51:21), 104
(56:25,26), 197;
(1vii. 25), 120; . . . . (57:25), 120
(1ix. 7), 185 . . . . (59:7), 185
(57:27), 243;
(1ix. 2), 107; . . . . (59:22), 107
(59:24), 226;
(59:523), 193;
(60:7,8), 197, 236
(62:10), 172, 182
(LXIV:2), 45; . . . . (64:2), 45
(67:1-2), 226;
(72:18), 234;
(1xxv. 8), 108; . . . . (75:8), 108
(1xxxv. 4), 113; . . . . (85:4), 113
(87:1-3), 226
(91:7-10), 225, 227
(95:4), 225, 227;
(civ. 1,2), 105; . . . . (104:1,2), 105
(civ. 2), 105; . . . . (104:2), 105
(109:6), 202;
(cxii. 1-4), 107; . . . . (112:1-4), 107

ABOUT THE AUTHOR

Professor Farooq Hassan was born in Pakistan and educated in England, principally at the Universities of Oxford and Cambridge. He is a Barrister of England and graduated in Law with Honors from Oxford and has obtained various other research degrees and diplomas from England, Europe, and the United States. While not quite the age of twenty-three, he appeared before an international court while internationally representing Pakistan in the Rann of Kutch case. He has written extensively both textbooks and articles and is regarded as one of the most outstanding experts in International Law from Asia. His views and opinions on important contemporary matters have been quoted by leading papers and journals. His accomplishments in the field of International Law and Diplomacy have been acknowledged by the White House and the State Department, in being referred to as "an internationally recognized scholar in the field of human rights and jurisprudence." In 1972, the President of the United States wrote of him while he was a fellow at the Academy of American and International Law, "You have helped Americans achieve a deeper, wiser understanding of our laws and of the legal systems of other nations. In so doing you have illuminated the meaning of the rule of law as the fundamental element of our civilization. You are today advancing our progress toward the just and lawful kind of peace we seek." Further, he is a member of the International Advisory Committee of the International League for Human Rights as well as a member of the Council of Experts of the World Peace Through Law Center. He is also associated with numerous internationally recognized world organizations and has taught extensively in the United States and abroad. Besides being a Professor of Law, he has taught in diplomatic academies as well as in the departments for humanities in various universities. Recently, he was engaged as a specialist by UNESCO to frame a new Human Right entitled, the Right to be Different; his paper and suggestions were subsequently adopted at an international conference in Mexico.